THE
SOCIOLOGY
OF BRITISH
COMMUNISM

by Kenneth Newton

Allen Lane The Penguin Press London 1969

63,470

For D.

CONTENTS

ACKNOWLEDGE-MENTS

This study is a revised version of a doctoral dissertation submitted to the University of Cambridge in 1965. A large number of people gave me invaluable help and advice during my three years as a research student preparing the dissertation. First and foremost, I am deeply indebted to Dr Philip Abrams who taught me what sociological research is all about and whose patient help and guidance has contributed enormously and immeasurably to the quality of the study.

I am most grateful to Dr Christine Craig and Mrs Dorothy Wedderburn for their help in drawing up the questionnaire, and to Dr Henry Pelling, Mr Maurice Broady, Mr Peter Cadogan, Mr Andy McKeown, and Mr Brian Pearce for their generous assistance.

I would like to express my deep gratitude to the staff of the Sociology Department at the University of Exeter who taught me as an undergraduate, and particularly to Mr Derek Crabtree. Like many other graduates of Exeter University I shall always remember his constant kindness and encouragement. But for him this study would never have been written.

I would also like to thank my colleagues in the Political Science and Sociology Departments of the University of Birmingham. Discussions with them forced me to re-think and re-write large portions of the manuscript. Special thanks are due to Dr Geoffrey Ostergaard, and to Dr Gi Baldamus who greatly improved the quality of Chapter 10, and who suggested that the method presented in the chapter should be called 'a method of dual analysis'.

My examiners, Professors E. H. Carr, and D. G. MacRae, suggested a number of valuable modifications to the dissertation.

My father read the manuscript with painstaking care, and I am happy that it was he who pointed out its illogicalities and corrected its worst abuses of the English language.

This study could never have been written without the help and cooperation of a large number of Communists and ex-Communists. I cannot mention them by name, and throughout the book I have taken care to obscure their identities, but I would like to thank them for giving me so much of their time and for showing so much patience in the face of an almost unceasing flow of questions. I have interviewed a large number of people in the past few years but none were as helpful as the Communists whose words are quoted in the following pages.

Finally, I would like to thank Miss Sandra Thory, Miss Jennie Peplow, and Mrs Bardell and her staff in the University's typing pool, all of whom took on the unenviable task of typing various drafts in a short period of time.

Birmingham University   KENNETH NEWTON
October 1966

ABBREVIATIONS

A.E.U.	Amalgamated Engineering Union
B.C.P.	British Communist Party
B.S.P.	British Socialist Party
B.U.F.	British Union of Fascists
C.D.R.C.U.	Committee to Defeat Revisionism, for Communist Unity
Comintern	Communist International
C.P.	Communist Party
C.P.G.B.	Communist Party of Great Britain
C.P.S.U.	Communist Party of the Soviet Union
C.P.U.S.A.	Communist Party of the United States of America
D.W.	*Daily Worker*
E.C.C.I.	Executive Committee of the Communist International
E.T.U.	Electrical Trades Union
I.L.P.	Independent Labour Party
Inprecorr	International Press Correspondence
I.R.I.S.	Industrial Research and Information Services
N.U.W.M.	National Unemployed Workers' (Committee) Movement
P.C.F.	Partie Communiste Français
S.P.G.B.	Socialist Party of Great Britain
S.W.F.	Syndicalist Workers' Federation
W.N.	*World News*
W.N.V.	*World News and Views*
Y.C.L.	Young Communist League

CHAPTER 1

INTRODUCTION: THE SCOPE AND METHODS OF THE STUDY

The British Communist Party commands less electoral support than any other Communist Party in Western Europe, with the exception of the Communist Party in Northern Ireland. It is tiny compared with the French or Italian Communist Parties, which each attract millions of votes and paid-up members in their tens of thousands. In contrast, the British Party has about 34,000 members and no representative in Parliament, so by the standards of electoral support and membership, it is a fourth party, and a relatively minute one at that.[1] Its standing in British politics is further reduced because it operates within a political system that weighs the balance of power heavily in favour of the two main parties.

Why, then, bother to write about a political party as small and seemingly insignificant as the British Communist Party? There are two main answers. In the first place, it is important that the politically concerned layman should have at his disposal a body of reliable information about the Party. And in the second place, the Party can be used as a case study against which the sociologist can test and improve his generalizations about political behaviour and political radicalism.

The B.C.P. is one small fragment of a vastly larger and more powerful complex of organizations, but quite apart from the immense importance of the international Communist movement, the B.C.P. is interesting in its own right. There is a whole battery of questions about Communism and Communists which the layman would like answered. The sociologist would seem to be in a good position to answer these questions, and yet the body of sociological literature about western Communism is unsatisfactory. As a result the layman and the sociologist alike harbour a number of misconceptions about it. Discussion about the nature of Communism in the Press is often unbalanced by a lack of hard fact and prejudiced thinking. Debate between politicians is often just as unreliable and emotionally blinkered, and some sociologists are little more dispassionate and scientific in their treatment of Communist movements. They have frequently arrived at sweeping generalizations on the basis of inadequate and suspect data, they have jumped to false conclusions, and produced unserviceable typologies.[2] This book, therefore, is written for the layman who is interested in British politics, and for the social scientist or the historian who is interested in the analysis of political behaviour. On the one hand it hopes to provide the layman with a systematic body of reliable data about British Communism so that he may arrive at an informed judgement of it. On the other hand the study adds this body of information to the existing information about other radical political movements and uses both sources as a basis for formulating sociological generalizations about political radicalism in general.

Communism and Communists are easy prey to popular myths and conventional stereotypes. For example, many people believe that British Communists would not stop short of using violence as a political means, and that they would resort to wholesale bloodshed to establish a totalitarian government. Are British Communists revolutionaries in the sense that they want the insurgent masses to arm themselves with guns, and rifles, and bombs in readiness for the day when the revolution comes? Certainly a large proportion of the population thinks that Communists are ruthless and Machiavellian fanatics. Side by side with this stereotype, there exists another which depicts Communists as humanitarian and idealistic liberals whose good intentions have somehow gone off the rails. Which, if either, of these stereotypes is accurate? It is also widely believed that a great deal of industrial unrest is engineered by a small group of tightly knit and well-organized Communist agitators who are somehow able to manipulate the mass of peace-loving and moderate trade unionists into following lines of industrial action which they neither want nor need. In the past few years there has been the E.T.U. ballot-rigging case, then the troubles at Ford's, which some attributed to a bunch of Communist wreckers, and then the Seamen's strike which, the Prime Minister himself implied, involved members of the Communist Party. What is the impact and influence of Communist Party activity on trade-union affairs? Can the Party dominate huge trade-union organizations against their will, or is it rather that militant trade unionists willingly and knowingly elect Communists into office?

Fascists are also given to believing, somewhat inconsistently, that both big business and the Communist Party are run by foreigners and Jews. What proportion of British Communists are Jews and foreigners? Is Communism in Britain some unnatural and imported artifact of alien agitators, or is it the uniquely British product of uniquely British conditions? Some observers, from a vantage-point outside the Communist Party and the Fascist parties, have formed the opinion that both movements are very similar in a number of important respects, and are happy to put them in the same category marked 'authoritarian' or 'totalitarian'. Can we usefully and accurately label the B.C.P. a totalitarian party, or is there some validity in its claim to be the most democratic political organization in Britain? There is also the view that a good proportion of people who are unhappy in the C.P. leave it to join a Fascist group. Is there a certain amount of traffic between the two movements? What does happen to ex-Communists?

There are a large number of other questions which any sociological study of the British Communist Party ought to attempt to answer. Why has Communism never taken firm root in British soil? Why do people join the Party? What kind of people are they and what political beliefs do they hold? What kind of jobs do they have? Are they miners and factory workers or does the Party contain a high proportion of alienated middle-class intellectuals? Are they completely committed to Communism in a blind and uncritical sort of way, or do they have certain doubts and reservations about Party policy and practice? In answering these and other questions it is hoped that the study will help towards an understanding of British Communism and British Communists, and also, though in a much smaller way, towards an understanding of world Communism.

Although it is useful to throw light on these questions, there are other, and perhaps sounder, reasons for studying the B.C.P. In this study it is treated as an example of a specific type of social organization – a radical political party. By formulating generalizations about the B.C.P. and comparing them with generalizations about other radical political groups, it is possible to arrive at higher order generalizations which are applicable to a wide range of radical political groups. In this way answers to questions about British Communism can help to produce answers to questions about political radicalism in general, irrespective of time or place, ideology or 'isms'. The two basic questions asked in this study are: Why do people join the B.C.P.?, and, conversely: Why do they leave it? Or, to put the questions another way, who joins the Party and leaves it, and under what circumstances? To answer these specific questions about a specific organization is to go part of the way to answering more general questions about the membership of all radical political groups.

Not only does the B.C.P. offer a convenient point of departure for tackling problems about radical politics, but it can also help the sociologist to understand moderate politics as well. For the usual can sometimes be better understood by looking at the unusual. The B.C.P. is a small, well-defined, sect-like group with an explicit and clearly defined ideology, upon whose members social forces have acted in a definite and observable way.

In other words the B.C.P. provides a small, relatively clear-cut and simple case for study which forms one of the sociologists' limiting cases. Treated as a limiting case it is perhaps as fruitful a subject for study as the much larger and more amorphous social groups upon whose members social forces and events have had a more muted and less observable effect. In plain words, when we are studying British Communists we know more or less who we are studying and what they believe, but the same would not necessarily be true of much larger organizations like the Conservative Party or the Church of England.

Yet research into politics is the art of the possible. In this respect the student of British Communism is at both an advantage and a disadvantage. He is unfortunate in so far as the Party, like so many other organizations, is suspicious of the motives of those who are studying it. It has little to gain from a sociological study, and perhaps something to lose, for every now and again in the past, a *poseur* sociologist has presented ill-founded and anti-Party propaganda as if it were a scientifically valid and detached summing up of what actually does go on inside the Party. However, the sociologist is fortunate because the Party publishes a fairly large quantity of information about itself, most of which has remained hidden away in back copies of Communist periodicals. This information is far from complete, and what is available is not entirely satisfactory since it is not presented in a systematic sort of way. Unfortunately, this has not prevented some sociologists from writing about British Communism as if they were in full possession of all the relevant facts. Much has been written about Western Communism although comparatively little is known about it.

At this point it would be as well to discuss in detail the sources and validity of the information used in this study. It must be unmistakably and clearly stated at the outset that there are very few hard data about the British Communist Party. Seldom does one come across any single piece of information which is conclusive in itself and which can be used to support useful and illuminating generalizations. There is no body of reliable and complete information about any single aspect of the Party's membership or activity. For example, the Party has never published a complete breakdown of its membership in terms of class, or age, or sex, or occupation, or geographical distribution. But the problem of fact-gathering is not completely discouraging by any means, for although 'hard' information is rare, there is a great deal of the 'soft' variety. It is possible, for instance, to piece together a rough picture of the occupational composition of the Party's membership by using a large number of little bits of information. The information certainly has large gaps in it, but what little does exist is internally consistent and points roughly to the same set of conclusions. This state of affairs is far removed from the sociologists' ideal, but the sociologist has to work with what data can be unearthed, and it has been possible to collect together a basis of information which is sufficiently reliable and complete to support some fairly well-substantiated general conclusions. Some of these conclusions throw doubt on existing statements and theories about British Communism and about political radicalism.

The Party's annual membership figures form one of the most complete, reliable, and useful bodies of statistics. Figures have been published in a variety of Party periodicals for almost every year since 1922. There is little reason to doubt their validity since the Party has made no attempt to disguise a large drop in membership. For example, it stated that its total registered membership fell from 33,095 in 1956 to 24,670 in 1958. However, there are some difficulties with the published membership figures. Ever since its formation in 1920 the Party has recruited a large number of people who have stayed in it for only a short time. Membership turnover is very high. The 1,200 recruits made between 1922 and 1924 were little more than sufficient to make up for lapsed members.[3] More recently the Party's General Secretary has written, 'To make a net increase of 3,406 in our membership we had to recruit 6,907'.[4] Because of this high turnover membership figures fluctuate quite considerably within any given year, and for this reason the most reliable figures are those given immediately after the period of annual re-registration, because they take account of both membership gains and losses. If the re-registration figures are accepted, the problem of large discrepancies and fluctuations is largely ironed out. There are two exceptions. The Party claims to have lost no members at the beginning of the Second World War, when Russia and Germany signed a non-aggression pact. Yet for years Communist Parties all over the world had been offering dire warnings about the Fascist threat, and a great deal of the attraction of the Communist Party in the 1930s lay in the fact that it was the most aggressive anti-Fascist political organization in Britain. It is most likely that some, if not many, members of the C.P. left after this reversal of policy towards Fascism and the signing of the Nazi–Soviet Pact. The other exception occurs in 1943, when one source states that the Party had 55,138 members, and another gives a figure of 46,643. It is quite possible that the higher figure is the more accurate. Apart from these two dubious cases it is fairly certain that the figures published by the Party are reliable, and far more so than the figures obtainable for the American Communist Party.[5]

One District official said in an interview that some younger Communists are members of both the Young Communist League (Y.C.L.) and the B.C.P., so that a few Communists will be counted twice and the total figures inflated a little. There may also be a number of crypto-Communists, who are fully paid-up members but who, for one reason or another, keep their membership quite secret. Although there is obviously no information about these crypto-Communists (outside the police files, perhaps) it is difficult to believe that they add up to anything like a significant number. There is a much larger number of fellow-travellers, but this term is a great deal more vague than the term crypto-Communist. It refers to those who are not actually card-carrying Party members but who nevertheless have strong sympathies for the Party's policy and join in some of its activities.

It is possible to gain some very rough idea of the number of fellow-travellers by comparing the number of Party members with the number who vote Communist in a general election, although there are some protest voters who vote Communist but are neither members of the Party nor part of that hazy and ill-defined group of fellow-travellers. There is a large gap between Communist electoral support and Party membership. One official estimated, in an interview, that a constituency in his area had 100 members whereas the Communist candidate received just over 1,000 votes in the general election of 1964. As one branch secretary has complained, the Party has many more friends than members.[6] This study is concerned primarily with card-carrying Party members, rather than sympathizers or fellow-travellers. The Party accepts applications for membership irrespective of race, religion or knowledge of Communist principles.[7] According to one District officer it

accepts Commonwealth members while resident in Britain but not members of the armed forces or members of non-Commonwealth countries. It is not in their interests because information might get back to their home country. I know one case of a man who lost his job because of this.

Information about the social composition of the Party is much more difficult to come by. There is little doubt that the Party's Central Organization Department is in possession of detailed information about the social composition of the membership of the nineteen Party Districts. However, the Department turned down a request for some of this information and so it was necessary to fall back on the analyses of the delegates to the National Party Congresses which are usually held every second year. The analyses are carried out by the Credentials Committees and are published in the Congress Reports. Although Congresses are held during the Easter holidays so that most members who are elected as delegates should be able to attend, there is no reason to believe that the delegates necessarily form an accurate cross-section of the total Party membership.

However, figures given by the Credentials Committees were checked against figures given by four District officials, and it was found that Congress delegates do reflect, roughly perhaps, the social composition of the total Party membership. Questionnaires were sent to all the nineteen District secretaries, but Party headquarters advised them 'not to cooperate'. Of the four District officials interviewed, only one would provide complete and detailed figures. The other three would (or could) give only estimated figures to some of the questions and would not answer some of the others at all. The Party also publishes, every now and again, statements about its social composition which can be used to cross-check the usefulness of the Credentials Committees' figures. In 1947, for instance, two per cent of all

Party members were students, while at the National Congress of that year the student group formed three per cent of the delegates.[8] Again, there were 11,978 (twenty-six per cent) women in the Party in 1944, while twenty-three per cent of the delegates to the Congress in 1944 were women.[9] This war-time figure was much larger than usual since many of the potential male members were in the forces. The post-war figure would be much nearer to fifteen per cent.[10] One group which is probably over represented among the Congress delegates is that of the paid Party workers. The C.P. does have a very large number of these relative to its overall size, but it is doubtful whether there are as many as 1,800 of them.[11]

District membership figures have been published in complete form for only five years – 1926, 1927 and 1942, 1943, 1944 – and are presented in Appendix 5.

General election statistics, together with District membership figures, give a good indication of the geographical distribution of the support for Communism in Britain. The Party has never contested more than fifty-seven seats (in 1966) except in 1950 when it put up 100 candidates. In most general elections since 1922 the Party has put up between ten and twenty-five candidates. Support is concentrated in urban and industrial areas. In 1943, for instance, South Wales had 2,579 registered members, while North Wales had 246.[12] The point is best demonstrated by figures from the 1950 general election results:

Constituencies with the Highest and Lowest Communist Party Vote (expressed as a percentage of the electorate) in the 1950 General Election

HIGHEST CONSTITUENCY	PERCENTAGE	LOWEST CONSTITUENCY	PERCENTAGE
West Fife	18·3	Wycombe	0·33
Rhondda East	11·1	Bedfordshire	0·40
Stepney	9·1	Shipley	0·51
Gorbals	4·5	Portsmouth West	0·43
Shettleston	3·2	Suffolk Eye	0·57
Springburn	3·2	Swindon	0·62
Govan	3·1	West Croydon	0·62
Neath	3·1	South Shields	0·62

Of the eight constituencies with the highest vote, four are in Glasgow, five in Scotland, one in the East End of London and two in South Wales. The six candidates in Glasgow in 1950 polled over three times the national Communist average. Much the same pattern of support repeats itself in those elections where the Party has polled over twenty per cent of the votes against Labour Party opposition.[13]

Greenock	1924, 1925		*Mile End, Stepney*	1945
West Fife	1929, 1931, 1935, 1945, 1950		*Hornsey*	1945
Rhondda East	1931, 1933 (by-election), 1935, 1945		*South Hackney*	1945

Of these, two are in Scotland, one in South Wales and three in the East End of London. Glasgow, West Fife, South Wales and the East End are the areas which have traditionally provided the Party with its most concentrated support and a large section of its membership. Support for the Y.C.L. is similarly distributed.[14]

The Average Vote for Communist Party Candidates in the 1950 General Election Ranked by District

DISTRICT	AVERAGE VOTE	NUMBER OF CANDIDATES
Wales	2,560	4
Scotland	1,720	16
London	900	36
Yorkshire	735	7
Lancashire	530	13
East Midlands	500	4
Kent	477	8
North East	453	2
Devon and Cornwall	423	1
Midlands	422	4
West of England	414	3
Teesside	367	1
South Midlands	263	3
South-East Midlands	282	2
East Anglia	277	1
Hampshire and Dorset	251	1

There is also a significant positive correlation between support for the Communist Party and support for the Labour Party. The correlation is, perhaps, higher than might be expected, and indicates that the Communist and Labour vote may well be the product of the same factors.[15]

C.P. VOTE	NUMBER OF SEATS	MEDIANS OF THE LABOUR PARTY VOTES
per cent		per cent
0–1	28	50
1–2	50	56·3
more than 2	22	60

Yet there are peculiar lacunae in the seats fought by the Party. Plymouth, Southampton, Cardiff, Swansea, Luton, Wolverhampton, Stoke, Derby, Bolton,[16] Hull, Salford, Bristol, Portsmouth, Leeds, Bradford, Newcastle, Leicester, Edinburgh and Liverpool have seldom if ever been contested. But for the 100 candidates in 1950 the list would be much longer. Liverpool offers a strange contrast to Glasgow which is similar in so many respects. Both are port cities, both have a large immigrant Catholic population from Ireland, and both divide their constituencies roughly equally between the Conservative and Labour Parties. Glasgow can be regarded as the most important city in the British Communist Party's history – London included – while Liverpool is of negligible importance. In Lancashire generally, as in the North-East, the Party fares rather badly.[17]

Besides the data collected from Party documents and periodicals, a number of Party members were interviewed. The questionnaire was pre-tested for intelligibility on a group of ten Communists, ex-Communists and non-Communists. It was designed to act mainly as a spring-board for an organized monologue. Respondents were never encouraged to keep to 'the point', but were allowed to talk as freely as they liked about anything they felt to be relevant to their political beliefs and behaviour. Interviews were conducted during the first half of 1964 when the Cold War was continuing to thaw. There were no political events at the time which made the respondents particularly reluctant to talk about their beliefs.

It was hoped to interview at least 100 Communists from different parts of Britain. In fact only twenty-seven were interviewed before the Party headquarters denied access to any more. One of the twenty-seven was a Y.C.L. member. Those who were interviewed were extremely helpful and cooperative and there is no reason to doubt that they answered even the most probing questions with complete honesty. However, the twenty-seven are in no way a sample of either the Party Districts or the branches. Many were selected by District or branch officials and the remainder were selected simply because they were available for interviewing. Nobody asked for an interview refused one, although one woman did say over the telephone that she had no time to spare. Of the twenty-seven there were four married couples. Only four had working-class occupations. Because the sample was in no way random or representative it was decided that it would be most misleading to place any emphasis on interview material and pointless to attempt a statistical analysis of the answers. Instead the interviews are used to illustrate points made on the basis of other evidence. The interviews suggest a number of conclusions, especially where almost all the respondents made similar points. On their own, however, the quotations neither verify nor refute anything. A general analysis of the respondents is given in Appendix 6.

There is some useful information about Party members in the thirty-six volumes of biography and autobiography. These include autobiographies of ex-Communists, which ought to be treated with certain reservations. Many ex-Communists tend to react strongly and emotionally against the Party in a way which makes the information they give unreliable. As Almond has said in his study of ex-Communists,

the former Communist is hardly an unbiased reporter of his own experience. To point out that the faithful Communist would also be a prejudiced informant, although in another direction, does not eliminate the problem, but merely underlines the difficulties of getting reliable first-hand information about the Party.[18]

It is worth underlining the fact that although there are gaps in the published data, there is still a great deal of information which can be used and which is reliable insofar as there are no major internal discrepancies or inconsistencies. Some of this data has already been collected together in three valuable secondary sources which treat the B.C.P. from a historical angle.[19] The more constrained political atmosphere of many other Western countries prohibits their Communist Parties from publishing much useful information about themselves, and consequently the large number of books and articles on most Communist Parties in Western industrial societies suffer from a lack of hard facts. But the works on Communism in America, Australia, France, Italy, Sweden, Finland and Holland do provide a pool of comparative data.[20] In addition there is the thorough study by Almond, and his colleagues, of ex-Communists in France, Italy, Britain and America,[21] Selznick's work on Communist organizations,[22] and Leites's two volumes on the Bolshevik ideology.[23] The present study is intended to add to this pool of comparative data about Western Communism, and to further a sociological understanding of political radicalism.

Both the Communist and the anti-Communist will find material in this study which they may feel they can use for their own political ends. Be that as it may, the study is in no way intended to be a piece of political polemics. The sociologist should try to treat his evidence in the same way as the natural scientist treats his. He should be concerned with showing only what happens and why it happens, and not with showing what ought or ought not to happen. It is most emphatically not the job of the sociologist to judge the people and institutions he examines. Sociologists of Communism have often broken this first rule of sociology by mixing scientific methods with explicitly value-loaded conclusions. As far as possible, I have attempted to eliminate all value judgements, explicit and implicit, and to present a fair and honest account of the sociology of British Communism. It is up to the reader to form his own value judgements about the Party. No one else can do that for him.

1. In the 1964 general election 44,567 people voted for thirty-six Communist candidates. This amounted to 2·4 per cent of the votes in the constituencies contested by the Party, and 0·2 per cent of the national poll. In the same year the Party's central office calculated that it had 34,281 members. By comparison the Labour Party had about three-quarters of a million individual members, and received forty-four per cent of the votes in the 1964 general election. The Communist Party is roughly the same size as the Society of Friends or the Salvation Army, which had 21,126 and 42,064 members respectively

2. For two notable exceptions see G. A. Almond, *et al.*, *The Appeals of Communism* (Princeton, N.J.: Princeton University Press, 1954), and N. Glazer, *The Social Basis of American Communism* (New York: Harcourt, Brace, 1961). The latter is probably the best study of any Communist Party in the West

3. Macfarlane, 1966, p. 55

4. *World News and Views*, vol. 9, no. 26

5. Glazer, 1961, pp. 207–10

6. *World News*, vol. 5, no. 25, 21 June 1958

7. Some left-wing parties, like the Socialist Party of Great Britain, demand a knowledge of socialist principles before they allow applicants to become members

8. *The 20th National Congress Report*, 1947, p. 12

9. *Report of the Executive Committee to the 18th Congress of the Communist Party*, 1945

10. See Appendix 2

11. See Appendix 2. It has been calculated that the C.P. has about sixty full-time organizers, or about one organizer for every 570 members, and that the ratio in the Conservative Party and the Labour Party is about one to 1,500 and one to 3,000 respectively

12. *World News and Views*, 19 February 1944

13. Butler, 1963, p. 156

14. *Communist Review*, vol. 5, no. 3, 1933, p. 149

15. Figures from Nicholas, 1951, p. 325.

16. The Bolton Communist Party branch had less than fifty members in 1960 and the Glasgow one had 1,815 in the same year – *World News*, vol. 7, no. 51, 24 December 1960

17. *Communist Review*, vol. 6, no. 12, p. 440; vol. 7, no. 11, p. 211

18. Almond, 1954, p. xv

19. Pelling, 1958; Wood, 1959; Macfarlane, 1966

20. For studies of American Communism, see Draper, 1957, 1960; Howe and Coser, 1957; Iverson, 1959; Shannon, 1959; Roy, 1960; Record, 1951, 1958, 1959; Nolan, 1951; Ernst and Loth, 1952; Lasswell and Blumenstock, 1939.
For Australia, see Webb, 1955.
For France, see Caute, 1964; Cantril, 1962; Einaudi, Domenach and Garoschi, 1951; Stoetzel, 1955; Rossi, 1955; Micaud, 1955, 1963.
For Italy, see Cantril, 1962; Einaudi, Domenach, and Garoschi, 1951.
For Sweden, see Phillips Davison, 1955.
For Finland, see Allardt, 1962, 1962, 1964, 1965.
For Holland, see Stapel and de Yonge, 1948

21. Almond, *et al.*, 1954

22. Selznick, 1952

23. Leites, 1951, 1953

CHAPTER 2

THE COMMUNIST IDEOLOGY

Sociologists and historians have often tended to treat the Communist ideology as if it were a single unchanging set of ideas which was formulated by Marx, Engels and Lenin, and which has been handed down unaltered to each generation of Communists ever since. In effect such an approach implicitly assumes that one has only to look at the classics of Communist literature to discover what is believed by the millions of members of the various Communist Parties the world over. From this assumption it follows that all Communists believe in essentially the same political programme whether they are South American peasants or high officials of the C.P.S.U. The development of the ideological differences in the Sino–Soviet dispute and the resulting split of the world Communist camp into two major factions indicates that such an assumption is not justified, and that Marxism –Leninism means different things to different people in different times and places. Although Communism does not mean all things to all people, and although there are consistent themes to be found in the policies and ideologies of all Communist Parties, the job of determining what the members of any particular Communist Party actually believe can only be carried out satisfactorily by interviewing them, and by reading the very large quantity of literature which they produce in the form of newspapers, weekly reviews, journals and political pamphlets and leaflets. The classics are not to be ignored, however, especially when they are quoted in the Party's Press.

For comparative purposes it would be useful to contrast the ideology of British Communists with a model of the 'classical' Communist ideology. Such a model is presented by Almond in the first section of his book *The Appeals of Communism*.[1] Almond's main theme is that there is a sharp difference between the exoteric ideology of the Party, the ideology it presents for public consumption in the mass literature, and the esoteric ideology presented in the inner-Party journals and the Communist Party classics, for the benefit of the 'steel-hardened cadres'. While Marx and

Engels saw the leadership of the Party as being not so very different from the ordinary Communist, Lenin insisted that the revolutionary working class had to be led by a highly trained and disciplined élite which was dedicated, indoctrinated and organized for the purpose of manipulating and mobilizing the working class towards their eventual aim of the dictatorship of the proletariat – the monopolization of power. The most distinctive feature of the esoteric ideology is its emphasis on power. Everything is reduced to a matter of power tactics. The struggle for the eight-hour day, or for increased wages, or unemployment benefits, or reduced rents, are not ends in themselves. They must be seen as a preliminary skirmish before the final battle for power, and as a stage in the struggle which has the important function of organizing the working class behind important issues and heightening their class consciousness.

Quantitatively, non-power themes are quite minor in the classics, while the tactical themes of militance, rationality, organization, discipline and leadership are heavily stressed. The tone of the American *Daily Worker*, and of the British *Daily Worker* as well, is moral, while that of the Cominform's periodicals is tactical. The *Daily Worker* concentrates on local and national issues; its enemies are the police, the bourgeois Press and big business. It has little to say about the power-oriented tactician. The Cominform's periodicals elaborate on the image of the power-oriented tactician at considerable length, while its enemies are more generalized – capitalism, imperialism and Fascism. It also stresses the international aspect of Communism much more than the *Daily Worker*.

The esoteric ideology *does* tend to be the same at any given time or place, though it varies a little during 'popular-front' periods and the more sectarian 'social–fascist' periods. The exoteric ideology varies according to the characteristics of the areas in which the Party is operating. In Britain this ideology is to be found in the *Daily Worker*, the Party pamphlets and such periodicals as *Comment, Workers' Life, Party Life, World News*, the *Communist Review, Challenge, Labour Monthly* and the *Marxist Quarterly* – and many others. The content of the exoteric ideology also varies with time as social conditions change. From the exoteric ideology I have picked out the themes which seem to be most important to the political sociologist – the Communist attitude towards the state and its democratic system, towards revolution and the distribution of power and property, and towards industrial relations and industrial policy.

The membership of the British Communist Party, however, has never really concerned itself with the disputes over ideological theory and interpretation that have figured so largely in the histories of other European Parties. In fact, Lenin believed that it was a reluctance to theorize which held the British Communist Movement back.[2] It was the proud boast of many British socialists before 1917 that their socialism was of a unique, pragmatic, British kind and not a European one,[3] and even after its formation in 1920, the C.P.G.B. persisted for a time in using an ideology and an organization that was more British than Bolshevik.[4]

The Communist Party was supposed to be a Marxist Party, but there were very few in it who had more than a nodding acquaintance with the writings of Marx.[5]

The denunciation of Trotsky in 1924 was the cause of a major upheaval in the French Communist Party,[6] but it had much less impact on British Communists.[7] In 1925 the E.C.C.I. criticized the C.P.G.B. for its aversion to Marxist–Leninist theory.[8] The characteristics of tolerance, compromise and pragmatism have always been reflected, sometimes dimly and sometimes with surprising clarity, in the orientation of the British Communists. It has been told how a British delegate to a meeting of the Comintern provided the laugh of the year in Moscow when he objected to a policy because it would require lying.[9] Yet, at the same time, the B.C.P. has retained something of a sectarian nature by using its own vocabulary and mode of address, and, although the average British Communist could scarcely be described as a sophisticated Marxist–Leninist, the Party is, at the same time, one of the most successful in Britain when it comes to educating its members in the ideological basis of its politics.[10] In its own eyes it is not successful enough, for the person most concerned with the Party's Educational Department has gone on record as saying that some of those who have climbed quite high in the leadership are more ignorant than they ought to be of Communist political theory.[11]

The C.P.G.B. was formed during a period in which widespread unemployment, rapid social change, the dislocations of the 1914–18 war, and the impact of the Russian revolution of 1917, all added up to produce a widespread demand in Britain for social, political and economic reform. The Russian revolution of 1917 had a particularly strong influence. G. D. H. Cole commented that

in 1914 socialism still seemed a distant ideal; after 1917 it presented itself to men's minds as a real, immediate possibility. The capitalist system lost its inevitability; the sense of a positive alternative sank deeply into the minds of the active workers of the Labour movement.[12]

The Comintern was established on the assumption that the European working class was revolutionary in temper and needed only a truly revolutionary leadership to attain its objectives.[13] While Lenin considerably over-estimated the depth and extent of this revolutionary feeling, perhaps intentionally for propaganda purposes, he was not the only one who believed that Great Britain was on the verge of revolution in 1919.[14]

There were also good reasons why the Party was formed in 1920, rather than one or two years earlier or later. Since 1910 the working-class movement had relied more on industrial action than on political action, but in the early 1920s emphasis shifted back to political action to counteract the control exercised by the government over the basic industries during the war, and the government's attempts to control the post-war wave of strikes.[15] On top of this, the failure of the government to create a 'land fit for heroes', and an intense disappointment with the Labour Party, created conditions ripe for the formation of a new radical left-wing political party. An observer concluded from an analysis of the political scene in 1920 that 'Britain is faced by universal unrest in the working class and by the demand that economic power shall be shifted from the owners of capital to the worker'.[16]

In this kind of atmosphere it is not surprising that British Communists took a more radical line in the 1920s than they do now (and election statistics indicate that the C.P.G.B. was closer to the mood of the ordinary workman in the 1920s than it has ever been since).[17] One speaker at the Communist Unity Convention in 1920 claimed that the revolution was too near to try to convert the electorate to socialism. The C.P., he said, would have to act in the revolutionary situation first and talk afterwards.[18] Another delegate at the same Convention pointed out 'the historical and revolutionary value of the gun in the hands of the working class'.[19] The overall tone of the Convention, however, was somewhat more moderate than these two delegates would have wished. But it did repudiate 'the reformist view that social revolution can be achieved by the ordinary methods of parliamentary democracy', and regarded 'parliamentary and electoral action generally as providing a means of propaganda and agitation towards revolution'.[20] The majority of Communists at this time (or, indeed, at any other time in Britain) were not in favour of violence as a means to an end, but believed, and believed very strongly, that the revolution would have to defend itself against the bloodshed started by the counter-revolutionary middle class.

There is no record in history [insisted one writer in one of the earliest C.P. periodicals] of a ruling class being persuaded to destroy its own economic and political supremacy . . . the ruling class will resort to savage butchery, armed force, and tanks to defend itself against the revolution.[21]

The transition to Communism would involve civil war of some kind but that war would be caused by the middle class and its military, and not by the working class or the Communists.

Together with the period of social disorganization following the 1914–18 war went a certain amount of ideological confusion. The various Communist groups were not clearly distinguished from the Anarchist movement. The Cowdenbeath (Scotland) Anarchist group, for instance, issued a revolutionary and anti-parliamentary manifesto with the local Communist League, and in May 1920, the same Anarchist group changed its name to the Communist Party. On the other hand, the Glasgow Communist group changed its name to the Anti-Parliamentary Communist Federation.[22] Lenin remarked that the position of the Socialist Labour Party was very close to that of the Anarcho-Syndicalists on a number of issues.[23] Lenin, however, insisted that the Communist Party of Great Britain should not only use the parliamentary system as a propaganda platform, but also should become part of the Labour Party and support it as 'the rope supports a hanging man'.[24] The aim of this participation in the parliamentary system was to make it obviously contemptible and fraudulent. But many of the English Communists and most of the Anarcho-Syndicalists were unsure of the advice of Lenin and the Comintern. They were suspicious of anything to do with elections, parliament, and most of all of anything to do with the Labour Party. Gallacher, later a Communist M.P. for fifteen years, wrote:

At that time the Shop Stewards' Committee was still comparatively strong and I had little regard for parties and still less for parliament and still less for parliamentarians. I was the outstanding example of the 'left' sectarian . . .[25]

'Communists', said Gallacher, 'had something better to do than waste time over parliamentary elections.'[26]

Even after Lenin had persuaded the C.P.G.B. to put up candidates in the general elections, many factions were still anti-parliamentary. The anarchist Guy Aldred claimed 'that persons who are standing really and truly for Communism and speeding the Workers' Republic, are the anti-parliamentarians'.[27] Two years later he was still attacking the C.P.G.B., now in the process of its Second Congress, on the basis that 'the real pioneering Communist Organization in this country [i.e. the anti-parliamentary, revolutionary movement which dated from 1907] was not represented'.[28] While the anarchists never changed their views about parliament, British Communists came eventually to see it as democratic in some ways, and as such, worthy of participation and development. Lenin's warnings about bourgeois democracy were almost forgotten.

The Party's policy began to change soon after 1920. As early as 1925 there were complaints that the tactics and ideology suited to Russian conditions in 1917 could not be applied indiscriminately to the British political situation.[29] Marx had held that the British workers might possibly be able to achieve their ends by peaceful means, and perhaps the failure of the General Strike convinced the British Party that even the most serious disruptions could not produce a truly revolutionary situation and that the Party would have to work for more immediate ends. Its chronic failure to gain anything that might be described as mass support may also have led it to change its policy in order to attract more members. But the greatest influences on ideology since 1920 must have been the vastly improved working conditions and standard of living, a relatively more efficient and generous welfare state, and the reduction of unemployment, all of which have had the effect of reducing the sense of alienation and bitterness against the State, employers and the government. At any rate the position of British Communists in the 1960s is different from that in the 1920s. The

British political culture has overwhelmed the British Party, which has been forced to accommodate to the country's political traditions.

The belief that the Party is prepared to wage violent civil war at a moment's notice is quite inaccurate. In fact, the Communist means by 'revolution' simply 'the transfer of State power from one class to another.'[30] Although this transfer of power may be peaceful, it will, nevertheless, be revolutionary.[31] Revolution for the B.C.P. does not necessarily imply armed conflict, civil war and bloodshed, but the process in which the working class assumes a monopoly of economic and political power.[32] It recognizes that social, economic and political conditions have changed since the early 1920s, and it has always believed that political tactics ought to change to suit social conditions.[33] As a result it now holds that violence is not only unnecessary but also that the counter-revolutionaries are unlikely to resort to it.

The people in different countries led by the working class have taken power into their own hands in different ways, according to the conditions of their country and in the world as a whole. So also will the people of our country take power in their own way, on the basis of their historical conditions and traditions.[34]

Those Communists who were interviewed had no doubts that the counter-revolutionary forces would not use violence in the face of a democratic change of government, and that the Communist revolution would be a peaceful and democratic one.

We don't want a revolution in Marx's sense. We don't want a bloody revolution. [Student]

We couldn't build socialism in Britain without mass support and this means building it by democratic methods. [Railway Worker]

The working class can gain power by democratic means in Great Britain, though in South Africa, for instance, it might be different. [Electrician]

The democratic heritage in Britain is valuable and therefore change must come by modification with mass support to back it up. There will be a gradual build-up to a situation in which the government cannot rule because of the strength of the opposition. Then the Communist Party will take over. [Student]

It is just possible that the reactionary forces might resist but I think this is unlikely. The Communists won't start anything violent. [Teacher]

We believe in a peaceful revolution – the less violence there is the better it is for everyone. [Full-time Party worker]

Communists are not in favour of violence as a principle. [Middle-class housewife]

The British working class is so strong that the ruling class will have to give way, but unwillingly. [Bank clerk]

Violence is not, and never has been, with a very few exceptions, an implicitly or explicitly stated means of the British Communist Party. The only record of it being used on anything like a wide scale is in the Olympia Rally held by the British Union of Fascists in 1934, and in the demonstrations which followed in the East End of London in the years leading up to 1939.[35]

On the industrial side too, the policy of the Communists has changed markedly since 1920. The early members were unwilling to settle for anything less than the total re-structuring of society. Reform of the existing structure was thought to be grossly inadequate, for the capitalist system, even an improved one, could produce nothing but misery for the working class. In such a system the ruling class and the employers allowed only minor concessions, and these only to distract the working class from their final aim of establishing the Communist society. It was written: 'It is militancy which is called for in the movement; the silly kids' game of negotiating and arbitrating and finicking with industrial councils all operate in one way, to lower the worker's standards.'[36] Another claimed that higher wages and improved conditions amounted to 'little more than gilt on the chains'.[37] A little later, in 1926, a pamphlet warned the workers that they should oppose reforms whose effects were always temporary and which were often traps.[38]

However, soon after the C.P.G.B. was founded, the militance of the British working class waned[39] and so did that of the C.P.G.B. The Party became more and more moderate as social conditions and the standard of living improved.[40] Were the B.C.P. now to pursue such an anti-reformist, 'gilt on the chains' policy, it would promptly lose a very high proportion of its membership and support. Most of the Party's industrial policy is now geared to the things that the early comrades despised; to negotiating and arbitrating with employers.[41] This shift from the demand for nothing less than worker's control to militant bargaining corresponds to a somewhat similar shift in general British trade-union policy,[42] although most Communist trade unionists have always been more militant than non-Communist ones. Far from dismissing demands for higher wages and improved conditions as reformist, the Party now rates these among its main aims. A leader column in the *Daily Worker* states its opposition to any form of wage restraint,[43] and another article expresses the opinion that any form of wage restraint is simply a mechanism for keeping wages low and profits high.[44] The British Communist Party, like most other Communist and Socialist movements in Europe, has come to accept the philosophy of gradualism and piecemeal reform,[45] though the reforms it demands are still more radical than those of other political parties in Britain.

In effect the B.C.P. has come closer to Stalin's definition of a reformist party – 'a party which denies the socialist revolution and tries to establish socialism peacefully',[46] or, according to Gallacher's scornful statement, one whose aims are 'to maintain the existing capitalist system by diverting the workers' struggle for socialism with the granting of small reforms'.[47] Certainly it still demands widespread nationalization, but, at the same time, it is now prepared to work within the existing political structure until it has sufficient means to reform it. These reforms, by its older standards, are fairly minor – the abolition of the House of Lords and of the Monarchy – while, at the same time, it intends to change the economic foundations of society in order to make them more democratic.[48] The author of one book on the British Communist Party has concluded that

British Communism might become a potent political force instead of a trouble-making propaganda sect. But such a consequence might mean an end to the careers of the present leaders and to the comfortable routines which they have made for themselves. Formerly radical, vigorous and imaginative, now they are none of these things. They have grown conservative defending revolution.[49]

This gradual reduction of militancy and changes of policy over the past forty-six years have produced their own reaction. In 1963 the Committee to Defeat Revisionism, for Communist Unity (C.D.R.C.U.) broke away from the B.C.P. The C.D.R.C.U. may be regarded as a group of political schismatics intent on returning to the ideological purity of the founding fathers of Communism. They are doctrinal purists who regard the B.C.P.'s programme, as contained in *The British Road to Socialism*, as a reformist one 'of Fabian imperialism foisted on the Communists of Great Britain'.[50] The C.D.R.C.U. is a pro-Stalin and pro-Chinese group which has denounced Khruschev as 'the arch-revisionist, the great friend of U.S. imperialism and the biggest traitor to Communism of all time'.[51] In particular, the Committee pours scorn on the belief that the revolution will be a peaceful one. 'The capitalist state', wrote its former leader [an old Etonian with an Oxford degree, and son of a general], 'cannot be captured and transformed, it must be smashed.'[52] And finally, it denounced the leadership of the C.P.G.B. as having 'complete and utter contempt for the working class . . . their appeal is to petty bourgeois elements'.[53]

> The people's flag is palest pink
> It's not so red as you might think,
> It's time you prolies realised
> That Marx and Lenin we've revised.
>
> We've put an end to all class hate
> For we can now transform the state,
> You'll find you'll tote a lighter load
> If you will take our 'British Road'.
>
> Nikita's praises loudly sing
> Heed not the Marxists of Peking,
> The promise falls from Khruschev's lips
> Of goulash with your fish and chips.
>
> (George Shaw, *Vanguard*, vol. 1, no. 6, p. 15.)

There are no membership figures for the C.D.R.C.U., but it is only a tiny fraction of the size of the B.C.P., and probably has a larger proportion of middle-class intellectuals among its members.

While changing social conditions over the past forty years have produced concomitant change in ideology, so, also, the different social conditions of working-class and middle-class Communists lead the two groups to focus on different facets of their Party's ideology. The average British working-class Communist, like the average British working man, is outstandingly pragmatic in his political outlook.[54] His political vocabulary is made up mainly of such words as wages, working conditions, prices, speed-up, redundancy, housing, cost of living, overtime and unemployment. It is the B.C.P.'s attitude towards unemployment, industrial relations and the standard of living which attracts the working man, and not, as is frequently believed, the utopia-building and abstract theorizing, of which there is very little in any case.[55] One ex-Communist succinctly analyses the appeals which Communism held for him:

To me Communism was simply a fight against low wages and high rents, against slums, tuberculosis, rotten schools, ignorance and exploitation. It was only many years after I joined the Party that I began to see Communism as something more than the attempt to raise the standard of living.[56]

The approach of the working-class Communist is even less theoretical than that of his middle-class comrades; he reads fewer of the Communist classics, understands less of them, and in many cases, is little more than a militant trade unionist. 'The Party does not appear before the workers as an organized, all round political force, but more typically as a group of workshop militants.'[57] As one District secretary of the B.C.P. said in an interview, 'There is a great gap between the support for a Communist as a militant trade unionist and support for the same man as a member of a political party with a philosophy and a world view of its own'. Phil Piratin, a successful Communist candidate in the general election of 1945, has gone as far as to say that although the Communist programme was an important factor in his election, it was, all the same, 'essentially, as understood by the electorate, not so very different from that of the Labour Party'.[58]

The middle-class members, though not much more concerned with the subtleties of Marxism–Leninism, tend to be more concerned than the working-class Communist with the moral and ideological facets of Communism; they use more abstract political slogans. They supplement the interests of the working-class Communists in purely economic matters and national problems by such notions as justice, human dignity, equality and freedom. The C.P. appeals to the idealistic and humanitarian strains of the middle-class social conscience. As Wood has said, 'Communism at least appears to offer something to men who can be moved by an appeal to the reasonable and humanitarian'.[59] A trenchant critic of Communism has allowed that 'there is no doubt that the Marxist ideology can appeal to men moved by a large and genuine compassion'.[60] Typical of this kind of approach to the Party is that of Freda Utley, whom Bertrand Russell described as 'a romantic about politics.[61] In her autobiography she writes,

The concept of human freedom formed the axis of my socialist beliefs. . . . I was in revolt against tyranny and oppression . . . in my mind Pericles' funeral speech, Shelley's and Swinburne's poems, Marx's and Lenin's writings were all part and parcel of the same striving for the emancipation of mankind from oppression.[62]

Such a Communist does not, of course, ignore the Party's programme on industrial and domestic affairs but is equally interested in, and moved by, international affairs and general political principles.

Between 1935 and 1942 the number of Communists in Britain increased enormously (from 5,800 to about 50,000) and a high proportion of these new recruits were middle-class. The Party had gained a large number of new members, mostly unemployed working-class people and especially South Wales miners, during the most acute period of economic depression between 1931 and 1932, but had lost these recruits almost as promptly when they became employed again. A new influx of members started in 1935 and the membership figures continued to climb steeply until 1942. That an unusually large proportion of these recruits were middle-class is indicated by the fact that the number of student Communist organizations and intellectual left-wing groups increased considerably in the 1930s. In 1931 Communist organizations were established at Cambridge University, at University College, London, and at the L.S.E.; Oxford's October Club was founded in 1932 and had 300 members a year later; by 1938 the Cambridge Socialists Club had 1,000 members, or one in five of the student population.[63] A year later the inter-university Student Labour Federation had 3,500 members.[64] The number and sales of left-wing intellectual journals increased as well. The circulation of the *Labour Monthly* expanded from 4,500 in 1934 to 6,500 in 1936.[65] The *Left Review*, standing for 'militant communism' first appeared in 1934 and a year later had a monthly sale of 3,000 copies.[66] The Left Book Club and its bulletin *Left News* was launched. In 1937 the *Modern Quarterly* was founded with five F.R.S.s on its Editorial Council.[67] Numerous other left-wing political and cultural journals sprang up – *Cambridge Left*, the *Week*, *Plan*, *New Verse*, *Storm*, Middleton Murray's the *Wanderer*, *Controversy* which became *Left* and then *Forum*, and *New Writing* which became eventually *New Writing and Daylight*.[68]

The interest of the middle class and intellectuals in left-wing radicalism coincided with the rise of Fascism in Italy, of Nazism in Germany, with the growing strength of the British Union of Fascists in Britain, and with the Spanish Civil War and the threat that it would spread. The Spanish Civil War crystallized many people's political ideas into a neat black and white, Fascist versus anti-Fascist pattern. It had the effect of polarizing the choice between the radical left and the radical right.[69] Many of the new Party recruits at this time were more anti-Fascist than they were Communist,[70] and they joined because the C.P.G.B., up until 1939, could claim to lead the anti-Fascist movement.

It is often found written that Communism has the appeal of a millennial religion.[71] It is difficult to judge whether this is true of the B.C.P.'s membership even after long interviews, but there seem to be very few who have a faith of a religious nature in Communism. Only one of the people interviewed seemed to come near to this religious style of adherence to Communism.

Joining the C.P. was the biggest step forward I ever made in my whole life. It was like going from darkness into light. [Office clerk]

Blind faith in scientific socialism is fairly rare in the British Party, for the working-class members are not interested in building a new utopia but only in improving their present standard of living. The middle class, with a few exceptions, are no more intent on 'the assault of heaven' although they do phrase their conversations about politics in more generalized terms than their working-class comrades. Lenin insisted that 'our teaching is not a dogma but a guide to action',[72] and most members of the B.C.P. will agree with Lenin.

There is a great deal of information in the interviews to support and illustrate this distinction between the working-class pragmatists and the middle-class idealists, but limitation of space will permit only two examples. The first is a graduate and teacher from a Conservative and middle-class family background. She said:

The first thing that interested me about the Party was the idea of a scientifically planned society, but now the emphasis of my interest has shifted and I'm more concerned with human happiness. I think the Party talks a bit too much about economics and efficiency and leaves ordinary human happiness out of things a bit. I want to see man rise to his full stature and to eliminate the barriers which prevent him from doing it in this society. People are stunted – literature and art should flourish freely – this is where I part company with the Russians. The idea of the full development of the individual is the main-spring behind all the little mundane tasks we undertake – struggles over wages and rents. It's so that people can have things that they are denied now – books, concerts, plays, sport, freedom, happiness. Understanding as well. This is our universe and we can explore it. That's what we're working for.

The second example is a full-time Party worker who had been an office clerk after leaving school at fourteen. His father had been a Party member for many years.

Until I was three or four our standard of living bordered on slum conditions. My father was a skilled engineer but he had one period of eighteen months' unemployment and other periods of some weeks or months. After that our conditions improved but only because of the sheer hard work and sacrifices of my parents.

I suppose we had an average standard of living for the pre-war working class. Standards improved a lot but not as much as they should or could have done. In 1945 I left the army but couldn't get into any apprenticeship scheme. From my own experience I knew that the system was wrong and the Y.C.L. was the only organization which offered plausible answers.

Besides the working-class pragmatists and the middle-class idealists there are also the Communist professionals – 'the steel-hardened cadres' – who have been exposed to, and assimilated, the esoteric doctrine. Their political vocabulary is made up of words like militance, tactics, strategy, discipline, leadership, organization, activism, élite, dedication and power.[73] Books such as Philip Selznick's *The Organisational Weapon*, and, to a lesser extent, W. Kornhauser's *The Politics of Mass Society* treat most Communists as if they were of this professional type. In fact the steel-hardened cadres seem to form only a small minority of the membership of the B.C.P., albeit the most influential section of its leadership. The difference between the pragmatist, the idealist and the professional is considerable. In the view of one ex-member,

The fact is that the average C.P. member was absolutely genuine in his devotion to socialism and really had no idea of what his leaders were up to. His world was vastly different from that of the regiment of full-timers concentrated in the Party headquarters in King Street, London. . . . It was assumed that the Party was pure and unspotted and, in fact, there were always enough people of that order in a local area to make this assessment convincing to those who were willing to take it as they found it.[74]

The professional, however, is quite willing to believe with Lenin that 'our morality is entirely subordinate to the interests of the class struggle of the proletariat . . . we subordinate our Communist morality to this task'.[75]

Lenin's comments on political morality raise the subject of the relationship between Communist means and ends. The Communist ideology is, above all, a this-worldly one and it uses the means of this-worldly politics. It is an 'ethic of responsibility', a *realpolitik*, and not an 'ethic of ultimate ends'. It does, of course, strive after an ideal and ultimate end, but in pursuing it, Communist leaders take into account the consequences of political actions, the motives of other political leaders and the deficiencies of human beings in their political roles, rather than aiming at morally ideal actions over a short period of time.[76] Such an approach to politics is incompatible with the political principles of the Communist idealists.

The problems which the use of this-worldly power tactics presents for the Party's idealists will be discussed in Chapter 8. Meanwhile it can be said that the way in which some Communist idealists structure their ideology helps them to accept those Communist Party actions which are based on the tactics of the 'ethic of responsibility'. The Communist ideology can easily become a 'closed' ideology which uses all political events as evidence to confirm the Marxist view of the world – even those events which seem to non-Communists to defy or contradict a Communist interpretation.[77] As one respondent said: 'In Marxism politics is total. And as far as I can see Marxism explains most things more or less satisfactorily.' Similarly, there are clauses in the ideology which can be used to justify all Communist Party action – even those actions which seem to most non-Communists to run against the grain of Communist beliefs. The crisis in Hungary in 1956 is an outstanding example, and put a great strain on the Communist beliefs of some of the idealists in the British Party.

The steel-hardened cadres, who have internalized the esoteric ideology, are more strongly committed to the cause than are the pragmatists and especially the idealists, who sometimes find it very difficult to accept Party policy and action. However, the Party leadership can always summon up a quotation from Marx or Lenin to explain that what it is doing is both inevitable and essential for the good of the movement. In particular, the leadership can reiterate Lenin's insistence that tactics must mesh with social conditions and that the Party must act according to particular political situations. In this way the Party can always vindicate its actions. This is the safety valve, the escape hatch of practical Communism. All successful ideologies, and especially those with as great a scope and pervasiveness as Communism, have such a safety valve in one form or another. By using it, the Party can claim Marxist ideological orthodoxy. In practical politics theorizing is rare, but as Rossi has said: 'Orthodoxy in the sphere of ideas is the counterpart of discipline in the sphere of action'.[78] The British Party, it has been argued, is more theoretically inclined than any of the major political groups in Britain. Nevertheless, among the small, radical left-wing groups in Britain there are several brands of revolutionary orthodoxy, each claiming a monopoly of the correct reading and interpretation of the authoritative sources.[79]

How does the average British Communist reconcile the somewhat grandiose aims of the Party's political programme with the comparatively tiny size of its membership? The average British Communist rarely asks himself this question. He spends much of his time with other Party members or with people who have very similar political ideas. Over three quarters of the respondents said that most of their friends were either members or sympathizers of the C.P. In this situation it is very easy to form a false picture of the power of the Party.[80] Realization that the Party is very small is usually accompanied by a belief that it takes only a small number of dedicated and active people to get things done.

The Party is the pinch of yeast which leavens the masses of the working class movement. [Research scientist]

The Party's influence on trade unions is quite considerable on some issues, though it is limited by bans on Communists, and right-wing obstruction. . . . Our influence on the country's foreign policy is quite significant, especially at times of crisis. We inspire much that finally appears as part of the Labour Party and trade-union official policy. . . . At times our influence on local affairs is very marked indeed – on issues such as housing and rates and bus fares, we have a lot to say. [Primary-school teacher]

Oh, we may be small, but we have a lot of influence on the trade unions and on the country's domestic policy. . . . Although we apply pressure on the country's foreign policy, it is not enough to alter it to any great extent. In this area the influence on local affairs is small, but in other places, where the Party is better organized, it is much, much bigger. [Office clerk]

The smaller the Party became the more we consoled ourselves with the *quality* that remained.[81]

Analytically, this reduction of interest in the main aims of classical Communism to small victories is equivalent to a shift of emphasis from the expressive to the programmatic elements of the ideology. This accommodation of ideology and activity to the real position of the B.C.P. is one aspect of the main movement of the ideology from a revolutionary one towards an innovationist one, with only comparatively minor revolutionary elements. It is also an aspect of the shift of the focus of interest of individual members to goals which, twenty years ago, would have been seen at best as fairly minor questions, and by-products of the surge towards the total proletarian victory which was expected and demanded. The Party leadership itself has encouraged this change of focus by publicizing and magnifying the importance of small successes and gains in Party support. Thirty-six *Daily Workers* were sold, it will say, at such-and-such a factory, or, this or that branch has recruited eight new members in the past few weeks, or, these candidates have increased their vote in the general election (though all the other Communist candidates may have lost votes on the previous election's showing).[82] On the other hand there is a strong consciousness of being one member of an international organization of millions, and this helps maintain morale at a tolerably high level.

Other members do come to see the Party as a powerless political sect, and, in some cases, they believe the solution to the problem to be not a further accommodation to the moderate views of the majority of working people, but the renewal of the old revolutionary policy. The members of the C.D.R.C.U. believe that the B.C.P. has failed to become a mass party because its policy is not distinguishable from that of the Labour Party. By returning to a militant and revolutionary ideology, it believes that it can successfully lead the masses back to the proper British road to socialism. The C.D.R.C.U. will also have to come to terms with political conditions, unless these change radically. At the moment the esoteric and the exoteric ideologies of the C.D.R.C.U. are the same, and they are much closer to Almond's model of the classical ideology than the British Communist Party has been for a long time.

How, then, does the British Party and the ideology of its members compare with Almond's esoteric model ? In its early years the Party was certainly less reformist than it is now. It believed in the possibility of, and was intent on pursuing, the final goal of the dictatorship of the proletariat. This was the essence of the revolutionary 'gilt on the chains' attitude which insisted that the state and its worthless pseudo-democracy had to be smashed. The Party now believes that the state can be transformed and that peace, democracy and freedom and the interests of the working class can be attained without substituting a new social system but by modifying the existing one. The contemporary working-class pragmatist and the middle-class idealist pick their own themes from the exoteric ideology. Few Party members have been exposed to, or understood, or assimilated the pure, esoteric ideology of the Communist militant.

Almond found that as Communist recruits were drawn deeper and deeper into the Party, so they were exposed to elements of the esoteric doctrine. They became ideologically sophisticated as they began to learn something of the rudiments of Communist political theory and analysis and of the Party's aims and methods. There is ample evidence in the interviews to support this picture of politicization. The respondents would say 'I joined for emotional reasons but now my understanding of society and of Marxism has increased', or, 'Being in the Party has done a lot for my understanding of things – it has broadened and deepened. I've more intellectual and solid reasons for being in the Party. I know more about scientific Marxism which has been a great intellectual liberator.' As the present General Secretary himself has said, 'Joining the Party is often only the first step in becoming a Communist'.[83] In fact the majority of members seem to be recruited on the basis of a single issue which the Party has fought with him and for him – unemployment, eviction, rent increases, racialism, victimization or 'a bastard of a boss'. The psychologist Hadley Cantril has suggested that 'an individual generally joins or votes for the [French or Italian] Party because of the concrete experiences he had had and not simply because he has intellectually arrived at a "logical truth".'[84] It is because the C.P. works harder for him than any other organization that he joins it. As one District secretary said, 'It is only to the extent that the Party is active that it is successful and is able to recruit'.

Frequently the new recruit loses interest in the Party when his immediate problem has been solved. Hence the Party's high membership turnover. But if the recruit stays in the Party he soon learns that his particular problem was only one aspect of the class struggle. If he joins because the Party has fought with him against a rent increase, then he begins to find out that an increase in bus fares is one way of 'keeping the workers down'. He learns how to fit his problem into a general plan which explains all social problems. Generally, he does not join because he is in sympathy with the Communist ideology – he may know little or nothing about it – but he learns about the ideology once he is in the Party. He joins as a result of an event in his personal life which has a traumatic effect, and he may leave only after another event which has as great a traumatic effect – Hungary, de-Stalinization, anti-Semitism in the Soviet Union, Inner Party Democracy. But his belief system may be so structured that all these events can be interpreted in such a way that they support the Communist view of the world. In this case he may accept the view that the events in Hungary were engineered by Fascist counter-revolutionaries, or that reports of anti-Semitism in the Soviet Union are capitalist lies. It is this 'closed' or 'come-what-may' element which helps to preserve the Communist ideology, and most other ideologies as well, as a major force in world politics.

Even so, few members who have been in the Party, even for a long period of time, come to understand the mentality of the power-oriented, steel-hardened cadres portrayed in the esoteric ideology. It is difficult to know how closely even the Party leadership conforms to the esoteric model. After all, their speeches and writings are intended for public consumption as elaborations of the exoteric ideology. One can only guess, and the writer's guess is that few of the B.C.P.'s élite conform to the classical, esoteric ideal.

It is easy to overstate the differences between the pragmatists and the idealists. Some working-class Communists are more typically idealist in their ideology, and some middle-class members are more like the pragmatists. Nevertheless, there is a tendency for the working-class members to cluster at the pragmatic end of the exoteric ideological continuum, and for the middle-class members to be distributed at the idealist end. The distinction between cadres, idealists and pragmatists suggests that these different types of Communist join the Party for different reasons. In this case, the original question which provided the main point of departure for the study should be broken down into two questions. The question of, 'Why do people join the C.P. and leave it?' must become firstly: 'Why do working-class people join the C.P. and leave it?', and secondly: 'Why do middle-class people join the C.P. and leave it?'

Although the B.C.P. is small, minute compared with some, it has all the same managed to operate continuously against considerable odds ever since 1920. Its imminent death has been forecast on a number of occasions when political events have chopped its membership figures to dangerously low numbers. Each time it has recovered. The main body of the study will be concerned with how and why the B.C.P. has managed to maintain itself.

1. Almond, et al., 1954, pp. 1–179. See also Leites, 1951, 1953, and Selznick, 1952
2. Lenin, 1959, p. 35
3. Bell, 1941, pp. 251–61
4. Klugmann, Marxism Today, 1960. In 1943, with the dissolution of the Comintern, the title of the Communist Party of Great Britain was changed to the British Communist Party
5. Murphy, 1941, p. 181
6. Caute, 1964, pp. 81–92

7. Pelling, 1958, p. 45; Macfarlane, 1966, pp. 92–3
8. H.M.S.O. Cmd 2682, p. 33
9. Silone, in Crossman, 1950, p. 109
10. Hobsbawm, 1954. See also, *Report of the Executive Committee to the 28th National Congress*, B.C.P. 1962, pp. 12–13, and Macfarlane, 1966, pp. 13–45
11. Klugmann, 'Education for the Main Debate of the Day', *World News*, 1960. See also Borkenau, 1962, p. 181
12. Cole, 1948, p. 282
13. Degras, in Footman, 1960, p. 9
14. Ransome, 1919, p. 79
15. Pribićević, 1959, pp. 162–3
16. Gleason, 1920, p. 15
17. In the general elections of 1922, 1923 and 1924, 23·2 per cent, 25·3 per cent and 19 per cent of the electorate voted for the Communist candidates in the constituencies in which they stood. The Party put up only seven, nine and eight candidates, however. See Appendix 4
18. *The Communist Unity Convention Report, 1920*, C.P.G.B., 1920, p. 7
19. *The Communist Unity Convention Report, 1920*, C.P.G.B., 1920, pp. 7–8
20. *The Communist Unity Convention Report, 1920*, C.P.G.B., 1920, p. 29
21. Paul, 1921, p. 14. See also Campbell, 1928, p. 14 and A. MacManus, *The Communist Unity Convention Report, 1920*, C.P.G.B., 1920, p. 5
22. Aldred, 1943
23. Lenin, 1959, p. 600. The S.L.P. was the largest of the various groups which came together to form the C.P.G.B. in 1920
24. Lenin, 1947, pp. 623–4
25. Gallacher, 1936, p. 253
26. Carr, 1950, p. 170
27. G. A. Aldred, the *Communist*, May 1919
28. G. A. Aldred, the *Spur*, 21 February 1921
29. Philips-Price, 1925, p. 12
30. Lenin, quoted in Morton, 1963, p. 72
31. Morton, 1963, p. 79
32. See, for example, *Communism and the World Today*, B.C.P., 1963
33. See, for example, J. Gollan, 'Which Road?' *Marxism Today*, July 1964, pp. 198–216. This article by the General Secretary of the B.C.P., together with its policy statement, *The British Road to Socialism*, are the two most important documents in the postwar history of the Party. The latter defines its attitude towards the Sino–Soviet dispute. Yet in spite of the belief that policies ought to be adapted to national conditions, the B.C.P. has probably never been given enough room to formulate its own policy to suit British conditions
34. *The British Road to Socialism*, B.C.P., 1958, p. 10. See also Gollan, 1963. Officially, the Party continued to believe in the inevitability of violent civil war until at least 1953 and most probably until the postwar period of reorganization
35. See Cross, 1961, and Piratin, 1948, for accounts of these events
36. Mann, 1923
37. Lawrence, 1923
38. *Communism is Commonsense*, C.P.G.B. pamphlet, 1926
39. Arnot, undated, p. 12, and Murphy, 1934, p. 209
40. Similar changes accompanying improved social conditions are noted by Lorwin, 1958, and by Legget, 1964
41. See, for example, Campbell, 1963
42. Knowles, 1952, p. xi
43. *Daily Worker*, 2 September 1963

44. Jarvie, 1963, p. 2
45. Lipset, 1964
46. Stalin, 1943, vol. 4, p. 133
47. Gallacher, 1949, p. 80
48. Gallacher, 1949, p. 206
49. Wood, 1959, p. 224
50. *Vanguard*, vol. 1, no. 1, p. 2
51. *Vanguard*, vol. 1, no. 5, p. 1C
52. M. McCreery in his introduction to Evans, 1964, p. ii
53. *Vanguard*, vol. 1, no. 1, p. 10
54. Almond and Verba, 1963, p. 253; Almond, 1954, p. 230
55. 'Marxism', claims the leading Party theorist, 'is always concrete; it deals with living, concrete situations and practical problems, never plays with formulas in a vacuum.' - Palme-Dutt, 1963
56. Darke, 1953, p. 21
57. *Comment*, 23 February 1963, Supplement, p. 1. See also, Almond, 1954, pp. 104–6, p. 230
58. Piratin, 1948, p. 79
59. Wood, 1959, p. 111
60. MacRae, 1961, p. 197
61. Utley, 1949, p. 11
62. Utley, 1949, p. 36
63. Wood, 1959, pp. 51–2. In 1935 the Cambridge University Party Branch was supposed to have had 180 members – *Communist International*, vol. 12, 1935, p. 809. It had about fifteen members thirty years later
64. Wood, 1959, p. 52
65. Pelling, 1958, p. 54
66. Wood, 1959, pp. 58–9
67. Pelling, 1958, p. 81
68. Wood, 1959, pp. 57–60
69. See, for example, Foote, 1953, p. 11. Foote, a Russian spy, was never a member of the B.C.P.
70. See, for example, Haldane, 1949, p. 269
71. Cf. MacRae, 1961, p. 185; Monnerot, 1953
72. Quoted in Pollitt, 1945, p. 1
73. Almond, 1954, Chapter 1. For what amounts to no more than a caricature of this type of Communist, see Hoffer, 1964
74. Cadogan, 1961. Barbu, who was acquainted with both Russian and Western Party members, was 'surprised how far the Western Communists differ from the true Bolshevik type' – Barbu, 1956, p. 193. See also Koestler, 1954, p. 382
75. Lenin, 1947, p. 667
76. Gerth and Mills, 1957, pp. 118–28
77. For a full discussion of the meaning of 'closed' see Rokeach, 1960, and Chapter 8
78. Rossi, 1955, p. 209
79. 'The C.P.G.B. has never *fully* mastered dialectical materialism, the Marxist view of the world, in the sense that it never proved itself capable of applying the generally agreed principles of Leninism to British conditions' (*Vanguard*, vol. 1, no. 1, p. 1). Besides the B.C.P. and the C.D.R.C.U., there is also the Trotskyite Socialist Labour League, the Socialist Party of Great Britain, the Syndicalist Workers' Federation, the Independent Labour Party, and a number of other smaller factions and splinter groups, often with a membership of tens rather than hundreds, including the Revolutionary Socialist League, the Revolutionary Workers' Party, the Socialist Review group and the Solidarists

80. This is probably true of most other people who are dedicated to a cause, whether political, social or religious, and who live most of their lives within a single organization or group of people

81. Murphy, 1941, p. 182

82. In some cases this magnification of small successes reaches the level of almost ludicrous distortion. 'Nothing has hit West Perthshire like Hugh MacDiarmid's campaign has done since the forays of Rob Roy. . . . People who sneered at the idea of a Communist campaign in this "safe" Tory seat and even those who considered it a brave but useless gesture are amazed at the growing support and the crowded lively meetings.' (*Daily Worker*, 3 October 1964, p. 5). On polling day Hugh MacDiarmid collected 127 votes

83. J. Gollan, *World Marxist Review*, August 1961

84. Cantril, 1962, p. 93

CHAPTER 3

THE INFLUENCE OF UNEMPLOYMENT

A principal claim of the Communist ideology is that capitalist systems produce increasingly disastrous economic crises and increasing misery for the working-class. Since Communists claim to have found a solution to economic problems of this kind, it might be expected that Communism will have an especially strong appeal for the unemployed victims of economic depressions. Not unexpectedly, sociological research has shown that support for radical groups of many kinds does grow during periods of widespread unemployment.[1] But research has also shown that although some of the unemployed do develop radical attitudes, others remain political moderates, or withdraw from social and political activity to become isolated and apathetic.[2] On the one hand it is said that:

Political action does not rank high among the tactics adopted by the unemployed as a means of solving their problems. In view of the limited part played by politics in the life of the unemployed this is not surprising.[3]

On the other hand, Almond reports that twenty-eight per cent of the British ex-Communists interviewed for his study joined the Party partly because of unemployment experiences.[4] The different reactions of the unemployed to their situation are described by Hilda Jennings in her study of Brynmawr, a South Wales mining village which suffered acutely during the depression of the 1930s.

One man will approach the [employment] Exchange with impatience and bitterness at his dependence and impotence to help himself; one in a mood to find cause of complaint and irritation with the officials; one with growing apathy and with no conscious feeling except when his pay is threatened; one, again, with each visit, feels a need for a change in the economic and social system; his political conscience is aflame, and he will fumble in his mind for an alternative, or shout the current formula at the next 'unemployment' or 'party' meeting, according to his mental outlook and capacity.[5]

After analysing over one hundred research reports on unemployment, Eisenberg and Lazarsfeld have argued that the unemployed pass successively through seven stages, or psychological states, in their adjustment to their predicament. They list the defining characteristics of the stages as: (1) injury, fear and anger; (2) apathy; (3) calming down and activity; (4) futility; (5) hopelessness and fear; (6) acquiescence and apathy; (7) fatalism and restrictions of desires.[6] An examination of these characteristics suggests that only two stages, the first and the third, are conducive to radical activity, and that people passing through the other five stages will tend to withdraw from political activity. Consequently it is reasonable to suppose that only a small proportion of the unemployed at any given time will be predisposed to join the Communist Party, or any other type of radical group.

The graph (p. 33), which traces the fluctuation of Communist Party membership figures against unemployment figures, shows that periods of high unemployment are usually accompanied by an increased rate of recruitment into the Party. One of the first circulars of the C.P.G.B. called upon its members to support the struggle of the militant organizations of the unemployed.[7] Much of the later history of the Party is bound up with unemployment, for five of the six main periods of increasing unemployment in Britain since 1924 (1924–6; 1929–32; 1937–8; 1945–7; 1951–2; 1956–9) have been followed very shortly afterwards by an accelerated rate of recruitment into the C.P. The larger and more sudden the increase, the more noticeable is the effect on the Party's membership figures. In 1932, with twenty-two per cent of the insured workers unemployed, Party membership totalled 9,000 but only two years earlier, with ten per cent of the insured workers unemployed, the membership was about 2,600. Other Communist Parties increased their membership during the depression also. The C.P.U.S.A. doubled its membership between 1930 and 1932,[8] and there were similar increases in Italy and France,[9] and Australia.[10] It has also been noted that industries which have a high proportion of Communists in their ranks tend to be economically unstable.[11] The Communists themselves have long recognized that periods of unemployment are favourable times for recruiting drives, and the Party has generally been more active among the unemployed than other political groups. In the post-First World War depression 'the bulk who threw their energies into their [the unemployed] protection were the Communists'.[12] In the 1930s the failure of the Labour Party to crusade militantly on behalf of those struck by the depression left the field free for the C.P. and its subsidiary organization, the N.U.W.M.[13]

Thirteen of the twenty-seven Communists interviewed had experienced some personal or family unemployment, mostly in the 1930s. In seven cases the respondents themselves had been unemployed, and in the remaining six it was the respondent's father. The periods of unemployment ranged from

Communist Party Membership and Unemployment

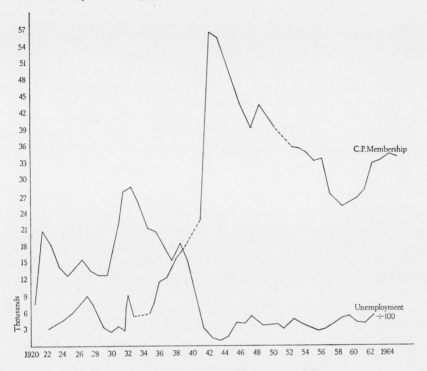

UNEMPLOYMENT FIGURES: SOURCES
1920–47, Cole, 1948, p. 481
1948–62, Min. of Lab. 1962, p. 471
– – – – Figures not available

4–8 months (in most cases) to 3–6 years. Two respondents believed that unemployment experiences had little or no effect on their political attitudes.

My father [who was a Party member for many years] was unemployed for about six months in the thirties, but I don't think it affected him at all. I'm fairly sure it didn't. [Teacher]

I was unemployed on three occasions for about three months each time, but I was a seaman and we expected lags between ships. I got away quite lightly, I suppose. [Journalist]

In other cases unemployment was a traumatic event which has never been forgotten and whose return is constantly feared.

My father was an invalid. He couldn't work. We lived in extreme poverty. I was always conscious of it. . . . I've been unemployed for three years altogether. My living conditions are better now than they've ever been before, but there's always the considerable degree of uncertainty. [Railway worker]

The first stage of analysis shows quite clearly that unemployment is closely associated with Communist attitudes and behaviour. But there are other figures which throw doubt on this bald conclusion. Although there is a high and positive correlation between the number of unemployed and the total number of Communists, the actual numbers of those involved with the C.P. is very small indeed compared with the total number out of work. At the end of 1930 the British Party calculated that nineteen per cent of its members were jobless.[14] In December 1932, sixty per cent were unemployed.[15] Some of these unemployed Communists were victimized – they had lost their jobs because of their political opinions[16] – but the majority had joined the Party because they had lost their jobs. From the 1930 percentage of unemployed Communists it can be calculated that only 3,140 of the unemployed had joined the C.P., whereas the total number of insured unemployed workers was 2,717,000. The available unemployment figures include only the insured unemployed. When the uninsured workers are added on, it is clear that an even smaller minority of the unemployed saw political action inside the C.P. as a viable solution to their problem. As the leader of the Comintern sadly commented in 1923:

If we take into account the great amount of unemployment and suffering of the English proletariat, the slow development of Communism in Britain is remarkable.[17]

The Communist-run National Unemployment Workers' Movement (N.U.W.M.), which was the largest organization for the unemployed, never had a standing membership of more than ten per cent of the total (insured and uninsured) unemployed at any given time, although its leader claimed that millions passed through the movement during its history.[18] At the end of 1921 the N.U.W.M. had a contributing membership of 100,000,[19] but at the same time about two million insured were unemployed. The great majority of the unemployed had little to do with political parties or the N.U.W.M.[20]

During periods of economic prosperity only a small proportion of the unemployed are Communists. According to the four District officials interviewed, the number of unemployed Communists in the 1960s is negligible. Using the reports of the Credentials Committees as an indicator to check their information, it can be calculated that only about one per cent of British Communists were unemployed during 1961 and 1962.[21] From the same source, it can be calculated that about 0·8 per cent of the unemployed were Communists in 1963. There were about ten times as many Communist school-teachers as there were unemployed Communists.[22]

So far it has been shown that only a very small proportion of the unemployed join the B.C.P., but the relationship between unemployment and radicalism has not yet been adequately explored. Perhaps the unemployed in Britain are more typically attracted by right-wing political radicalism or religious radicalism. The figures, however, suggest that this is not the case. Sir Oswald Mosley's British Union of Fascists was the largest and most active right-wing party during the thirties, and it was smaller even than the C.P.G.B. It probably never had more than 5,000 members.[23] Similarly there was no great increase in the membership of at least two radical religious sects. A period of successful revival for the Elim Foursquare Gospel Church coincided with the depression, but at the same time, it recruited fewer members than it had done in the 1920s.[24] The increase in the number of Christadelphians in the 1920s and 1930s does not seem to have been affected by widespread unemployment.[25] In fact, comparatively few of the unemployed resort to political or religious radicalism. This is because the frame of mind of the recruit to a radical organization and that produced by a long spell of unemployment are at the polar ends of the apathy-activism continuum. While the Communist ideology is based on the firm belief that man can and must control completely his own social affairs, unemployment tends to reduce an individual's desire and belief in his ability to determine his own destiny.[26] Consequently apathy and withdrawal are the typical modes of response.[27] It has also been suggested that trade-union and unemployment benefits have served to reduce the susceptibility to radical appeals,[28] although in America it has been found that discontent was greater among the unemployed receiving public relief than among those without it.[29]

Although the majority of the unemployed may not become active political participants, they do tend to change their political attitudes,[30] and become more class-conscious.[31] Left-wing political parties did not recruit a high proportion of the unemployed, but they did increase their election votes. The average vote for the Labour Party parliamentary candidates increased from 12,900 in 1931 to 15,500 in the general election of 1935.[32] In the latter election, the C.P., following a united front policy of support for the Labour Party, contested only two seats. In both constituencies an increased percentage of the votes went to the Communist candidates compared with 1931, and Gallacher was elected for West Fife.

Unemployment seems to be an important factor creating the social basis of radicalism, but there are others which, under certain circumstances, may override or cross-pressure the effects of economic depression. At the end of the Second World War unemployment figures were the lowest for the century in Britain, yet purely political events pushed the B.C.P.'s membership figures to the highest of the century. There were 45,435 Communists in 1945, but only 9,000 in January 1932. On the other hand, in 1956 when unemployment figures were rising to a post-war peak, political events in the Communist camp at home and abroad cut the Party's membership by approximately one third. Yet the B.C.P. started increasing its membership again in 1959, which was surprisingly soon after Hungary, the C.P.S.U.'s Twentieth Congress and the B.C.P.'s Inner Party Democracy controversy.

It may be that the continued and comparatively high unemployment figures were partially responsible for this increase.

Other than Eisenberg and Lazarsfeld's own evidence, there is no data which is directly related to the suggestion that the unemployed pass successively through seven fairly well-defined and separate stages of adaptation to unemployment. But the data collected does support the hypothesis that the psychological states produced by unemployment in Britain are more typically ones of apathy than of radicalism, and that unemployment results in withdrawal more frequently than in activism. Assuming, therefore, that the unemployed do pass through a number of stages of adaptation, some of which are conducive to radicalism and others not, it might also be argued that different individuals pass through the stages at different rates, and consequently that there will be no widespread convergence of a large number of people at a radical stage. On top of this, periods of unemployment begin for different people at different times and so the whole unemployed group will not pass through the stages in phase. As a result the stages of adaptation of the whole unemployed group will be 'scrambled'. Some will be disposed towards radicalism and others towards apathy. Lastly; most studies of unemployed men show that they tend to withdraw from social and political activity, and thus become socially isolated. In this case their psychological predisposition towards apathy will be strengthened because their social isolation will make it difficult for radical groups to contact them and organize them.[33]

What distinguishes the politically active unemployed from the unemployed apathetic? Most sociologists would argue that the degree of relative deprivation is the distinguishing factor – 'the more severe the economic crisis the greater the extremist response'.[34] The main blocks of evidence which may be brought to bear on this hypothesis are the various studies of South Wales and North-East England. In her study of Jarrow, a town in the north-east of Durham, Ellen Wilkinson points out that eighty per cent (more than 7,000) of the insured population was unemployed in 1932, and that the local C.P. branch had only seven members.[35] Though it was terribly badly hit by the depression, and was officially recognized as a 'special' or depressed area, the North-East as a whole suffered in silence and, in general, has most usually been conservative.[36] The Pilgrim Trust's study of unemployment in this area found a 'determination to make the best of things'.[37] The C.P. itself dismissed the North-East with one bitter sentence. 'The North-East coast has been in a sectarian rut for years.'[38] There were only 'a handful of members in Durham' in 1934.[39]

On the other hand, Brynmawr, a South Wales mining village, experienced large-scale unemployment for over ten years, and although this produced only a little social uprooting and atomization, it did produce fairly widespread radicalism.[40] In 1931 the highest proportion of unemployed Communists in any of the Party Districts was in South Wales.[41]

The demographic and occupational characteristics of South Wales and the North-East of England were not dissimilar,[42] and the one significant difference between the two areas seems to have been that the North-East, and particularly its coal-mining industry, had been depressed ever since the end of the nineteenth century. Unlike South Wales, it did not enjoy the pre-war boom, and therefore its relative deprivation was less severe.[43] Also the miner in the North-East feels himself to be the aristocrat of workers, and he has the steadying influence of long-established trade unions behind him.[44] South Wales and the North-East of England are the only well-documented case studies relevant to British Communism, but this small body of data suggests that the greater the relative deprivation the more widespread the radicalism.

A further examination of Eisenberg and Lazarsfeld's seven stages of adaptation to unemployment suggests that the radical stages are the early ones. This is because, perhaps, the initial shock of unemployment produces acute relative deprivation, which wears off as the unemployed become accustomed or resigned to their situation. From this statement it may be deduced that Communist radicalism will be more widespread at the beginning of a depression than at the end. The national data about the Party support this hypothesis. For example, in January 1932 the Party had 9,000 members but the membership started to decline rapidly even before the most acute period of economic crisis had passed over. By November 1932, it had lost 4,000 members.

On the other hand, regional data seem not to support the hypothesis. Radicalism was not uniformly distributed throughout the country in 1931 and 1932. There was, as has already been pointed out above, no great increase in revolutionary feeling in the North-East. This might have been because the relative deprivation in the initial stages of adaptation to unemployment was not acute enough to draw people into the C.P. Or it might have been that the particular pattern of unemployment in the North-East produced a 'scrambling' of stages, so that few unemployed individuals arrived at the radical stages at the same time. A third possible explanation is that the depressed condition of the area before the industrial crisis had the effect of speeding up the rate of movement from one stage to another, so that workers in the North-East arrived at the fatalistic stage more quickly than workers in most other parts of Britain. The lack of detailed information makes it unwise to draw even a tentative conclusion about the hypothesis.

Besides Communism, there are other types of radicalism which might attract the unemployed. What factors influence the unemployed man's choice of radical movement? Class variables seem to be the most important. Information about Fascist, Communist and radical religious groups outside Britain shows that these three types of radicalism attract different social strata. Fascism draws the bulk of its support from the middle class.[45] In

Denmark, Norway, Finland, Sweden, and Canada,[46] and in France,[47] Communist support is strongest among the skilled and semi-skilled workers. Most radical religious sects in America are populated by unskilled workers.[48] It would seem, then, that of those who become radicals as a result of unemployment experiences, the unskilled workers will tend to turn to religious radicalism, the skilled and the semi-skilled to Communism, or some other radical, left-wing political group, and the middle class will lean towards Fascism.

In Britain, radical religious groups of the type which often increase their membership during periods of unemployment find most of their members among the unskilled sections of the working class – 'the low, the lost, the least, and the last'.[49] The B.C.P., on the other hand, attracts only a small proportion of the unskilled workers. The largest section of its membership is made up of skilled and semi-skilled workers.[50] There is some considerable doubt about the predominant social and economic status of British Fascists in the 1930s. Colin Cross, the historian of the B.U.F., has written: 'There is no 1965 counterpart of the lower-middle-class white-collar workers who formed the backbone of Sir Oswald Mosley's pre-war Blackshirts.'[51] On the other hand, he has pointed out in an earlier publication that the B.U.F. drew most of its support in the 1930s from the working-class communities in the East End of London. 'It was in the East End of London, principally in Bethnal Green, Shoreditch and Stepney, that the British Union from 1936 onwards at last found a mass following.'[52] There was a large number of financially unstable small businesses in the area,[53] and the owners of such marginal small businesses do usually provide the bulk of the support for the radical right.[54] But these small businesses were mainly tailoring and furniture-making businesses,[55] and it seems most likely that most of them were Jewish-owned since a quarter of the area's population was Jewish,[56] and since also a large proportion of Anglo-Jewry is concentrated in the tailoring and furniture-making trades.[57] The East End Jews, of course, were solidly anti-Fascist and supported the B.C.P. because of its militant stand against Fascism and anti-Semitism.[58] The Communist Party was also very strong in the East End.[59] Although the evidence is far from conclusive, it seems, therefore, that the B.U.F.'s support in the East End came not from the owners of the small businesses, as 'classical' sociological theory has it, but from the working class. In America it was found that those with incomes of less than $1,000 or more than $5,000 before becoming unemployed tended to become Fascists rather than Communists.[60] It is possible that the same pattern was repeated in Britain, that the B.U.F. had a large proportion of both unskilled and middle-class supporters, and that, like the B.C.P., the middle class and the working class were attracted by different aspects of Fascism. The working class was perhaps attracted by simple and emotional anti-Semitism, and the middle class by the economic aspects of the Fascist ideology. At least, the

B.U.F. did not gather up its East End support until 1936 which was after it had adopted an explicitly anti-Semitic policy at the end of 1934. Up to 1934 the B.U.F. had not been anti-Semitic.[61] Robb has pointed out that 'unemployment is rather likely to be associated with some degree of anti-Semitism'.[62] In 1965 the appeal of the radical right is mainly a racialist one and its main support comes from the unskilled working class.[63] It would seem that the standard sociological theory of Fascism fails to explain British Fascism insofar as the evidence available suggests that the B.U.F. was mainly successful in recruiting working-class members and not middle-class members. However, the evidence is quite inadequate to support any firm conclusions.

The largest part of the most recent discussion of unemployment has been in terms of the theory of mass behaviour and mass politics.[64] Many of the activities of the unemployed in the 1930s may be accurately characterized as 'mass'[65] – e.g. the Hunger Marches, the clashes with the police, the demonstrations, the publicity stunts. They are mass activities in that they are 'direct and activistic modes of response'.[66] On the other hand it is not true to say that 'the focus of attention was remote from personal experience and everyday life'.[67] On the contrary the policy of the Communist-backed N.U.W.M. was pragmatic and practical. There was little attempt to act or think in terms of Marx's theory of 'the reserve army of the unemployed' and the final collapse of the capitalist system. As a C.P. organizer said, it was an error to brandish the slogan of 'the struggle for power' before workers whose main interest was in gaining some improvement in their immediate economic situation. Kornhauser writes that 'mass movements are not looking for any pragmatic solution to economic or any other kind of problem',[68] but both the Communists and the members of the N.U.W.M. were almost exclusively concerned with the immediate and practical ramifications of the government's unemployment policy.[69] They were decidedly uninterested in the remote goal of bringing the capitalist system to an end, and substituting a Communist society. In his study of a Communist campaign in an election in Greenwich at the height of the unemployment problem, Bakke was struck by the way in which speakers emphasized bread-and-butter slogans, although, at the same time, he noted the element of idealism which could not 'be overlooked in assessing the real place which such movements as Communism have in the lives of the workers'.[70]

The N.U.W.M. was a mass movement insofar as it was involved in politics in a direct and activistic manner, but not insofar as its activities were oriented towards immediate and practical problems. There seems to be no reason why all mass movements should necessarily respond only to remote and abstract symbols, though it is true, of course, that some of them do. However, we shall return to the theory of mass society and mass movements in Chapter 9.

1. Hall, 1934; Rundquist and Sletto, 1936, p. 248
2. Pelling, 1963, p. 166; Eisenberg and Lazarsfeld, 1938; Hallgren, 1933, p. 269
3. Bakke, 1940, p. 46
4. Almond, 1954, p. 198
5. Jennings, 1934, p. 139
6. Eisenberg and Lazarsfeld, 1938. In their list of characteristics, the authors mix psychological states and the probable behavioural consequences of psychological states
7. Klugmann, *World News*, 1960
8. Glazer, 1961, p. 92
9. Einaudi, Domenach, and Garoschi, 1951
10. Webb, 1955
11. Lipset, 1960, p. 114
12. Cole and Postgate, 1961, p. 361
13. Cole, 1948, p. 148
14. *Communist Review*, December 1931, p. 378
15. *Communist Review*, December 1932, pp. 577–8. Four fifths of these unemployed members were in the Liverpool and Tyneside districts
16. Hannington, 1936, p. 9; Hyde, 1952, p. 24
17. Zinoviev, 1923, p. 489
18. Hannington, 1936, p. 323
19. Murphy, 1934, p. 217
20. Hannington, 1937, p. 248
21. See Appendix 2
22. See Appendix 2 and Chapter 3
23. Cross, 1961, p. 131
24. Wilson, B. R., 1963, p. 42
25. Wilson, B. R., 1963, p. 262
26. Bakke, 1940, p. 253
27. Bakke, 1940, p. 46
28. Hutt, 1937, p. 66
29. Rundquist and Sletto, 1936, p. 369
30. Hall, 1934; Rundquist and Sletto, 1936, p. 248
31. Legget, 1964
32. The Labour Party increased its individual membership from 297,000 in 1931 to 371,000 in 1932. (Pelling, 1962, pp. 127–8)
33. Kornhauser, 1960, p. 166
34. Kornhauser, 1960, p. 161
35. Wilkinson, 1939, pp. 159, 192
36. Mess, 1925, p. 25
37. The Pilgrim Trust, 1938, p. 78
38. *Report of the Fourteenth Congress of the C.P.G.B.*, May 1937. Earlier the Central Executive Committee reported that Tyneside was 'the weakest and least satisfactory of all Party Districts'. (*Report of the Central Executive Committee to the Annual Party Congress*, 1925, p. 7)
39. *Communist Review*, December, 1934, vol. 7, no. 11, p. 211
40. Jennings, 1934, p. 54
41. *Report of the Twelfth Congress of the C.P.G.B.*, November 1932
42. Knowles, 1952, p. 190
43. Knowles, p. 190
44. Muir, 1936, pp. 32–3
45. Lipset, 1960, Chapter 5; Kornhauser, 1960, pp. 179, 194–211
46. Lipset, 1960, p. 125. Lipset also includes Britain in his list but offers no evidence to back up the inclusion

47. Rossi, 1955, pp. 34, 111, 225
48. Clark, 1959, p. 230
49. Wilson, 1951, p. 107
50. See Chapters 4 and 5
51. Cross, 1965, p. 12
52. Cross, 1961, p. 149
53. Cross, 1961, p. 150
54. Lipset, 1960, Chapter 5; Kornhauser, 1960, pp. 179, 194–211
55. Cross, 1961, p. 150
56. Cross, 1961, p. 151
57. Neustatter, in Freedman, 1955, p. 254
58. Cross, 1961, p. 151; Hyde, 1952, p. 178; Darke, 1953, p. 45
59. Hyde, 1952, p. 178; Darke, 1953, p. 20
60. Stagner, 1930
61. Cross, 1961, p. 119
62. Robb, 1954, p. 143
63. Cross, 1965
64. See especially Kornhauser, 1960, pp. 159–67
65. There is a difference between the meaning of the word mass as it is defined by Kornhauser, and as it is used by the Communists. The latter mean by it a large and popular movement
66. Kornhauser, 1960, p. 46
67. Kornhauser, 1960, p. 43
68. Kornhauser, 1960, p. 233
69. Cf. Hannington, 1940, and Pelling, 1958, p. 64
70. Bakke, 1933, pp. 230–33

CHAPTER 4

THE INDUSTRIAL ROOTS OF BRITISH COMMUNISM

In Chapter 2 it was argued that the typical working-class Communist is as much an industrial militant as he is a political militant. The content of his ideology suggests that the conditions of his working life are important causes of his political sympathies. What are the industrial sources which nourish British Communism? Before an answer to this question can be attempted, it is necessary to establish the occupational composition of the Party's membership, and the proportion of Communists in different industries and occupations.

Only twice has the Party published occupational analyses of its membership; neither are terribly useful because on both occasions a high proportion of the members were unemployed. (See table on page 43.) The figures given for 1930 and 1931 are similar to those in 1925, when it was calculated that sixty-nine per cent of the delegates to the Party Congress were employed in the coal, iron, steel, engineering and ship-building industries.[1]

A rough indication of the occupations of Party members over a period of time can be gained from the analyses of delegates to national Party Congresses. The delegates do not necessarily form a cross-section of the whole Party, although the Congresses are held at Easter when most members could attend if they were elected to do so. The Congress figures can be cross-checked for representativeness against figures occasionally given in Party journals, and against exact figures obtained, from a District official, for the occupational composition of the South Midlands District in 1964 (see Appendix 3). Three other District officials were interviewed but they either refused or were unable to answer most of the questions. None of the mail questionnaires sent to the remaining District secretaries were returned. The South Midlands District (which includes Oxfordshire, Buckinghamshire, Berkshire and parts of south Warwickshire) is mainly agricultural and has no mining or textile industry. It has a greater concentration of middle-class and retired people than most parts of Britain, but it also has the Oxford industries of Morris Cars, Pressed Steel and the Oxford University Press. In spite of these demographic and occupational peculiarities, the occupational composition of the District membership and of the Congress delegates is strikingly similar. In both cases the percentage of builders, schoolteachers, clerical and administrative, distributive, and transport workers is almost the same, if not identical. There is a ten-per-cent difference in engineers, but in both cases they are easily the largest occupational group.

Occupational and Industrial Composition of the B.C.P., 1930,[2] 1931.[3]

1930	PER CENT	1931	PER CENT
Unemployed	49·0	Unemployed	60·0
Miners	11·0	Women	14·3
Textile workers	7·0	Housewives	10·7
Metal workers	7·0	Metal workers	5·5
General labourers and clerks	4·0	Building Workers	4·4
Railway workers	4·0	Miners	3·6
Clothing workers	2·5	Railway and transport workers	2·8
Dockers	2·5	Textile workers	2·7
Bus and tram workers	2·5		
Distributive workers	1·7		
Building workers	1·7		
Furniture workers	1·3		
Printers	1·3		
Iron and steel workers	1·0		
Seamen	1·0		
Shipyard workers	0·8		
Electricians	0·5		
Chemical workers	0·2		
Total 99·0		*Total* 104·0	

Like the Congress delegates, most South Midlands Communists are engineers, school-teachers and builders. Few of them are unemployed or medical, agricultural, printing or paper workers. In 1945, engineers and aircraft workers were the largest single occupational group in the whole Party.[4] Between a third and a half of British Communists are engineers, school-teachers and miners, and only about five per cent are professional, clerical or administrative, textile, or distributive workers. In Scotland and South Wales, two of the strongest Party Districts, the main support comes from the miners,[5] and in 1932 more than half the Party's members lived in the Scottish and South Wales coalfields.[6] This evidence suggests that it would be most dangerous to treat the Congress delegates as anything more than a rough indicator of a cross-section of the total membership, but the delegates do seem to be fairly representative, and sufficiently so for an analysis of the occupational forces underlying British Communism.

The percentage of Communists in different industries and occupations can be calculated from the figures provided by the Credentials Committee, and those given by the Central Statistical Office for the total number of employees in each major British industry.

Percentage of Communists in Different Occupational and Industrial Categories, 1963

Teaching	0·73	Unemployed	0·08
Mining	0·34	Public Employees	0·05
Engineering and Shipbuilding	0·34	Power	0·04
Students	0·22	Agriculture	0·04
Building	0·18	Professional and Technical	0·03
Transport and Rails	0·12	Chemical	0·03
Health Services	0·10	Self Employed	0·02
Printing	0·09	Distribution	0·02
Clothing and Textiles	0·08	Clerical and Administrative	0·01

The overall rank ordering of different occupations in the table is most probably fairly accurate, but specific figures for the percentage of Communists in different occupational categories may be misleading, for there is a possibility of compound errors in the calculations. The Congress delegates are only an extremely rough indication of the occupational composition of the whole Party, the occupational categories used by the Credentials Committees are vague and not clearly defined, and these categories may not correspond to those used by the Central Statistical Office. For example, the Party uses 'engineers' as a category to cover skilled, semi-skilled, and unskilled factory operatives, but not white-collar technicians with degrees or similar qualifications in engineering or applied science. Even so the category is too broad to be of great use because it could cover an enormous variety of occupations and industries, from highly-skilled workers like maintenance men or tool-makers, to the unskilled men who themselves may work in any one of a diverse range of occupational situations which fall within the broad category of 'the engineering industry'. Nevertheless, all the information indicates that the Party attracts a relatively high proportion of school teachers, miners, engineers and students, but can count on relatively slight support from agricultural, chemical, distributive, and professional and clerical workers. What variables account for this pattern of support?

It has already been seen that some workers become radicals as a result of their unemployment experiences. The engineering and mining industries are both prone to high unemployment rates during periods of economic depression, and builders suffer from seasonal unemployment.[7] The wage bargaining situation of an occupation may also be an important determinant of industrial radicalism.[8] Piece-rates, widely used in the engineering industry, are a source of constant friction. From the very start the engineers were faced with the problem of changing production techniques, and with the threat of new materials, machinery, and work routines being used to undermine their standards of life and work.[9] The complicated wage structure which they developed to prevent any such possibility demands, in turn, close contact between the local union leaders and the rank-and-file, who must be permanently watchful and militant if they are not to run the risk of wage cuts or speed-up. Thus the shop-steward is given an important place in the trade-union structure,[10] and there is room for an active, militant Communist to make his mark. The strength of mining union has been accounted for by the fact that certain groups of miners are constantly thrown into a bargaining position with the employers.[11]

The work pattern of many miners and engineers is determined for them by the machinery they use. Unlike bricklayers, truck drivers, or agricultural workers, the limits within which they can set their own pattern and pace of work are comparatively narrow. In America, Chinoy found that assembly-line work is avoided because its coerced rhythm and the inability to pause at will makes it exacting and strenuous work.[12] Marshall has also pointed out that poor industrial morale in large factories may well be the consequence of the organization of the work pattern, rather than the result of the size of the factory.[13] The frustrated desire of the worker to control his own working life, to use his own initiative, needs and moods, to decide when and how he works, may be extremely important in the development of industrial and political attitudes. The pressure of production-line work and constant supervision was given as one of the major bones of contention behind the recent troubles at Ford's. 'Increased work has meant the worsening of conditions and constant pressure on our members taking the form of people being penalized, policed by supervision, and moved from job to job.'[14]

Closely connected with the problem of the 'imposed' authority of the mass-production line is the distribution of authority in the factory hierarchy. Four writers have found a close connection between work satisfaction, alienation, and the authority situation in the workshop.[15] Lipset has also stressed the idea that there is some connexion between the structure of authority in a factory, and political preference.[16] In the early part of the century 'shop discipline' was one of the problems which had to be faced by the 'red' shop stewards' committee of the engineers.[17] More recently the change from the older conventional system in the mining industry to a more technological and rigid system has brought with it an increased possibility of management–worker conflict over supervision and discipline.[18]

Closely related to these problems are those raised by automation and redundancy. The *Daily Worker* devotes considerable space to a discussion of automation and its possible consequences. It could, its writers say, be used to shorten hours, increase wages and improve working conditions, instead of which there is a grave danger that it will result only in unemployment and increased profits.[19] 'Automation, and all its techniques, instead of being something to be welcomed by the workers becomes something to be feared, to make us unsure of the future.'[20]

Figures have been collected to show that there is a positive correlation between industrial plant size and the size of the left vote in the plant.[21] Even early on in this century forty-eight per cent of engineers were concentrated in 1·6 per cent of the total number of engineering establishments.[22] More recent figures show that about forty-five per cent of federated establishments employ more than 150 workers.[23] Good industrial relations are difficult to maintain in large factories. The size of some South Wales coal and anthracite mines correlates positively with industrial unrest, strikes, and absenteeism.[24] However, the Party is not very informative about the size of its factory branches relative to the size of the factories. The best information given is that most industrial cells are in factories which employ less than 2,000 people, and that the rest are in factories of between one and two thousand strong.[25] But only a small number of factories employ more than 1,000 people,[26] so it seems that a disproportionately large number of Communist factory cells are in large factories.

Industrial accidents and disease are also likely to create a militant working force.[27] Few miners are able to avoid injury altogether, and a high percentage have 'serious' accidents.[28] Though the number of miners is decreasing, the *Daily Worker* states, the number of mining accidents is increasing.[29] The building industry contains just under seven per cent of those in civil employment but it suffers almost forty per cent of fatal industrial accidents.[30] The *Daily Worker* also gives quite a lot of space to the problem of industrial accidents and disease. 'What is required,' says one article, 'if accidents are to be substantially reduced is that an effective safety organization must be established on the factory floor, and workers should have statutory power that will provide them with the right to set up safety organizations in the workshop.'[31] Such a demand, of course, gives increased weight to the demand for workers' control in the factory.

It has been found that limited prospects for upward social mobility tend to generate class consciousness and favourable attitudes towards collective action.[32] Both the mining and the engineering industries are 'closed' in the sense that the unskilled have little chance of reaching the skilled ranks, and that the skilled have little chance of promotion to a higher level.[33] In this way many miners and some engineers are tied to their occupational positions. Furthermore, mining skills are not transferable to other industries and, in South Wales in the 1930s, many miners had bought their own cottages, so that they were unable or unwilling to move to less depressed areas or industries. Thus the radicalism of the South Wales miners, generated by unemployment and a high rate of accidents and diseases etc., was 'contained' because the escape routes of geographical mobility and vertical and horizontal social mobility were closed. Miners were forced to remain in a highly unsatisfactory occupational situation, and hence the probability of widespread radicalism was increased. In addition, miners work in what are probably the worst conditions of any industry.[34] More than half of all British Communists in 1932 lived in the Scottish and South Wales coalfields.[35]

To join together the threads of the chapter so far, it may be said that a high proportion of British Communists (about forty per cent) are miners, builders and engineers, and among working class occupations these three have the highest proportions of Communists in their ranks. The three industries are marked by all or most of the variables which are thought to be the causes of political and industrial radicalism in the industries of other countries. Communist support is very weak in agriculture and the chemical industry, which are not usually marked by these variables. This is not to say that all engineering factories use mass production techniques, or that they are all large, but compared with chemical factories or farms, many of them are large mass-production units.[36] Many of the variables tend to cluster in the one industry or factory. In the engineering industry, the introduction of automation or highly mechanized mass-production lines tends to disorganize the work force, to produce management–worker conflict over wage rates, and to increase the size at which a plant may operate with maximum efficiency.

Some of these factors have been integrated into the mass theory of industrial and political militance. The theory was given a first simple formulation by G. D. H. Cole in 1923, when he drew attention to the density of coal miners living similar lives and in close contact with one another, yet separated from the wider society.[37] One of the main themes of mass theory is that homogeneous work groups or communities which are separated from their wider society tend to form socially distinct and isolated masses, which are well disposed towards industrial and political radicalism. Such working and living conditions often produce intense solidarity and class consciousness.[38]

Mass theory does help to explain the radicalism of some occupational groups. It has been said that London busmen are militant because good communications between depots foster industrial democracy, and because the spread-over of duties allows them to congregate in canteens and games rooms where they can discuss their grievances and organize their colleagues.[39] The same is true of firemen. Their unusual job and the length of time they have to 'waste' together create among firemen a consciousness of a separate identity from other workers. Their formal discussion groups, organized to pass the time, became at one period 'demonstrations for the political left'.[40] The National Fire Service and the Fire Brigades Union were successful areas for Communist recruitment during the Second World War.[41] Similarly, large industrial units, like a mass-production factory or an aircraft factory, tend to collect together a large number of people who live rather similar lives and who are in close and constant contact with one another. These conditions sustain collective and radical action, and also help to keep working-class traditions alive. The miners still remember and act upon memories of 'the bad old days'.[42]

However, there are significant exceptions to the mass theory of industrial and political radicalism. In the 1920s and 1930s the textile communities in Lancashire and Yorkshire were similar to the mining communities of South Wales, because textile workers often lived in undifferentiated and isolated masses.[43] Yet although they were almost as strike-prone as miners, they were also politically conservative.[44] On the other hand, the textile industry employs an unusually high proportion of women, and as a rule women are not as politically radical as men. Only about fifteen per cent of British Communists are women. Because of the high proportion of women in the textile industry, it does not form a clear exception to the mass theory of radicalism. A better example of an exception to the theory is provided by the mining communities in the North-East of England, which are more conservative than those in Scotland and South Wales. The strike histories of North-East miners and South Wales miners are very different.[45] This seems to suggest that the mass conditions of mining communities do not always produce militance.

Rimlinger has discovered significant differences in the international strike patterns of miners. He suggests that the sources of discontent and tension inherent in mining work, such as unemployment, great physical danger, and acute physical discomfort, must be moulded by the separatism of the miners, their habit and intensely felt need for cooperation, and the psychological burdens and anxieties of their job, before they produce a strong feeling of common destiny which can be translated into collective action. The industrial and political radicalism of mining communities, he concludes, may be either activated or dampened depending on the nature and impact of the larger socio-cultural environment.[46]

In his book *The Politics of Mass Society*, Kornhauser suggests that the mass conditions of merchant seaman and dockers generate radical attitudes. In Britain neither the merchant seamen nor the dockers give much support to the C.P. The latter have swung away from the Party for purely historical and political reasons, although most of them remain very left-wing, but the extreme mass character of a merchant ship leads sailors to avoid discussion of religion and politics because it might lead to bad feelings and conflict.

In 1960 the leaders of a seamen's strike would tolerate no 'Communist interference' and very, very few British merchant seamen are Communists.[47]

Some doubt is thrown, then, on the theory that work groups forming largely undifferentiated and isolated masses are usually radically disposed. In Britain and in other countries these conditions have been accompanied by radical attitudes and behaviour in some cases, but not in all cases by any means. Mass conditions are closely associated with an absence of cross-pressures and the presence of strong intra-group or class communications. These conditions may sustain an ideology and reinforce it once it has emerged but it is difficult to see how they can determine the content of the ideology as being either collectivistic or individualistic, radical or moderate, right-wing or left-wing.

There seem, also, to be purely organizational reasons for the concentration of Communist support in a small number of industries. The Party finds radically-minded workers who are geographically stable or who work in large factories much more accessible than geographically mobile workers or workers in small factories. The floating population of builders and labourers is difficult to contact and organize, and so are agricultural workers because of their geographical dispersion.

It's very difficult to contact people in agriculture – you can't reach them through their trade union unless you are in the union yourself. . . . The same goes for the Irish. You can never tie them to a branch even if you can contact them in the first place. They're always off on some other job in another part of the country. You have to work through some other organization. We are making a drive for members through the Irish Anti-Partition League, and in fact have recruited two members in this way. [Communist Party official]

The problem of contacting recruits is a tough one for the Party. It probably contacts most of its working-class members, and a considerable proportion of its middle-class members, through a large factory or some other stable industrial unit.

The number of builders is not up to the national level in this District. Mostly the building firms are small. It's easier in London where there will be upwards of a hundred men on the site at one time or another. . . . Most of our Clerical and Administrative group are in the offices of the factories. . . . Most of the truck drivers work for a factory. Not like the people in road haulage firms. They're all over the place. . . . Workers on the building sites have done a lot to recruit the contracting electricians. [Communist Party official]

Thus there are three analytically separate elements in the organization of a large industrial unit which help create the conditions necessary for an individual to join the Communist Party. The pattern of industrial relations tends to generate management–worker conflict; the high degree of intra-group communications helps spread and sustain militant worker attitudes towards this conflict; and the fact that a large working force is collected together in one place helps the Party in its efforts to contact and organize the militant workers.

The same factors also help to explain why Communists are concentrated in certain trade unions. Over the past two decades or so the Party has come to concentrate more of its energies in trade-union affairs and elections, rather than in national politics and elections – perhaps because of its lack of success in the latter. 'The factories', states the Party Handbook, 'are the centre of the class struggle . . . and winning the support of the workers is decisive for the advance of socialism.'[48] In the twenties and early thirties it aimed at building up a working-class organization outside the established, 'reformist', trade-union movement. It now aims at using the existing machinery rather than replacing it. The Minority Movement, the instrument of the earlier policy, was thought to be too sectarian and recognized as a failure[49] when the 'Class Against Class' policy of 1929 was replaced by united front tactics.

Although they are stereotyped as 'trouble makers', Communists often follow a moderate industrial policy both in America and in England,[50] where, to quote Ross and Hartmann, 'disinterested in ideological unionism, members have expected a bread-and-butter approach'.[51] One unusually militant Communist shop-steward was disliked by his fellow Communists because they considered him 'an unreliable factory worker'.[52] More recently, the industrial correspondent of the Sunday Times has expressed surprise at the moderate policy of a leading Communist miner:

As an executive member of the Communist Party, and the acknowledged symbol of the Welsh miners, Mr Paynter was making a remarkably open confession to the Lancashire miners of just where his sympathies lie. For he not only told the men not to strike, but warned them of the dangers of attempting to adopt an overtime ban as an alternative.[53]

In some cases Communists have been used as scapegoats by industrial and trade-union officials. In the 1920s, for instance, they were used by non-Communist miners' leaders as an excuse to attack any form of industrial militance.[54] Arthur Deakin who seemed, in public, to have an anti-Communist phobia was less inclined, in private, to see the hand of the Communists in all industrial unrest.[55] Sometimes the Party may not deny responsibility for a strike if it wants to foster the idea that it is a powerful force in industrial affairs, and the spearhead of the working-class movement. In fact the strikes are most frequently the products of social forces which are way beyond the Party's control.

An analysis of the history of strikes shows that there is little that the Party can do to foment industrial unrest on its own. Strikes are not the only consequence of bad industrial relations, and all strike data must be treated with certain reservations, but together with lock-outs, absenteeism, and accident rates they give a quantifiable indication of the state of industrial relations. As expected, though with certain significant exceptions, Communists tend to be concentrated in strike-prone industries, but this is not to say that Communists necessarily cause most strikes. There has been a general downward trend in strike participation and loss of working time through strikes since 1915 in Britain,[56] and yet the overall tendency of Communist Party membership has been to increase. At the same time, strike-participation rates are significantly higher than elsewhere in Northern Europe,[57] while the industrial power of Communists in Britain is considerably less than in almost all other European countries. Communists cannot provoke strikes unless the right industrial foundations are already laid for them. There was, for example, no appreciable increase in the number of strikes between 1945 and 1947,[58] when Communist influence in the trade unions was reaching its peak. Again, the Party could do little to restrain strikes in the 1941–5 period of the war, when Communists played the role of strike-breakers and blacklegs,[59] although there might have been a larger number of strikes but for Communist influence. The heaviest annual strike rate after the war occurred in 1957,[60] which was a time when post-war Communist influence and stature was at a minimum. Communists have never gained even moderate support from the textile workers in Britain, though textile workers are second only to the miners in Knowles's table of strike-prone industries.[61] Although the Communists have, no doubt, been responsible for a number of strikes and have created other forms of industrial conflict, it is doubtful if they can act, in the majority of cases, as anything more than what Knowles calls 'midwives of strikes'.[62] Tom Bell berated his fellow comrades for failing to do what social conditions prevented them from doing.

Our experience in strike movements has shown that the Party came to the strikes centres from outside, like an ambulance corps; that the Party was still a propaganda sect, and did not play a leading role in economic or political struggles.[63]

In many cases the Party has taken up the cause of a militant movement after it has started; it has played upon and used the militance rather than created it itself. Such was the case with the Minority Movement which managed, with qualified success, to canalize pre-existing militance,[64] and which had to be wound up when this militance expired. In fact, the Party itself was born during a period of aggressive working-class political and industrial action. The industrial groups which have provided its main support, the miners and engineers, were revolutionary long before the C.P.G.B. was formed.[65] Now that Communist industrial policy is becoming more and more moderate and failing to satisfy the demands of the uncompromising revolutionaries, there are signs that its role is being taken over by the younger Trotskyists in the Socialist Labour League.[66]

The Communist Party, then, is not responsible for most industrial unrest, but rather industrial unrest and Communism are partly the common products of the same underlying factors.[67] Thus, say Cyriax and Oakshott,

the Communists can thrive when they can identify themselves with particular industrial conditions; they may try to make industrial relations worse,
but they are successful only within narrow limits when they try the more
difficult task of making good relations bad.[68] Even when they have gained
control of important trade union offices they have not always been able
(or wanted) to change union policy completely.[69]

To explain why a large number of Communists are concentrated in one
industry is quite a different matter from explaining why Communists are
able to gain influence in, or control of, a particular union. The former
requires a general sociological analysis of social and working conditions,
while the latter demands, in addition, an analysis of the power structure
and organization of trade unions. Some types of organization will be more
susceptible to Communist influence than others. A frequently cited cause of
conflict within trade unions is the geographical distance between, and
different attitudes of, trade-union leaders and rank-and-file members. This
is not a particularly new problem. In 1916 one revolutionary trade unionist
wrote: 'We hold the view that trade-union officials are the servants and not
masters of the rank-and-file.'[70] The same complaint was echoed a few years
later in the journal of the Communist-backed Busmen's Rank-and-File
Movement, when union leaders were compared with a fat and lazy dog,
which was incapable of looking after its master's property.[71] Many authors
have since pointed out that unofficial strikes are as much a protest against
the leadership of the unions, as they are a sign of conflict between management and workers.[72] Almost invariably, though not on issues such as
demarcation disputes, the Communists support the strikers. There is a
strong opinion among them that the shop stewards' position within the
union should be revised, because shop stewards have detailed knowledge of
trade-union affairs at the local level, and because they are the elected
representatives of the men.[73] And, of course, many shop stewards are
Communists.

Communist leadership in the unions is often ascribed to the apathy of
the rank-and-file, which has allowed a dedicated, vigilant and hard-
working minority to elect its own men into positions of power. This is not
always the way things have worked, for the more militant unions have
elected more militant officers. In such cases Communists can be the obvious
candidates. The Communists have been strong in the E.T.U. and the
A.E.U. In both unions militance is regarded as a special virtue.[74] The
former has been under Communist control at almost all organizational
levels as a result of careful ballot-rigging,[75] but also as a result of democratic election as well. In the thirties the militant London busmen supported
the Communist-backed Busmen's Rank-and-File Movement.[76] In many
cases militant unions have given at least passive support to Communist
trade-union leaders.

Nor is there any evidence to show that attendance at branch meetings is low where the branches are dominated by Communists,[77] and nor can the Communist minority be held responsible for non-attendance at branch meetings, as the Trade Union Congress has suggested.[78] The rank-and-file member, though he may not be a Communist, a fellow-traveller, or even a left-wing sympathizer may see the Communist as a hard-working, extremely well-informed trade unionist who is 'on the right side', and more able to carry out trade-union business than most, since he had probably attended a Party evening school, which has trained him in book-keeping, minute-taking, chairmanship, and public speaking.[79] The attitude of, 'Oh, I know he's a Communist but all the same he's the right man for the job', may well be more widespread than, 'Oh, I know he's a Communist, but I can't be bothered to go and vote for the other chap'.

1. *Workers' Weekly*, 23 October 1925, p. 4. In 1932 the occupational composition of the C.P.U.S.A. and the B.C.P. appears to have been similar – the *Communist International*, 1932, vol. 9, p. 516

2. *Communist Review*, January 1931
3. *Communist Review*, December 1932
4. *World News and Views*, 20 January, vol. 5, no. 3
5. Gollan, 1964, p. 2
6. *Communist Review*, December 1932, vol. 4, no. 12, pp. 577–8
7. Knowles, 1952, pp. 171, 180, 247
8. Dennis, Henriques, and Slaughter, 1956, p. 87
9. Jeffreys, 1945, p. 205
10. Marsh and Coker, 1963
11. Dennis, Henriques, and Slaughter, 1956, p. 87
12. Chinoy, 1955. See also Blauner, 1964
13. Marshall, 1945
14. The Joint Ford's Shop Stewards' Committee, *What's Wrong at Fords*, undated pamphlet
15. Nettler, 'The Alienated Man Revisited', mimeo; Pearlin, 1962; de Grazia, 1948, p. 126; Blauner, 1964
16. Lipset, *et al.*, in Lindsey, 1959, p. 1139
17. Jeffreys, 1945, p. 174
18. Goldthorpe, 1959; Wilson, 1951; Trist and Bamforth, 1951; Wellisz, 1953; Rimlinger, 1959
19. Paynter, 1963, p. 2; Tighe, 1963, p. 2. See also Gouldner, 1955
20. *Ford's – Whose Hands at the Wheel?*, B.C.P. undated pamphlet
21. Lipset, 1960, p. 249
22. Jeffreys, 1945, p. 211
23. Marsh and Coker, 1963
24. Revans, 1956
25. *Communist Review*, December 1932, vol. 4, no. 12, pp. 577–8
26. H.M.S.O., 1964
27. Knowles, 1925, p. 249
28. Dennis, Henriques, and Slaughter, 1956, p. 42
29. Francis, 1963, p. 2
30. Weaver, 1963, p. 2
31. Prince, 1964, p. 2

32. Landecker, in Freeman, 1952, p. 246
33. Pribićević, 1959, p. 26; Brennan, Cooney, and Pollins, 1954, p. 56
34. Rimlinger, 1959
35. *Communist Review*, December 1932, vol. 4, no. 12, pp. 577–8
36. Blauner, 1964; Allen, 1961, pp. 219–28
37. Cole, 1923, p. 7
38. Cf. Kornhauser, 1960, Chapter 12
39. Clegg, 1964, p. 136
40. Spender, in Sansom *et al.*, 1943, p. 60
41. Wood, 1959, p. 163
42. Dennis, Henriques, and Slaughter, 1956, p. 42
43. Zweig, 1952, p. 40; Knowles, 1952, p. 167
44. *Communist International*, 1935, vol. 12, p. 132; *International Press Correspondence*, vol. 8, no. 3, pp. 86–7; Turner, 1962, pp. 29–30, 319
45. Knowles, 1952, p. 186
46. Rimlinger, 1959
47. Foulser, 1961, pp. 187, 189–90
48. *Handbook for Members of the British Communist Party*, 1962, p. 5
49. J. R. Campbell, *Communist International*, vol. 12, no. 16, August 1935
50. Taft in Kornhauser, Dubin and Ross, 1954, p. 253; Chester in Kornhauser *et al.*, 1954, p. 464; Moore, 1957, p. 339
51. Ross and Hartmann, 1960, p. 66
52. Goldstein, 1952, p. 191
53. A. Coulton, *Sunday Times*, quoted in *Vanguard*, July 1964, p. 12
54. Williams, 1962, p. 740
55. Allen, 1957, p. 288
56. Ross and Hartmann, 1960, p. 89
57. Ross and Hartmann, 1960, p. 89
58. Knowles, 1952, p. 56
59. Pelling, 1963, p. 215
60. *I.R.I.S. News*, December 1963, vol. 8, no. 4, p. 4
61. Knowles, 1952, p. 203
62. Knowles, 1952, p. 65
63. Bell, 1937, pp. 136–7. See also Piatnitsky, 1933
64. Knowles, 1952, p. 51
65. Evans, 1961, pp. 7, 215; Jeffreys, 1945, p. 174
66. Cyriax and Oakshott, 1960, p. 122
67. For a different view of the role of Communists in strikes see Wigham, 1961, Chapter 6
68. Cyriax and Oakshott, 1960, p. 122
69. Clegg, Killick, Adams, 1961, p. 12
70. *The Worker*, 8 January 1916. Intra-union conflict was prevalent in the Amalgamated Society of Engineers – Pribićević, 1959, pp. 30–31
71. *Busmen's Punch*, May 1933, no. 7
72. Cf. Ross and Hartmann, 1960, p. 94
73. Williams, 1963
74. Pelling, 1963, p. 240
75. Rolph, 1962
76. Clegg, 1954, p. 108; Allen, 1957, p. 66
77. Goldstein, 1952, p. 260
78. *Report of the Proceedings of the 81st Annual Trade Union Congress*, Bridlington, 1949, pp. 274–9
79. Cf. Allen, 1957, p. 277

CHAPTER 5

COMMUNISM
AND THE
WORKING CLASS

People with working-class occupations make up by far the largest proportion of the members of the British Communist Party and always have
done, even in the late 1930s when the Party attracted a large number of
people with middle-class occupations. This predominance of working-class
membership in the Party is to be expected, yet compared with the absolute
size of the British working class, the size of the Communist Party is tiny.
Manual workers amount to about seventy-four per cent of the men in the
country as a whole,[1] but in 1965 the total Party membership was only
33,734, of which about seventy-five per cent were working class.[2] The class
composition of the Party is thus roughly similar to the class composition of
the country as a whole.

The question arises of why a left-wing political group can attract so few
members from a large working-class population. The Labour Party is also
small compared with the size of its possible working-class membership, but
there is less support for the B.C.P. than in any other Western European
country where a Communist Party is not suppressed in practice, or where it
is not formally prohibited by statute.[3] Even allowing for the absence of a
British peasant class (a class which produces a number of Communists in
the rest of Europe[4]) there must still be something in the British working-
class culture which accounts for the small size of the British Party. In the
mining, engineering, and building industries alone a large number of
workers are directly affected by many of the occupational variables discussed in the previous chapter. Yet only a minute proportion of them become members of the C.P., for even a short time. Since the working man's
attitudes towards unemployment and his work situation are moulded by
the culture in which he lives, it can be hypothesized that the British working-

class subculture is not conducive to Communist radicalism, and directs the activity of the working-class man into other channels.[5]

There is no single work on the British working-class culture as such, although there are a number of relevant studies. Some of these – Hoggart's,[6] and Zweig's,[7] – are impressionistic and based largely on the writers' personal experience, others, like Robb's,[8] deal only with a small section of the working-class, and others deal only with working-class people living in a small geographical area, like Kerr's,[9] and Spinley's.[10] But for the most part the findings of these writers are consistent, and may be fitted together to form a more complete picture of the British working-class sub-culture.

Britain, though a highly industrialized and urbanized country, has returned a left-wing party to political power with a working majority on only three occasions. First and foremost, the British Communist Party, like any left-wing political organization, has to combat the apathy of the working class which, compared with the middle class, is not interested in politics. British Communists recognized this problem of political apathy from the start. Within one year of the Party's formation a member had written:

Of all the difficulties that confront the Communist movements in the English-speaking countries, particularly in Britain and the United States, one of the hardest is that of the political indifference of the wide masses.[11]

A few years later one of the Party leaders echoed his words when he wrote: 'It is true that the British workers have not bothered themselves very much over parliamentary affairs.'[12] Awareness of this problem for the Party in the 1960s was shown in the interviews, when respondents answered the question 'Would you say that ordinary people have any influence over the way the country is run?' Typical of a certain group of responses were the following:

Yes – if only they would get off their hind legs.

If they take the trouble to exert their influence which, I'm afraid, they don't do as often as they should.

People have the power to influence events when they are prepared to use it. But they don't realize the power they have and don't use it.

Yes – people do have power to influence events – more than they realize.

Working-class apathy is not limited to politics. It is found in almost all other spheres of social life as well, and not least in the 'fringe' political activities which take up a considerable portion of the average Party member's time, energy and interest – activities like trade-union affairs, peace committees, and the local educational and social welfare pressure groups. A number of ex-Communists have suggested that the Party loses a high percentage of its members not long after they have joined because it tries to make them work too hard. In the early years the Party was made up predominantly of hard-working, dedicated activists, but more recently it seems that the hard work has been done mainly by core members while the rest do much less work. If the new recruit is not much more interested in politics than the average working-class man, he is not likely to tolerate this encroachment on his time. This disinterest in political activities may partly account for the very high turnover of Party membership. It is significant that the Party engages in a big drive each year to re-register those members who have joined in previous years.

In spite of his being apathetic, the average British workman retains a fairly well-developed sense of political competence in comparison with his counterpart in Germany,[13] and probably in France and Italy as well.[14] He is comparatively happy with the existing political system and is unwilling to subscribe to an organization which aims at changing it. As Almond and Verba say, 'in many ways, then, the belief in one's competence is a key political attitude . . . the self-confident citizen is also likely to be a more satisfied and loyal citizen.'[15]

There is also a large element of fatalism in the British working-class culture which conflicts with the Communist belief that political, economic and social affairs can and ought to be consciously controlled and directed. Kerr,[16] and Spinley[17] both comment on the fatalism and belief in luck of the working man, while Robb found that working-class people who were not anti-Semitic believed that the future is to some extent controllable, and that 'it is worthwhile making an effort to achieve one's ambitions'.[18] Communists are neither anti-Semitic nor fatalistic and therefore the Party will gain no support from a considerable proportion of the working-class which is anti-Semitic and fatalistic. Unemployment seems to be an experience which usually strengthens feelings of fatalism, but for the Communist it is an experience which seems to reinforce the belief that society must be re-organized along different lines. Similarly the working-class fatalist is likely to accept, with a great deal of grumbling perhaps, the unsatisfactory aspects of his work situation and use 'the dogs', 'the boozer', or a tranquil week-end's fishing to escape. Fatalism is directly connected with a willingness to accept things as they are, and a tendency to escape from an undesirable situation by ignoring it or trying to avoid it rather than trying to change it.[19] This attitude is expressed in the frequently voiced view that 'there's no use not liking it if you've got to put up with it'. Hoggart documents this tendency of the British worker to put up with things rather than trying to change them.[20] Such attitudes will not lead people to consider joining a group which claims that things ought to be changed, and that to do so demands a great deal of hard work, sacrifice, and self discipline. Spinley found the inhabitants of an East London slum to be essentially ill-disciplined, unable to postpone satisfactions, and unable to look ahead.[21] Others have found that working-class people lack drive and ambition,[22] qualities which are at a premium for the potential Communist.

Most British working people are also 'non-metaphysical' in their out-look.[23] One of Zweig's respondents is quoted as saying, 'Don't you think we'd all feel better with some cash in our pockets instead of slogans in our mouths!'[24] Such a man is unlikely to be much impressed by Communism if he believes it to be a complicated political theory. In most cases this belief will be quickly and easily dispelled if the man comes into contact with the pragmatic talk and action of Party members on the factory floor. Never-theless, the average workman is somewhat suspicious of anyone crusading for a cause, and is likely to dismiss him as 'a little touched', or 'cranky', or 'barmy'.

There are other elements in the British Communist's ideology which are alien to some sections of the working class. While the Communists believe very strongly indeed in the equality of all human beings, no matter what race or colour, many of those to whom they appeal for support are racially prejudiced. Abrams found that the 'pragmatists of the left' (those of the working class who describe themselves as working-class and vote Labour) are egalitarian in the sense that they favour the abolition of class differences, but at the same time, they are also nationalistic and ethnocentric.[25] While the C.P. opposes the Immigration Act, many working-class men give it their support, fearing that coloured immigration might threaten their job security.

I get my vote next time, and I don't vote for that let-down lot [the Labour Party]. You can't stick up for the niggers and then pretend to be for the working classes. . . . If they said 'kick the soots out' they'd have the biggest majority they've ever had. . . . What's it going to be like for us young ones when we get to forty? The bosses will take a young black before they take my man, won't they?[26]

There are no exact figures which show how widespread this racialism is, but studies by Eysenck, Cross, and Robb suggest that it is fairly widespread in a mild or extreme form.[27] Much of the support for racialist groups in Britain in 1965 comes from the unskilled working class.[28] Also, while unemploy-ment may draw some workers to the left wing, it is 'rather likely to be associated with some degree of anti-Semitism'[29] – a prejudice which cannot be tolerated in the Communist Party. Linked with this egalitarianism is the Communists' internationalist outlook, but the British worker tends, if anything, to be nationalistic. One miner is described as mixing 'retro-gressive, mindless, anti-foreignism' with his views on the defence of miners' rights.[30] The working-class nationalist is likely to react strongly against the B.C.P. if he believes it to be run from Moscow.

In the working-class subculture there are, then, a whole range of beliefs, attitudes and personality characteristics – apathy, lack of drive, ill-discipline, fatalism, unwillingness to make sacrifices or to think of the future, national-ism, and ethnocentricism – which are not merely irrelevant to Communist Party membership but which actively militate against it. The activism, drive, discipline, ability to make sacrifices and to think of the future, which are characteristic of the Communist Party member, show themselves in his attempts at self-education. One of the most striking patterns to emerge from the Communist biographies and autobiographies is the persistent attempt at self-improvement through self-education. The number of quotations and the strength of feeling behind them speak for themselves. They mark Communists as being very different from most working-class people.

Kipps and Tono Bungay contain autobiographical experiences not dissimilar from my own, with their characters' gallant and pathetically comical efforts at self-betterment and self-education, in a hostile environment, and without the help of influential friends or patrons.[31]

When I left school I continued to read a great deal, particularly scientific and philosophical works.[32]

That love of literature which I regard as being as important for a man's soul as food and drink are for his body.[33]

I was book hungry and found a land where books were as accessible in a quantity and variety sufficient to satisfy even my uncontrolled voracity.[34]

By this time David was nearly nine and a prolific reader of books and newspapers.[35]

It was the knowledge and the sacrifice made, and the self-denial endured by his mother and his sisters that enabled him to be educated, that made him resolve to use his education in the service of the workers.[36]

Until I was twenty-one I never missed attending night school four nights a week and doing all the home work that was given.[37]

I always did an enormous amount of reading . . . especially Dickens.[38]

My parents both passed on their love of learning to us. . . . I was fascinated by ancient myths, so much so that by the time I was eleven I was already something of an authority on Greek Mythology. This I achieved by simply swallowing all the books in the local library on the subject . . .[39]

I turned to the philosophers to see if they could resolve the problems for which, as yet, I found no answer. I read Thales and Lucretius, Pythagoras and Aristotle, Spinoza and Kant, Locke and Hume, Berkeley and Hegel and Spencer.[40]

. . . he became an omnivorous reader. . . . His thirst for knowledge led him to Geology, Astrology and Literature classes (one year we actually ventured to think of pure science) held at the Technical School in Glasgow.[41]

Already before I left school I would often call in the Public Library on my way home to read the newspapers and try to understand something about the war that was going on and I kept up this habit of going to the library in the evenings.[42]

Three evenings a week for five years I attended classes in connexion with the Science and Art Department . . .[43]

At eight or nine he began reading Henty's historical stories, and was so much interested that he started reading history and biography to learn more . . .[44]

Douglas Hyde, at one period in his life, cut down his sleep to two hours a night so that he could read more and still more books.[45] Of six Communists in one branch, three are mentioned as having extensive reading habits.[46] Looking at some of these biographies is not unlike reading J. S. Mills's autobiography, for every few pages or so the writer lists a few books which he thinks to be especially important in his intellectual development. Only two of the eighteen quoted above (David Guest and John Cornford) had a middle-class background which favoured an intellectual curiosity and a love of reading and knowledge, and the rest all write of their desire to pull themselves out of the poverty which their parents endured. Although such poverty may be rarer now, Communists are still required to read much of the vast quantity of Party literature.

. . . get the habit of reading – do it for yourself and don't leave it to others – study for yourself those brilliant ideas, theories and approaches, which have helped so many millions to understand the world in which they live in order to transform it.[47]

The Communist Party is much concerned with education.

The only permanent, guaranteed solution [concludes the author of one article in the *Daily Worker*], to the problem of higher education is not only that of providing more universities and teachers, but creating the kind of society which provides ever widening opportunities for everyone to aim at the stars – and reach them.[48]

This emphasis on the importance of education contrasts sharply with the more usual working-class attitudes to education. Spinley found that the parents of her sample of slum children took little interest in their children's schooling,[49] while Jackson and Marsden deal with the general social factors which prevent the working class from valuing the benefit of education as much as the middle class.[50] This pattern of self-education seems to have important implications for political activity, for although education does not determine political outlook, the educated are more likely to participate in political affairs. The better educated are more aware of the impact of governments on individuals, are more interested in political campaigns, are better informed on political matters, and are more likely to engage in political discussion.[51]

There are, however, elements in the British working-class culture which can be tapped by the B.C.P. Outstanding among these is the powerful class consciousness which is to be found in almost any working-class community.[52] Jackson and Marsden found that 'Many of the parents thought that to talk of class and to talk of politics was merely to approach the same subject from a different angle.'[53] Alford has concluded a study by saying that Britain has relatively 'pure' class politics.[54] The Party thrives in this atmosphere of class consciousness and antagonism, and does its best to use it and develop it. 'I and my family', writes an ex-Communist, 'had felt the rough edge of capitalism, I hated it for its exploitation, its bitter cruelty and its relentless persecution of the unfortunate.'[55] From his early childhood Arthur Horner, the Communist miners' leader, was conscious of the bitter hatred between the worker and the factory owners.[56] Class conflict in

South Wales was heightened by Welsh Nationalist feeling against the British owners of Welsh industry.[57]

But even this strong sense of class consciousness is mitigated by patterns of deference.[58] Almond and Verba record that:

> Despite the spread of political competence and participation orientations the British have maintained a strong deference to the independent authority of the government.[59]

Other writers have also commented on the somewhat curious, but not infrequently found, combination of class consciousness and deference.

> There is an accepted – but not imposed – hierarchy at the top, which is material-ized in the aristocracy. There is much real, profound, traditionally embedded sense of fraternity and equality in the masses.[60]

This pattern of deference is a very real obstacle to widespread Communist success in Britain. The Party would abolish the monarchy if it came to power,[61] but there is no indication that this would strike a sympathetic chord among British workers. On the contrary they take considerable pride in their monarchy.[62] This is a feeling which cuts across class divisions, prevents class polarization, and to some extent, acts as a moderating influence on class conflict. The British working class was given certain civil rights shortly after its emergence. It can be suggested that these civil rights gave the working class a feeling of belonging to society, of being included as part of it, and thus the working class developed a sense of allegiance to society and the apparatus of the state. So also, it came to believe that the state should be changed from within, and not destroyed by revolutionary activity from outside.[63]

Most working-class people support the Labour Party, which they see as an adequate, if not fully viable and effective, organization for the expression of their political interests. The Labour Party had the inestimable advantage of gaining the support of many working-class political organizations long before the B.C.P. was ever formed. Quite possibly the more timid of those who are dissatisfied with the Labour Party are not prepared to endure the social sanctions which they believe accompany membership of the B.C.P. The remaining working-class, left-wing political radicals are divided be-tween the B.C.P. and a number of smaller political organizations. The C.P. takes the largest number of them, but the Trotskyite Socialist Labour League is expanding, and there is also the C.D.R.C.U., the Syndicalist Workers' Federation, the Independent Labour Party, the Socialist Party of Great Britain, the Revolutionary Socialists' League, the Forum group, and International Socialism, and a number of even smaller groups.

At the trade union level, rather than at the national political level, class consciousness expresses itself in a 'one for all and all for one' union solidarity, a hatred for the 'blackleg', and a long memory for industrial grievances.[64] There is no mitigating feeling of deference on the factory floor over trade-union affairs, and it is here that the Communist Party is most successful. At the purely local political level, class conscious 'them' and 'us' awareness is expressed in the strong community spirit which is remarked on by almost every writer on working-class communities.[65] The C.P. is fairly successful where it can draw on this expression of class consciousness, and it carries not inconsiderable weight in some areas in local tenants' associations, committees, councils, and educational and social pressure groups.

In particular the B.C.P. appeals to skilled workers. A number of sociologists have already pointed out that, for some purposes, it is necessary to draw a distinction between the skilled, the semi-skilled, and the unskilled groups within the working class.[66] As far as the C.P. is concerned the potentialities of skilled workers are very different from those of the unskilled. Skilled workers were the first to establish successful trade unions; they are the most militant section of the working class, and, by and large, they provide the working-class movement with most of its active workers and convinced socialists. Skilled workers tend to be less deferential in their voting habits than unskilled workers,[67] and, in England and America, the comparatively well-off sections of the working class appear to experience a more intense sense of common destiny with other workers.[68] Much of the Labour Party's local working-class leadership has come from the craft and Section 1 members of trade unions, who have felt that their comparative material success provided them with added responsibilities for securing the well-being of their less fortunate workers.[69] This is partly the consequence of skilled and semi-skilled workers having higher educational and vocational qualifications, which make them more readily available for political mobilization.[70]

It is not surprising, therefore, that most working-class Communists are members of the skilled unions. In 1963, for example, the A.E.U. provided twenty-two per cent of the Congress delegates, while the larger T. & G.W.U. provided seven per cent. The N.U.M. and the E.T.U. provided 5·5 per cent each. The South Midlands District official calculated that the skilled, the semi-skilled and the unskilled formed one third each of the working-class membership. Other District officials said that the 'bulk' or 'the biggest part' of the District membership was either skilled or semi-skilled. Estimates ranged from eighty-five per cent to 'sixty per cent at least – probably more'. Party officials gave various reasons for this preponderance of skilled workers.

The skilled worker has more education and has achieved certain things in life which open his mind to new ideas. The engineers, for instance, play a big part in setting the pace for the standard of living of other workers.

They have better paid jobs and they think for themselves a bit. They struggle and have a wakening social conscience. We don't have many members in the slums or the depressed areas – these people are prey to all sorts of prejudices.

Much of this boils down to the fact that the higher one goes up the social scale the greater is the tendency to be politically active. Skilled workers have more money, more time, and, in many cases, more initiative and political energy than unskilled workers. They tend to be able to express their ideas more coherently than the unskilled, and they are better at organizing collective action, just as their greater geographical stability makes them more accessible for organization, especially if they work in a large factory.

Although the bulk of the working-class membership is drawn from the better-off sections of the working-class population, the role of poverty should not be underestimated as an incentive to join the Party. Relative deprivation can be a traumatic experience in the same way as unemployment or eviction, especially, it seems, where an acute sense of social stigma is attached.

Both my parents were born in one of the poorest working-class districts in Birmingham. . . . Both of them had been compelled to seek work when twelve years old. . . . The class struggle has always been for us, as for others of our kind, a real and personal thing, in the shape of low wages, bad working conditions and periods of unemployment. . . . My mind was a mass of confused bitterness and fury and little else – as much against the apparent apathy of the people as anything else . . . every man for himself was the callous and brutal formula for life.[71]

I am a Communist because I have experienced poverty in Wales.[72]

My early life was full of the things common to most working-class children – a home whose outstanding characteristics were poverty, sickness and death; the dread of getting into debt and the struggle to keep everything so clean that people thought you were better off than you ever dared hope to be.[73]

We were desperately poor . . .[74]

Of the twenty-seven interviewed for this study, only four had working-class occupations, but five had experienced an uncomfortable and distressing financial shortage or hand-to-mouth living. One reflected angrily on acute poverty.

We lived in extreme poverty. We were always extremely conscious of it. I'll give you two examples. I remember going one day to some better-off relations. My mother took some jewels with her – worthless trinkets – hoping that they would buy them. It was a very humiliating experience. The other one – we had to make frequent visits to the local poor relief for clothing. My mother was in tears for days before we went. Everybody knew you had parish clothes. A terribly humiliating experience. [Railway worker]

Most Communist autobiographies and biographies begin with an account of poverty-stricken childhood conditions.[75] Most of the authors are self-educated, skilled workers whose writing is coherent and articulate. Unlike less intelligent and ambitious workers, Communists are able to fit their own experience of poverty into an elaborate ideological frame of reference. They are capable of organized political analysis and criticism, and of organized political action, and, since their economic expectations are relative to the standard of skilled workers, this political action is rather more likely to be radical than moderate.

In Glasgow particularly, the standard of living falls far short of that expected by skilled workers. Not only does Glasgow have some of the worst slums in Britain, but Glasgow is known all over Britain for its notorious slum conditions, so that feelings of relative deprivation in the area are particularly acute. One half of the workers in the Hutchestown–Gorbals area are skilled workers, one third semi-skilled and only one sixth are unskilled.[76] Although the city built a very large number of houses between 1939–45, it was calculated in 1946 that 100,000 individuals needed re-housing.[77] In 1932 between a half and a third of the city's working population was registered as unemployed.[78] In 1950 the average vote of the six Communist parliamentary candidates in Glasgow was over three times the national Communist average.[79] In 1960 Glasgow had 1,815 party members. Bolton, a city one fifth as big as Glasgow, had only fifty members.[80]

Far from being the natural and inevitable, if extreme, product of the working-class sub-culture, there is little in the average working man's make-up that will lead him to give either his vote or his name to the Party. There is something in Communism which appeals to the skilled worker but little that attracts the unskilled. A number of cultural elements tend to cluster together in a single syndrome. Unemployment, fatalism and a degree of anti-Semitism tend to go together, while working-class interest in politics in Britain tends to strengthen class feelings.[81]

The C.P. has to compete for members with a large number of other, but usually very much smaller, political groups. Most important, it has to compete with the Labour Party which was well-established before the C.P. was founded. Most working-class people see no reason to vote for or support the C.P., when they have a vastly larger and more powerful political machine which they believe looks after their interests. They will only turn to the C.P. when some quite out of the ordinary event like unemployment disrupts their life, and then often only for a short period of time. In sum, the Communist Party is at odds with the way of life of those it most wishes to attract. For this reason it is one of the smallest in the world compared with the size of the group which it claims to speak for and lead.

1. Willmott, 1963, p. 14
2. See Appendix 2
3. U.S.A. Department of State, Intelligence Report no. 4489, R–15
4. Mitrany, 1961; Einaudi, Domenach, and Garoschi 1951, p. 216; Rossi, 1955, p. 34
5. This hypothesis is at odds with Lipset's basic assumption that Communism, among

other 'authoritarian' ideologies, is the natural and inevitable, if extreme, outcome of the working-class way of life in Western industrial societies – Lipset, 1960, Chapter 4

6. Hoggart, 1959
7. Zweig, 1952
8. Robb, 1954
9. Kerr, 1958
10. Spinley, 1953. Klein (1965) ties together and summarizes many of these studies
11. Whitehead, 1921, p. 290
12. Paul, 1925
13. Almond and Verba, 1963, pp. 105, 111, 153
14. Cantril, 1962, p. 48
15. Almond and Verba, 1963, p. 257
16. Kerr, 1958, p. 130
17. Spinley, 1953, p. 76
18. Robb, 1954, p. 140
19. Spinley, 1953, p. 60
20. Hoggart, 1959, pp. 69, 71
21. Spinley, 1953, pp, 59, 84
22. Hoggart, 1959, p. 62; Kerr, 1958, p. 116
23. Hoggart, 1959, p. 79. This is one aspect of what has been termed working-class cognitive poverty – Klein, 1965, p. 95
24. Zweig, 1952, p. 228
25. Abrams, 1961, pp. 342–50
26. Gosling, 1962, p. 10
27. Eysenck, 1958, Chapter 14; Cross, 1961, 1965; Robb, 1954; see also Segal, 1958, p. 440, and Lipset, 1960, Chapter 4
28. Cross, 1965
29. Robb, 1954, p. 143
30. Segal, 1962, p. 25; see also Degras, 1960, p. 195
31. Haldane, 1949, p. 15
32. Piratin, 1948, p. 4
33. Bell, 1941, pp. 15–16
34. Jackson, 1953, p. 12
35. Guest, 1939, p. 23
36. Bell, 1944, pp. 2–3
37. Pollitt, 1950, p. 31
38. *World News and Views*, vol. 27, no. 13, 2 April 1947
39. McCarthy, 1953, p. 34
40. Murphy, 1941, p. 28
41. Bell, 1927, p. 2
42. Davies, 1961
43. Mann, 1923, p. 15
44. Sloan, 1938, p. 20
45. Hyde, 1952, pp. 20–21
46. Broady and Mack, undated manuscript. Pye (1956, p. 124) notes that members of the Malayan C.P. show a similar thirst for knowledge
47. Klugmann, 1963, p. 2
48. Baker, 1963, p. 2
49. Spinley, 1953, pp. 53, 59
50. Jackson and Marsden, 1962
51. Almond and Verba, 1963, pp. 380–83
52. Hoggart, 1952, p. 53; Zweig, 1952, p. 34; Willmott, 1963, p. 106; Brennan, 1959, p. 125

53. Jackson and Marsden, 1962, p. 174
54. Alford, 1963, p. 290
55. Darke, 1953, p. 36
56. Horner, 1960, pp. 10–11
57. Coupland, 1954, Chapter 8
58. McKenzie and Silver, 1962; McKenzie, 1963
59. Almond and Verba, 1963, pp. 105, 111, 455
60. Blondel, 1963, p. 47
61. *The British Road to Socialism*, British Communist Party, 1958, p. 23
62. Shils and Young, 1953; see also Birnbaum, 1953
63. Marshall, 1963, pp. 67–127
64. Zweig, 1952, p. 212
65. Brennan, 1959, p. 110; Hoggart, 1952, pp. 41–5; Robb, 1954, p. 55; Way, 1959; Young and Willmott, 1962, pp. 104, 116; Segal, 1962, p. 21; Almond and Verba, 1963, p. 144; Kerr, 1958, p. 103
66. Lockwood, 1960; Miller, 1964; Miller and Riesman, 1961
67. McKenzie and Silver, 1962
68. Manis and Meltzer, 1963
69. Abrams, 1961
70. Almond and Verba, 1963, p. 382
71. *World News and Views*, 1947, vol. 27, no. 13
72. *Daily Worker*, 5 July 1963, p. 1
73. McCarthy, 1953, p. 35
74. Pollitt, 1950, p. 18
75. Moffat, 1965; Gallacher, 1936; Horner, 1960; Piratin, 1948; Bell, 1941; Bell, 1944; Mann, 1923; Copeman, 1948; McCarthy, 1953; Jones, 1937
76. Glasgow Corporation Architectural and Planning Department, *City Redevelopment 2*, undated pamphlet
77. J. McInnes, *Glasgow's Housing, Labour's Achievement and Future Policy*, undated pamphlet
78. W. Glen, *The Glasgow Council for Communal Services in Unemployment, 1932–50*, undated pamphlet
79. See Appendix 4
80. *World News*, vol. 7, no. 51, 24 December 1960
81. Benney and Guise, 1950; see also Glantz, 1958

CHAPTER 6

COMMUNISM AND THE MIDDLE CLASS

There is less information about middle-class Communists than about working-class Communists, although certain tentative conclusions can be gleaned from the data available. First of all, there is the obvious statement that the British middle class is overwhelmingly conservative in its politics, and therefore the Party will find it hard to recruit middle-class members. But it did attract a higher proportion of middle-class members in the 1930s than it had ever done before or since,[1] and it seems clear that this middle-class influx can be attributed to a certain set of political events which differed in character from the events which resulted in an increased working-class membership.

In 1926, the year of the General Strike, there was a sudden upswing in Party membership. Between October and April in 1926, 4,700 people joined – a forty-per-cent increase in the total membership. During the same period the Young Communist League doubled its membership to reach the 3,000 mark,[2] and the sales of the *Workers' Weekly* rose from 48,000 to 80,000.[3] Recruitment was mainly of working-class people, and was especially heavy in mining areas.[4] This was in spite of, or perhaps partly because of, the arrest of the twelve C.P.G.B. leaders, the police raid on the Party headquarters in King Street, and the subsequent publication by H.M.S.O. of 'Selected Documents'. When the General Strike began on 4 May 1926 many leaders were in prison and many more were arrested within the next few days. With the General Strike over, membership figures sank back to 7,000 – the loss being greatly due to defection of members in the mining areas, it was claimed.[5] The claim seems rather dubious since the main mining District, South Wales, actually increased its membership by 800. The loss seems to have fallen mainly in the Lancashire, Yorkshire, and Tyneside Districts.[6] But, since the Party had changed some of its District boundaries between the publication of the 1926 and 1927 figures, it is difficult to say more exactly where and why the membership figures fell. However, the rise in unemployment figures in 1931 and 1932 pulled the membership figures after them, until there were 9,000 registered members, more than half of whom were unemployed. But as people found work again, so they forgot about the Party that had tried to do so much for them, in the same way as the miners had forgotten all the efforts of the Communists to help them when most of the general strikers had gone back to their jobs.

The social forces behind middle-class membership are different. Middle-class members have more ideological, humanitarian and altruistic reasons for joining the Party. Bonham has suggested that the working class is attracted by 'industrial socialism', while the middle class is attracted by 'welfare socialism'.[7] Its better standard of living together with its higher standard of education gives the middle class a deeper and broader set of political perspectives.

Perhaps the most characteristic property of the socialist intellectuals is their attitude towards problems of international policy. In contrast, the attitude of the manual wage class appears insular, and at times, parochial.[8]

Bonham's point is well illustrated by the following extracts from interviews with middle-class Communists.[9]

I joined the C.P. over matters of principle. I knew the history of the C.P. and its internationalist record. I was an emotional sort of anarchist at the time. It was nothing to do with the C.P. policy on housing or education. That didn't come till later. [Student]

I joined because of an accumulation of events – Spain, the invasion of Czechoslovakia and Poland. The C.P. warned against Fascism. I thought they were exaggerating, but they were right. [Teacher]

Peace is the world's main problem, and that boils down to international co-operation. I can't stress that enough. [Architect]

The Growth of Fascism first prompted my interest in Communism. That had a tremendous impact on me. [Solicitor]

I happened to read a friend's Daily Worker which reported Mussolini's invasion of Abyssinia. That converted me to Communism. The world needed to be put right and I felt that the Communists were the only ones with an answer. [Middle-class housewife]

The Party attracted a higher proportion of middle-class members in the 1930s because of international events. While purely industrial matters drew some sections of the working class to Communism in the 1920s and 1930s, it was the Spanish Civil War and the rise of European Fascism and Nazism which led middle-class individuals to join the C.P. in the 1930s. As the international situation grew from bad to worse, so sections of the middle class shifted their political allegiance further to the left,[10] and so also a smaller number moved far enough left to become Communists. For the first time the Party could identify itself with, even claim to lead, public opinion on an issue that was thought to be crucially important – the growth of the radical right. In Britain, Mosley's B.U.F., formed on 1 October 1932, appeared to be flourishing. In 1934 it had over 100 branches, 5,000 members, and a hard core of vociferous activists.[11] In the same year it held its much publicized Olympia meeting. There was a strong feeling, especially among some sections of the middle class and intellectuals, that the Communist Party was the best answer to Fascism. 'Marxism soon became the fashion, not only in poetry and literature, but also in other fields of endeavour.'[12] Keynes was reported as saying that 'There is no one in politics today worth sixpence outside the ranks of the liberals, except the post-war generation of intellectual Communists under thirty-five.'[13]

Many middle-class Communists in the 1930s were more anti-Fascist than they were convinced Communists. 'I was not a politician, I was an anti-Fascist', wrote Charlotte Haldane in her autobiography.[14] Others like her were less convinced of the appeals of Communism than they were horrified by the events in Spain, Italy, and Germany, and by the upheavals which followed Mosley and his British Union of Fascists as they pursued their campaign for Fascism and anti-Semitism in Britain. The anti-Fascists felt that if Communism was not right it was at least on the right side, and more decidedly and determinedly so than any other political party in Britain – until the non-aggression pact between Germany and Russia.

Reaction against Fascism and Nazism can best account for the increased number of middle-class Communists in the 1930s, but there are other more minor factors to consider. In the 1920s and the 1940s the majority of intellectuals who joined the Party were occupied with the arts – writers, journalists, historians. In the thirties Communism attracted a larger number of scientists.[15] As Polanyi has written, Marxism appeals to the scientist with a social conscience because it claims to be scientific humanitarianism.[16] In the thirties the scientists in the Party hoped or believed that Communism could solve the world's problems scientifically and rationally, and in doing so would produce a new world in which the scientist would have a great deal of influence at the top political levels. 'In a world in which science alone seemed to know what it was about, Communism held the hope that the rule of the scientist–king might become more than a dream.'[17]

The intellectual subtlety and internal elaboration of the Communist ideology also makes it attractive to some middle-class members. In his survey of ex-Communists Almond found, not surprisingly, that the middle class had read more Communist classics than the working class.

The intellectuals based their confidence more often on historical materialism, while the working class tended to be more pragmatic, relying on empirical evidence that Marxism was right. . . .[18]

And as Reinhold Niehbuhr has suggested, the intellectuals seemed to be more easily swayed by the subtleties of Marxist dogma, than the working man.[19] In Communism, particularly in the thirties, they found an approach to the world which helped towards an understanding of it, and which indicated a way in which a new and better one might be constructed.

Unemployment might also help to explain, in a few cases, why middle-class individuals joined the Party. It has been estimated that 300,000 of the insured black-coated workers were unemployed in 1934, and that they 'suffered as acutely as any other group due to the lack of communal provision for their plight and the conventional expectations of their position.'[20] However, few middle-class people seemed to have joined the C.P. in the 1930s because of their own unemployment experiences.

Almond also discerns psychological reasons for becoming and remaining a member of the British Communist Party, especially among the middle-class members. While it would be incorrect, Almond says, to hold that the emotionally maladjusted are susceptible to Communism,

those people who found affiliation a means of coping with emotional difficulties may cling to the Party long after it conflicts with their ideals, their career, or other personal interests, or when leaving the Party, they may experience the most extreme suffering and disorientation.[21]

It may be true that the B.C.P. acts as a shelter for the neurotic and emotionally unsettled, but this is not an entirely satisfactory explanation of why people become Communists since a whole range of other groups may also function as emotional shelters, in which case it is still necessary to discover why certain unstable people pick the Communist Party rather than any other group. However, this psychological factor may help to explain why certain people decide to stay in the Party, even when continued membership conflicts with their material and ideal interests.

Almond has also suggested that:

Most of the middle-class intellectual neurotics who joined the Party did so because it provided them with an opportunity to express destructive and negative impulses in an intellectually and morally satisfying setting. As the movement has been stripped bare of its moral trappings, it no longer satisfies this peculiar combination of needs.[22]

Taking 'destructive and negative impulses' to mean diffuse, neurotic hostility, hate, bitterness, and *ressentiment* against the established social order, there is little that is either destructive or negative discernible in most of the interviews with middle-class Communists. Rather the general tone was idealistic and constructive, positive and pragmatic. It is true that the movement loses its moral appeal every so often (in 1956, for example, or at the time of the Moscow Trials, or the Soviet-Germany Non-Aggression Pact), although middle-class people continue to join the Party for moral and humanitarian reasons.

I suppose I'd describe my living conditions as 'perfectly adequate'. They always have been. It was really a sense of social injustice that brought me into the Party. At first it was a romantic view – the two nations. The Hunger Marches tipped the balance. I think lots of people join because of an idealistic notion of a reasonable, humane world. I knew jolly little about Communism at first, but I did know that people were being exploited. . . . Perfect justice just isn't feasible, but the C.P. is on the right lines. . . . It's a strange thing to say I suppose, but one of the things I like about the Conservatives is their politeness. [Publisher's reader]

I sat on the fence for some time before joining. . . . The last straw was seeing a policeman hit an old lady on the head in a demonstration. . . . I think the working class join for the simple reason that they want better conditions. The middle class have more intellectual reasons. That's only to be expected, isn't it? I mean they join for things like justice, freedom, education. . . . Communism will produce a more efficient society but also it will allow individuals to fulfil their potential as human beings. What I'm saying is that Communists have a humane ideal – a society where everybody can get their full social rights. And when I say social rights I mean a hell of a lot, not just good houses – education, art, beautiful surroundings. And small things too, that you and I take easily for granted – cleanliness. I've always been attracted by the way that Barker writes about justice – you should know it better than I – something about the maximum development of individual capacities.[23] [Teacher]

I model my ideal society (that's an impossibility itself but it's no reason for not trying to improve the existing one), along the lines of what I like doing best, which is only natural – reading, going to the theatre, meeting friends, gardening. But most people can't do these things. They've no time or money to. And they didn't have the chance to be taught to enjoy the theatre and things like that. But you have got to raise the standard of living first. Theatres aren't full of people with empty stomachs. (Teacher)

Only one respondent gave vent to occasional bursts of anger.

The Tories? I hate the bastards. Yes, put that down. Mind you I don't hate them (if hate *is* the word) as much as I used to. I used to be committed to revolution in an emotional sort of way. You know, the blow'em-all-up kind of attitude, but I changed my mind as a result of an understanding of Marxism-Leninism. . . . Socialism is the only answer to the cruel, ridiculous, limited world in which we live. Capitalism stunts people. It makes competition the be-all and end-all of existence – reduces everything to a cash nexus. [Teacher]

With the exception of the period between about 1934 and 1944, however, the B.C.P. has attracted few middle-class individuals or intellectuals – no matter how 'intellectuals' is defined. Wood has taken pains to point out that it is easy to overestimate the size and strength of the group of Communist intellectuals in the 1930s.[24] Although there was an unusually large number of intellectuals inside the Party there was a much, much larger number outside. But it is quite possible that the Party usually has a larger proportion of intellectuals among its members than most political parties. Again, there is no direct evidence, but indirect evidence suggests that the Party has never had a great deal of difficulty in finding people to write for, and read, its intellectually demanding journals, of which there is a large number for so small a party.[25] For a newspaper intended primarily for working-class readers the *Daily Worker* has an arts page of a high standard. On the day that this was being written it carried reviews of a ballet, Schoenberg's 'Moses and Aaron', and of books on Bizet and Tchaikovsky. The most significant indicator is the number of intellectuals who left the Party in 1956 and 1958. Some of these defectors produced the *Reasoner* which became the *New Reasoner* before it merged with *Universities and Left Review* to become *New Left Review*. Wood mentions twenty eminent academics, writers and artists who left the Party as a result of the C.P.S.U.'s Twentieth Congress, the events in Hungary, and the Inner-Party Democracy controversy,[26] and there were many other intellectuals who left the Party whose names were not publicized because they were not known to the general public. There are also the quotations from Communist biographies (pp. 59–60) which indicate that a sizeable proportion of working-class members have gone to great lengths to educate themselves. All this suggests that although only a very small proportion of British intellectuals become Communists, quite a high proportion of British Communists were intellectuals before 1958. At present, those with middle-class occupations form about 20–25 per cent of the total membership.[27]

The middle class is more susceptible to open disagreement with the Party line on some issues, and often leaves for this reason. They find the various actions of the world Communist parties more disturbing than the working-class membership. Claude Cockburn quotes an eminent Frenchman as saying, 'If the Communists are right I am the loneliest madman alive. If they are wrong there is no hope for the world.'[28] This dilemma is fairly typical of those who have experienced what Sidney Hook termed 'the drama of doubt'.[29] The convert might be willing to give the Party his full faith, or to believe that 'on balance the Soviet regime was, so to speak, on the side of the Angels',[30] but in the past his faith has been shattered by some event in the Communist world – Stalinization of the C.P.G.B., Hungary, the Twenty-ninth Congress of the C.P.S.U., reports of anti-Semitism in Russia, Lysenko, Inner Party Democracy, the Nazi–Soviet pact. The list is a long one and is sufficient to keep the Party middle-class membership at a high rate of turnover.

Another reason why the Party fails to attract a large number of middle-class intellectuals is the fact that Britain has produced comparatively few alienated intellectuals.[31] The British intellectual has always been curiously well-integrated into society compared with his European counterparts.[32] Wood offers a number of other explanations. The colonies and the Commonwealth, he suggests, have provided a convenient outlet for the disgruntled activist, and the Labour Party has offered a better ladder for the ambitious left-wing politician.[33] Since, also, the average man is disinclined to 'waste his vote' he is more likely to vote Labour than Communist, if he is going to vote for the left wing at all.

Anti-intellectualism is not uncommon in the working class as a whole,[34] and it is also to be found in the C.P. – even when the Communist is, himself, an intellectual. This feeling manifested itself in the first year of the Party's existence.[35] This is not anti-intellectualism in the proper sense of the word (a low valuation of the products of the intellect) but an anti-individualism and a distrust of a group which has tended in the past to go its own way rather than the way of the Party. 'If a Bourgeois wants to join you,' warned August Bebel, 'look him over closely; if he is an intellectual twice as closely.'[36] One ex-Communist tells how a teacher was 'astute enough to show the proper humility before her proletarian comrades'.[37] Whether an antipathy towards the individualism of the intellectual is to be found in the Party or not, or whether it is rare or prevalent, it is sensed by some of the middle class. Of six Cambridge undergraduates who were asked, 'What do you think is the attitude of most Communists towards the intellectual members of the Party?', five answered that they thought that there was some antagonism ranging from an almost imperceptible and unconscious suspicion to a strong distrust.

The working-class members are suspicious when they hear the intellectual talking of the factories and the C.P.'s industrial organization. I'm a bit suspicious too – during a crisis they might break away from the Party.

There isn't much conflict between the two groups though the working class is a bit suspicious of the middle-class talk about trade unions and factories. The middle class tend to be 'proletentious'.

Very strong suspicion – we had our experience of the intellectuals in the 1930s and in the 1950s when the intellectuals walked out.

The working class doesn't like the intellectuals certainly. I know from the Southampton dockers. This explains the tendency towards anti-intellectualism in the student branch.

Many distrust the intellectuals who have no experience of the factories. Student Communists feel this a bit too, I think – hence their 'donkey-jacketism'.

And one District official, also middle class, said:

McCreery, for instance, is not working class – a Communist who has been romanticized by left-wing slogan-shouting. There's a lot of that in British working-class history. The problem is to act, not to talk and McCreery knows very little about the actual problems of everyday work in the working-class movement. . . . Peter Fryer, there's another middle-class man who is part of the middle class which is romanticized about politics – thought he knew all the answers to everything.

All the respondents who thought that there was some feeling against the intellectuals were themselves middle-class. This distrust is not unfounded. The history of the B.C.P. shows that the middle class is less faithful to the Party than the working class. The main Party theorist, Palme-Dutt, has required of the intellectuals that they join the Party on its own terms and not on their own as 'a heaven-sent teacher of superior wisdom'.[38] For the most part the intellectual or the middle-class member is unwilling to join the Party completely on its own terms – not for any length of time, anyway. But such an anti-intellectual attitude can easily be over-emphasized. Most respondents thought that intellectuals and middle-class members were not treated in any special way, that they were accepted in the same way as anyone else, and that there was no feeling of antagonism towards them. Nevertheless, anti-intellectualism, should the intellectual ever meet it, is one of the factors which keeps the 'worker by brain' from the Party, and might encourage him to leave it should he experience it from the inside.

Of middle-class Communists in the period after 1945, teachers seem to provide about seven times more than any other middle-class occupational group. As an occupational group within the Party they are as large as, if not larger than, the miners, and probably a higher proportion of school teachers than miners are Communists. Very roughly, about 0·7 per cent of British teachers are Communists, and 7·0 per cent of British Communists are teachers. Teachers also form a large section of the Labour Party's office-holders in the local branches.[39] Communist teachers seem to show the same pattern as the working-class Party members who were so intent on self-education. Of the five teachers who were interviewed, one had paid his way through art school by working at night as a kitchen porter, another was studying for a degree by attending evening lectures at a London University college, although he was forty and had two children, another was still attending evening classes although she had retired. The last had attended evening classes on educational theory and on 'subjects of general interest'. One of the District officers suggested that many middle-class Communist teachers had working-class origins and brought their politics with them. This was true of four of the five interviewed.

In the case of teachers and perhaps in the case of the middle class as a whole, it seems more likely that their politics determine their occupation than their occupation determines their politics. This is not to deny the view that man's social being determines his consciousness, but a suggestion that extra-occupational factors are more important in determining the middle-class individual's political perspectives, while purely occupational factors are far more important when it comes to considering the social origins of working-class political ideas.

Teachers are subject to only one of the eight occupational factors (see Chapter 4) which tend to create radical political attitudes, which is that of vertical occupational immobility. There are only limited opportunities for promotion within the profession, and inadequate teaching facilities and the teachers' belief that they are deprived of their proper status and salary have helped create a low occupational morale. Yet these factors do not seem to be of principal importance. The Communist is unlikely to be attracted to the capitalist world of the business man and industrial executive or industrial white-collar worker, and prefers what he feels to be the more socially useful job of teaching the young. A teacher who has worked with Communists has also suggested that they have an urge to expound and explain – not only politics but anything that is interesting, important or problematical. One of the Communist teachers interviewed said: 'Teaching kids helps them to know and claim their social rights.' Another, a Y.C.L.

member who was studying at night school to get the required teaching qualifications, said:

I like children. I've always liked children and most of all I'd like to teach them. At the moment I'm studying educational theory on my own. It's the human aspect I suppose. Besides teaching is a useful job.

All the five teachers interviewed like their job 'very much', or had liked it in the case of one who had retired. Of the five, four had joined the Party before they took up their profession, and the parents of the fifth were both Communists, so that joining the Party 'seemed the natural and logical next step to take'. Of the six students interviewed, four wanted to become teachers.

After the teachers, the clerical and administrative, and the professional and technical categories are the next largest middle-class occupational groups in the Party. They make up about five per cent and three per cent respectively of the total membership. There is no information about them other than that given by one District official who said that most white-collar workers were attached to factory offices. Here they would be exposed to some working-class Communist influence, and the Party organizations would find them more accessible than white-collar workers who spent their days in blocks of offices separated from most working-class or Communist contacts.

There is little information about the self-employed group in the Party apart from the fact that they constitute about one per cent of Congress delegates, and the information supplied by one official about the members of his District. Most of them, he said, had been Communists before setting up their own business, and most had been employed in industries which usually produce a high proportion of Communists, especially the building and engineering industries. Almost all were marginal middle-class business men who were running their own small plumbing, electrical, building or tailoring concerns. Of the twenty-three self-employed members in the District, there was one market gardener, but no farmers and no service industry workers in shops, cafés, or taxi businesses. The wealthy business man with a social conscience does not seem to figure at all in Party life.

As the study has proceeded the original distinction between the working-class pragmatist and the middle-class idealist has become clearer. It is evident that the two types have a somewhat different approach to Communist politics and join the Party for rather different reasons. The working-class individual, could he be persuaded to work for a political organization, would favour a left-wing one, and most probably the Labour Party. Though a higher proportion of middle-class individuals join and work for political organizations, most of them favour right-wing or moderate left-wing ones. This is the dilemma of the Communist Party. It cannot interest many working-class people in politics, and it cannot interest many middle-class people in radical left-wing politics.

1. Wood, 1959. The C.P.U.S.A. also attracted a larger proportion of middle-class members in the 1930s – Glazer, 1961, p. 114
2. *Eighth Congress Report*, 1926, p. 35
3. *Eighth Congress Report*, 1926, p. 49
4. *Eighth Congress Report*, 1926, p. 31
5. *Ninth Congress Report*, 1927, p. 16
6. See Appendix 5
7. Bonham, 1954, p. 182
8. Bonham, 1954, p. 194; see also Knupfer, 1947
9. Lipset and Hayek define the intellectual in terms of his function as creator or distributor of culture. 'I have considered as intellectuals all those who create, distribute, and apply *culture*, that is, the symbolic world of man' [Lipset, 1960, p. 311]. 'What qualifies him for his job is the wide range of subjects on which he can readily talk and write, and a position or habits through which he becomes acquainted with new ideas sooner than those to whom he addresses himself' [Hayek, in *Huszar*, 1960, p. 372]. The intellectuals in the Party, then, include the theorists who have Oxford Firsts and those who are largely self-educated, those who write in, or regularly read, one of the large number of intellectually demanding Communist journals, the artists, musicians, and academics, and many of the professional workers, lawyers, scientists, teachers, students and doctors
10. Bonham, 1954, p. 163
11. Cross, 1961, pp. 107, 131–2
12. Wood, 1959, p. 42
13. Keynes, 1939, p. 122
14. Haldane, 1949, p. 269
15. Wood, 1959, pp. 79–80
16. Polanyi, 1958, pp. 226–48
17. Wood, 1959, pp. 150–5
18. Almond, 1954, p. 165
19. Niehbuhr, in de Huszar, 1960, p. 303
20. Lockwood, 1958, p. 57
21. Almond, 1954, p. 294
22. Almond, 1954, p. 395
23. '. . . the development of the capacities of personality of its members is the ultimate purpose served by the State and its final political value.' Barker, 1961, p. 136
24. Wood, 1959, p. 69
25. They include *Our History, Music and Life, Realm, Modern Quarterly, Mainstream, World Marxist Review, Labour Monthly*, and *Marxism Today*
26. Wood, 1959, pp. 196–213
27. See Appendix 2
28. Cockburn, 1958, p. 178
29. Hook, in de Huszar, 1960, p. 359
30. Cockburn, 1958, p. 174
31. Wood, 1959, p. 28; Aron, 1957; Lipset, 1960, Chapter 10
32. Bradbury, 1965
33. Wood, 1959, pp. 27–8
34. Hoggart, 1959, p. 149
35. Jones, 1937, pp. 193–4
36. Quoted by Golo Mann, 1955, p. 45
37. Darke, 1953, p. 28, also p. 61
38. Palme-Dutt, 1932
39. Blondel, 1963, p. 102

CHAPTER 7

ETHNO-RELIGIOUS AND IMMIGRANT GROUPS

Not unexpectedly, none of the Communists interviewed were members of any religious organization. Nineteen were unable to name any church or denomination which lay close to their sympathies. Four respondents named the Quaker church in this context, and the remaining four named the Baptist, Presbyterian, and Methodist churches and the Church of England. All the respondents followed the official Party policy of tolerance for all religious beliefs.

I view them with a tolerant smile – I've no objection, but they are peripheral to my interests. [Student]

I've been more tolerant of them since joining the C.P. Perhaps because I'm a bit older. Before I dismissed them as cant and humbug. [Student]

Religion can make me angry, but mostly it's meaningless or of no importance. [Full-time Party worker]

I'm militantly opposed to religion in most forms, but I'm not active. It all goes on in the philosophical plane. One of the few things that can still astonish me is that people still believe. [Student]

Religion is doing a good job in some cases, especially for old people. It gives them something to hold on to. I don't think the C.P. and religion are incompatible, and I'm not anti-religious. [Architect]

Religion is misguided and sometimes it does a lot of harm. [Student]

I'm a third-generation rationalist, and I've an instinctive prejudice against religious people, but it doesn't stop me from cooperating with them and working with them on a number of different social problems, although we don't share the same fundamental beliefs. [Publisher's reader]

I've simply no attitude towards them. [Teacher]

I'm an atheist but I've really no pronounced views on religion. I mean I don't get heated about them or anything. I've known a number of very religious people with very good intentions but I steer clear of them. [Teacher]

Religion has a very strong basis. It's not phoney or artificial – it attempts to explain what some people can't understand. We must respect the genuine religious sentiments of millions and millions of people. But our inability to understand is decreasing and therefore religion is becoming less and less necessary. [Railway worker]

I'm an atheist but I respect religious beliefs. I know quite a lot of left-wing progressives who are Quakers. I wouldn't attack religions now as I used to once. [Bank clerk]

My parents weren't religious though I was taught at a Convent. But I'm not like some others. I haven't reacted against Catholicism. I don't hate it at all. [Housewife]

I'm a Marxist, though one can be religious and a Communist. I agree with a policy of complete tolerance for all religions except state-organized ones. [Office clerk]

Atheism is one of the basic feelings in my character. Religion gives a false impression of human dignity. It thwarts the destiny of man. [Teacher]

There are, in fact, about six ministers of religion in the Party.[1]

While the religious affiliations and attitudes of Party members are clear, their ethno-religious and immigrant background are difficult to establish. In the early years, it has been suggested, there was quite a high proportion of foreign-born people in the Party,[2] but a more recent and more detailed analysis of the delegates to the first conferences suggests that very few of the founder members of the Party were immigrants.[3] However, there is no direct evidence about the size of its present ethnic or immigrant membership. The most that can be said is that, unlike the American Party, the numbers are small and probably always have been. It is known that in 1961 the London District of the B.C.P. had 6,682 members and that 752 of these were Cypriots.[4] In 1957 there were 435 Cypriots out of a total London District membership of 7,186.[5] In 1961 the Y.C.L.'s London District had 722 members, 154 of whom were Cypriots.[6] Most likely they are Greek Cypriots, for the Party regards the Turkish claim to Cyprus as imperialist sponsored, and sees the plans for partition as a tactic used by the British government to preserve its hold over Cyprus as a military base.[7] Quite a number of Cypriots in the Party may have brought their politics with them when they immigrated, and there may also be organizational reasons for their comparatively large numbers. The Party will find it much easier to recruit Cypriots if they live in only a few geographical areas, than if they are thinly dispersed all over London. One Cypriot Communist will be a valuable asset in the campaign to recruit more.

There is slightly more information about Jewish Communists, who are interesting to sociologists for two reasons. In the first place, they probably form the largest and oldest ethno-religious group within the Party, and in the second, their reasons for becoming Communists are, in part, different from the reasons of non-Jews. The left-wing and, in some cases, radical political attitudes of Jews have already been well documented, but there are, unfortunately, no figures which can be used to estimate the number of Jews in the B.C.P. Their numbers probably increased in the thirties when the Party attracted a number of people who were not so much convinced Communists as they were anti-Fascists. Of the twenty-seven Communists interviewed five had Jewish blood (one or both parents were Jewish), but only in two cases were both parents practising Jews. Only two of the five seemed to be influenced in any way by their ethnic origins. The father of one was a non-practising Jew.

The headquarters of the British National Party were near my home and I can remember the slogans 'Juden Raus' and 'Communists are Jews' painted on the walls. My sisters were Presbyterians and under their influence I used to go to church classes. It didn't go on very long and I wasn't confirmed, and I left because I disagreed with the theology. When I was thirteen, I remember, I wanted to be English rather than Jewish. I didn't want to go to Israel but I was very impressed by the Kibbutzim when I got there. . . . In the last three or four years I have felt myself increasingly Jewish, but it's not the religion which gives me this feeling of belongingness. . . I didn't join the Party because of a desire to belong. There is some connexion between the community spirit in the Party and this belonging- ness. The C.P. is no more idealistic and happy than any other group – some of the members get in your teeth – but you can find friendship in the Party and other people who have the same ideas. I value the intellectual ability and the community spirit of the Communists I suppose. [Journalist]

Both parents of the second were practising Jews who were active in a Jewish good-works organization in the East End of London.

I'm not now a member of any religious organization, though I was once a member of the Habonim – a Jewish semi-political organization. Religion is like the curate's egg. It's good in parts, but in general rather bad. There's a lot in the 'opiate of the masses' statement. . . . The attitude towards minority groups of the Party appealed to me – particularly anti-Semitism. Though I'm not a practising Jew I feel conscious of not being part of British life. Not fully a part. I feel my cultural home is in Europe – in France or Italy. [Teacher]

The widespread sympathy for the C.P. among Jewish East Enders in the thirties and after was due to the combined effects of a number of factors. The slum conditions and economic instability of the area contrasted strongly with the wealth of other parts of London, and provided a firm base for both left-wing and right-wing political radicalism. After adopting an anti-Semitic policy, the British Union of Fascists gathered up a considerable number of followers in the East End who used the high proportion of Jews in the area as scapegoats, thereby forcing the Jews to sympathize with, if not join, the C.P.

We regarded the racial problem as the key-plank of our peculiar problems in

Hackney. There was a high percentage of Jews in our ranks, but they did not predominate. Indeed I believe Central Office would have frowned on our becoming a predominantly Jewish branch.

Emphasis has been placed on winning Jewish sympathy during the anti-Fascist activities of the inter-war years. That emphasis is still maintained. There are few Jews in the East End who are hostile to the Party, whatever their standing, and that is an important measure of the Party's success in this sphere. East End Jews never turn down requests to buy Party literature or support Party activity. This is not because they are Communists or even potential Communists. It is a recognition of the work the Party puts in against anti-Semitism. Anti-Communist propaganda since the war which has attempted to prove that the Soviet Union has been itself guilty of anti-Semitism has had little success among East End Jews.[8]

Another ex-Communist makes substantially the same points, and adds that the branch in Stepney, an area with a large Jewish population and also considerable support for Fascism in the thirties, was one of the C.P.'s strongest branches. It had over 1,000 members.[9] It is not insignificant that two of the Party's leaders in the East End, Phil Piratin and Solly Kay, are both Jewish.

Even without the pressures of Fascist anti-Semitism, it is probable that a number of Jews in the East End would have joined the Party, for there are certain affinities between Communism and Judaism. Fuchs suggests that there are three dominant characteristics in the Jewish culture which are responsible for Jewish left-wing voting patterns.[10] They are learning (Torah), social justice (Zedakeh), and non-asceticism. Communists and Jews have something in common in that both tend to think in materialistic terms. Communism is undoubtedly a this-worldly ideology and so also, as religions go, is Judaism. 'For the Jewish entrepreneur it is clear that the very circumstances of his existence foster a very strong desire for success over and above an undoubted appreciation of the things that money can buy.'[11] Although Communism contains something of an ascetic work ethic, not unlike that of the Protestant ethic.[12] Communists do, at the same time, expect that mankind will benefit at some future date from a thoroughly efficient economic system, which will produce the ultimate in a high standard of living with the minimum of effort and work. Jews and Communists do not correspond completely in their this-worldly, materialistic and non-ascetic outlooks, but they do have something of a common basis for a similar ideological frame of reference.

To this common basis may be added a similar desire and reverence for learning. It has already been seen that many Communists have gone to considerable lengths to educate themselves in order to understand the world. The Communist ideology has a strong appeal for those who want to understand the world as a first step to controlling it. It may also have a strong appeal for the Jew, who, as Strodbeck has written, has always expected that everything might be understood if not, perhaps, controlled.[13] Lastly, the Jewish reverence for privately organized charity can easily be turned into a highly favourable attitude towards the welfare state. It is a principle of Jewish religious teaching that people should have a stable occupation.[14] Fuchs concludes an article by saying:

By the Jewish emphasis on this-worldliness and the enjoyment of life here and now, Jews have been made more receptive to plans for a better life, for reconstructing society, for re-making man's environment, for socialism and millenialism.[15]

The three characteristics of learning, social justice and non-asceticism are strongly activated if they are threatened by a wider culture which is anti-Semitic.[16] As a result Jews are often especially concerned with the equal treatment of all social groups. In America it has been found that Jews favour free speech for Communists, and even for Fascists, more frequently than non-Jewish Americans.[17] Yet it has been said that the most contemptuous anti-Semitism is to be found among the members of the British Communist Party and particularly among its Jewish members.[18] However, none of the Party literature betrays such feelings and nor did any of those Communists who were interviewed. It is easy to see how this belief in Communist anti-Semitism arises. A high proportion of Jews are capitalists,[19] and thus the anti-capitalism of the Communist can easily be mistaken for anti-Semitism. It is sufficient to point out that Communist hatred of Jewish capitalism is a hatred of capitalism and not of the Jew.

Anti-Semitism in Russia is quite a different problem. There is some evidence to show that there was a state policy of anti-Semitism in Russia which stemmed from a 'grass-roots' anti-Semitic tradition,[20] but few Communists knew this during Stalin's time, and most were ignorant of it until well after. Many Jews joined the British Party in the 1930s because of its philo-Semitic policies, and it was easy for them to dismiss reports of Russian anti-Semitism in the same way as they dismissed other criticisms of Russia which were patently false. If some Communists are disposed to believe that everything about Communism and Russia is good, it is equally true that some anti-Communists believe that everything is bad. Both sides reject each other's valid objections along with the manifestly false ones. One set of haloed beliefs is reinforced, in this case, when it conflicts with another set of haloed beliefs. Other Party members were sufficiently convinced that anti-Semitism was practised in Russia,[21] and in some cases left the Party for this reason, particularly after the Twentieth Congress of the C.P.S.U.

Both Communism and Judaism are cast within an internationalist framework. The Jewish race, culture and language is international. This internationalism and the other factors discussed above lead to the conclusion that the Jewish culture, like the British middle-class culture, will produce the idealistic, humanitarian type of Communist, if it produces Communism at all, rather than the pragmatic type of Communist. This is well-illustrated by the remarks of one respondent who had a Jewish background.

Communism will produce a more efficient society but it will also allow individuals to fulfil their potential as human beings. What I'm saying is that Communists have a humane ideal – a society where everybody can get their full social rights. And when I say social rights I mean a hell of a lot – not just good houses – education, art, beautiful surroundings. [Teacher]

Jewish left-wing radicalism would seem to stem more from a status struggle than from a class struggle. Jews have a high-class rating in many cases, but insofar as they are denied, or feel themselves to be denied, equal status with non-Jews, they are a subordinate group.[22] Even though they may be economically stable as individuals their social insecurity as an ethnic group may produce a strong desire for social change and also an ability to empathize with other ethnic groups, which may have the added disadvantage of a low social and economic status.

In their efforts to explain Jewish left-wing attitudes most writers have overlooked some of the factors in the Jewish culture and social position which are not conducive to left-wing affiliation and particularly to Communist affiliation. Anglo-Jewry, like the membership of the B.C.P., is concentrated in urban and industrial areas,[23] but, unlike the bulk of Party members, few Anglo-Jews are factory workers. They do not see themselves fitting easily into a society of industrial workers.[24] Again, the strong individualistic economic element in the Jewish culture[25] is in no way compatible with Communism.

I sat on the fence for a long time before joining. In fact I almost joined unwillingly because of my religious background, I suppose, which militated against collective action. [Teacher]

This economic individualism results in Anglo-Jewry being concentrated in the middle class, and although Jews may not identify with the middle-class culture they do gravitate to industries like clothing, tailoring, and the furniture and food trades, and to professions like medicine, law, and accounting.[26] None of these occupations is marked by many of the industrial factors which tend to generate a radical political consciousness. These industries and occupations also tend to be split into small units, which makes for organizational difficulties in Party recruiting. The stress on economic independence leads to a general lack of trade-union organization, although it is true that Jewish trade unions have been remarkably effective in some cases.[27] Also, the combination of individualism, charity, and materialism may result more readily in a nineteenth-century liberalism than in a twentieth-century Communist collectivism. Finally there is an anti-authoritarian element in the Jewish culture,[28] which makes the Jew a deviationist in thought and action, and an independent in politics rather than a party supporter.[29]

It must be reiterated yet again that there is only a small quantity of information about the ethno-religious and immigrant membership of the

Party. Much of this information has only an oblique bearing on the subject matter, and hence it is difficult to produce anything but tentative suggestions, and almost certainly impossible to produce firm conclusions.

1. Information given by a Party official
2. Pelling, 1958, pp. 15–16
3. Macfarlane, 1966, p. 59. Kendall (1963) adds weight, in a somewhat oblique manner, to Macfarlane's conclusion, when he says that the British Socialist Party had few immigrant members, even though these few may have had some considerable influence over the B.S.P.'s policy. The B.S.P. was one of the largest of the groups which came together to form the C.P.G.B. in 1920
4. *London District Committee Bulletin*, 14 December 1961
5. *London District Committee Bulletin*, April–May 1957
6. *London District Committee Bulletin*, 14 December 1961
7. *Daily Worker*, 18 August 1964, p. 1; *Finish With Colonialism!*, Communist Party pamphlet, 1963
8. Darke, 1953, p. 45
9. Hyde, 1952, pp. 178–9
10. Fuchs, 1956
11. Aris, 1964
12. McLelland, 1961, p. 413; Kerr, Dunlop, Harbison, and Myers, 1962, p. 43
13. Strodbeck, in McLelland *et al.*, 1958, p. 155
14. Aris, 1956
15. Fuchs, 1955
16. Litt, 1962. The extent and strength of anti-Semitic feelings in Britain is irrelevant. It is sufficient that they have existed at one time, and not so long ago in a highly organized form, and that they still exist now among certain sections of the population, even if in a latent form.
17. Fuchs, 1956, p. 190
18. Hyde, 1952, pp. 178–9. It is a poor argument, but one worth mentioning, that just as Hyde believes that some Jewish Communists become anti-Semitic, so also it can be said that ex-Communists who become Catholics become anti-Communist. Hyde left the C.P. to become an active member of the Catholic Church.
19. Aris, 1964; Freedman, 1962; Krausz, 1962
20. Nove, 1961
21. See, for example, Levy, 1956, p. 2
22. For a discussion of the concept of subordinate group, see Lloyd Warner and Srole, 1945
23. Neustatter, in Freedman (ed.), 1955, p. 77
24. Parkes, 1964, p. 232
25. Lipman, 1960; Krausz, 1962
26. Freedman (ed.), 1955, p. 254; Freedman, 1962
27. Brotz, in Freedman (ed.), 1955, p. 109. The Jewish trade unions in Leeds were very successful – Krausz, 1964, pp. 30–31
28. Brotz, in Freedman (ed.), 1955, p. 159; Parkes, 1964, p. 232
29. Fuchs, 1956, p. 131

CHAPTER 8

THE AUTHORITARIAN STRAINS

The concept of the authoritarian personality has received a great deal of attention since the publication of the book *The Authoritarian Personality* in 1950, for as one writer has put it, the concept has the greatest possible relevance to the social issues of the day.[1] The main purpose of *The Authoritarian Personality* was to delineate the characteristics and ascertain the socio-psychological origins of a cluster of psychological characteristics called 'authoritarian'.[2] The authors of the book, however, are careful to emphasize that they deal mainly with the psychological aspects of authoritarianism and not with its historical, economic, or sociological aspects. That is to say, they are concerned with attitudes and not so much with the behaviour which may result from these attitudes. For at least two reasons it ought not to be assumed that there is a simple, direct, and necessary connection between attitudes and behaviour.

Firstly; a person may not act out his attitudes because certain variables may intervene between attitudes and behaviour. For example, proportionately more middle-class than working-class individuals join political organizations and so, other things being equal, it might be expected that proportionately more middle-class authoritarian personalities than working-class authoritarian personalities will join totalitarian movements.[3] On the other hand, the middle-class authoritarian may feel that it is 'not nice' to express or act out his attitudes, while the working-class authoritarian may feel less inhibited about them. Again, it is more difficult to organize strong social movements in rural areas than in urban areas because the population is thinly dispersed and because communications may be poor. It follows that the authoritarian personality in an urban area is more likely to find a number of suitable social movements to join, while the authoritarian in a rural area may not join any social movement for the simple reason that there may not be a suitable one available. For organizational reasons among others, proportionately more people working in large factories or cities join the Communist Party than people working in small factories or villages. The Party finds it difficult to contact, recruit, and organize potential members who are thinly dispersed over a large area.

The second reason for doubting a simple connection between authoritarian attitudes and authoritarian behaviour has considerable implications for the concept of the authoritarian personality. It was one of the main conclusions of the book that the various characteristics of authoritarianism are generally to be found in a single configuration.

The most crucial result of the present study, as it seems to the authors, is the demonstration of close correspondence in the type of approach and outlook a subject is likely to have in a great variety of areas, ranging from the most intimate features of family and sex adjustment, through relationships to other people in general, to religion and to social and political philosophy.[4]

This implies that there is only one type of authoritarian personality. One of the main arguments of the present chapter is that the various aspects of what is known as the authoritarian personality are not always to be found in a single configuration of personality characteristics, but may be permutated in different ways to give different types of authoritarianism.

For the moment, however, the opposite argument will be explored; the argument that there is only one type of authoritarian personality in which a whole range of co-variant attitudes are clustered together. If this is true it might also follow that a whole range of totalitarian movements will function as alternative and equally suitable vehicles for authoritarian personalities. There is certainly some evidence about Communism and Fascism to support this view, and therefore both movements have been labelled 'authoritarian' or 'totalitarian'. Borkenau has described Nazism as 'Brown Bolshevism',[5] and Gurian has written: 'What matters is not the content of the totalitarian doctrine; its function of establishing total dominance by the totalitarian leaders and its élites is decisive.'[6] The British Union of Fascists and the British Communist Party gathered considerable support in the same place and at the same time – in the East End of London in the thirties. It seems also that they drew the bulk of their support from the same section of the population – from the working class. It is quite a common belief that authoritarians who are dissatisfied with the Communist Party find a fitting home within a Fascist movement, and that many ex-Communists join a Fascist group, or an authoritarian religious group.[7]

But a further examination of British Fascism and Communism shows that the views of Borkenau and Gurian break down completely. Many people joined the Communist Party in the thirties because they were anti-Fascist. There is no possible question of Fascism serving as an alternative ideology for them. This suggests that there are different types of authoritarian personalities who distinguish clearly between, and are attracted by, different types of authoritarian movement – assuming that both the British Communist Party and the various Fascist organizations were authoritarian in the same way. It is this assumption which needs to be questioned.

Harold Lasswell has written that 'the concept of the authoritarian personality is, in some ways, too general to provide a developmental model of *homo-politicus*'.[8] In making this observation Lasswell highlights one important deficiency in the concept; namely, that it is scarcely discriminating enough to handle the wide range of empirical data and types to which it has been applied. Support for Lasswell's view is provided by Harris, who found that 'within groups of working-class respondents . . . authoritarianism does not seem to correlate with observed variations of political behaviour and attitudes'.[9] The concept is too broad because it fails to distinguish between various types of authoritarianism. This becomes apparent when one lists the words which have been equated with authoritarianism, or which have been treated as being single aspects of the total range of behaviour, attitudes, and opinions which have been labelled 'authoritarian'. This list would include extremism, intolerance, illiberalism, ethnocentricism, tough-mindedness, anti-democratic feelings, dogmatism, rigidity, and non-humanitarian feelings.

For present purposes, therefore, it is intended to break down the concept of authoritarianism into three component dimensions. The first has been called the open–closed minded dimension, and refers to the way in which an ideology may be structured and organized irrespective of its content. The second two dimensions refer to the content of an ideology; they are the degree of authoritarianism or liberalism on economic issues, and the degree of authoritarianism or liberalism on non-economic issues. It is probably possible to isolate other important dimensions of the concept, but these three are sufficient for the present task of distinguishing between Fascist, Communist, and Social Democratic ideologies. When Fascism and Communism are compared on the three dimensions, certain similarities and differences appear. But when Fascism and Communism and social democracy are compared, a different set of similarities and differences appear.

Communism and Fascism are very different ideologies, although Communists and Fascists may structure their different belief systems in the same way. Rokeach has developed a dogmatism and an opinionation scale to measure the degree in which an individual structures his beliefs in a closed minded manner, whether the beliefs are left-wing or right-wing, liberal or illiberal, conservative or radical, progressive or reactionary. He defines a belief system to be structured in a closed manner

to the extent that there is a high magnitude of rejection of all disbelief subsystems, and isolation of beliefs, a high discrepancy in the degree of differentiation between belief and disbelief systems, and very little differentiation within the disbelief system.[10]

The dogmatism scale measures the degree of openness or closedness of the belief system, while 'the purpose of the opinionation scale is to serve as a measure of general intolerance'.[11]

For instance, Marx and Spencer could be grouped together as authoritarian and this would be an accurate grouping in so far as both were dogmatic in a way that J. S. Mill, for example, was not. Neither Marx nor Spencer could tolerate even mild criticism of their own ideas, and both were extremely agressive in their reaction to such criticism. This aspect of Spencer's personality is described by one of his contemporaries.

One of Mr Spencer's most marked characteristics was his extreme impatience, not to say irascibility, in discussion. The smallest difference of opinion in the most deferential of his admirers would produce a state of irritation alarming to witness, threatening, even, it used to be said, to the action of his heart. Therefore, for all conversational occasions he had equipped himself with a pair of earclips, which, as soon as danger point was neared, he clapped on firmly, and thus immediately put an end to the discussion.[12]

Marx was similarly, if not as extremely, intolerant of the views of others, and in this sense both he and Spencer could be called authoritarians. Compared with them J. S. Mill was not dogmatic but open-minded, and in this respect he was not authoritarian. Yet in another sense it is patently wrong to group Marx and Spencer together. Spencer was an authoritarian individualist. But, as Plamenatz says,

Whatever he may have been by temperament, Marx was not by doctrine illiberal; he believed that every man in the classless society would be as free as social institutions could make him, and merely denied that, while society remained divided into classes, this freedom was possible. Marx's avowed purpose was to work for the coming of the classless society, the only society where the rights of man so dear to the liberals would not be the privilege of the minority.[13]

From Le Gallienne's description one would expect Spencer to score the highest possible marks on the dogmatism and opinionation scales, while someone like J. S. Mill would score low marks. Of Rokeach's respondents, the British Communists turned out to be the most closed minded. He interviewed no Fascists but one would expect them to be similarly closed minded. Arthur Koestler describes how the Communist ideology has the effect of reinforcing the initial psychological tendencies of some Communists towards closed mindedness.

My [Communist] Party had equipped my mind with elaborate shock-absorbing buffers and elastic defences so that everything seen or heard became automatically transformed to fit preconceived patterns.[14]

Another characteristic of the closed minded is 'the isolation of parts within and between belief–disbelief systems'.[15] This is well-illustrated by the ex-Communist Douglas Hyde, who describes how, when he was transferring his allegiance from Communism to Catholicism, he kept his old and emerging beliefs rigidly segregated 'into water-tight compartments'.[16] The closed minded also take longer to construct new belief systems than the open minded.[17] A good illustration of this trait was given by one of the Communists interviewed in his description of a member of the C.D.R.C.U.

He reads a tremendous amount but is very slow to make up his mind. He had doubts about the Party and its policy a long time before he made the final break – perhaps for about ten years. But he took a long time to collect them together and really only arrived finally at his present position last year. But once he's made up his mind he won't change it. Not quickly anyhow.

The dogmatism and opinionation scales were not administered to the Communist respondents of this study, but their comments indicate that some of them might have been surprisingly undogmatic.

You can't be certain of anything. That's what the scientists tell us, isn't it? And it's true of everything – as much of Marxism as anything else. [Housewife]

Communists have a lot to learn from reading The God That Failed. I wish they would read it. It would do some of them a lot of good. It has a lot that is valuable for us. [Student]

This suggests that although the average dogmatism scores of Communists might be high, the spread of scores might be as great as that for any other group.

Moving from the structure or organization of an ideology to its content, it is useful to distinguish between the economic and the non-economic aspects. Economic liberals and illiberals hold opposite views on such matters as progressive taxation, unemployment benefits, free hospitals, a centrally regulated economy, and the welfare state in general. The non-economic aspects of an ideology are concerned with such matters as civil liberties, capital punishment, minority groups, coloured immigrants, internationalism, and the disciplining of children. In their economic aspects the ideologies of British Fascists and Communists in the thirties were partly similar. Both believed in a centralized economy tightly controlled by the State, and a State organized system of social security which would eliminate unemployment and other social problems. The Fascist economic ideology was much less detailed and sophisticated and more utopian than the Communist one.[18] It is in their economic facets that the extremes touch and hence, partly, the attraction of Fascism for some of the unemployed in the thirties.[19]

The non-economic aspects of the two ideologies are totally dissimilar however. Fascists are most frequently ethnocentric – both anti-Semitic and colour prejudiced. In both America and Britain Communists were found to have low scores on the F. and E. scales.[20] It could be argued that they simulated these low scores in order to create the desired image of themselves, but no one who has any contact with British Communists could believe that there is a glimmer of truth in the argument.[21]

The Communist Party stands against all forms of racial and colour descrimination, and pledges its full support to every progressive measure to combat racialism in Britain. . . . Every step taken to end the menace of racialism and to ensure that coloured immigrants are guaranteed equality of treatment with British workers, will assist and strengthen the bonds of solidarity in the common fight.[22]

The orthodox Marxist believes that all forms of racialism are foisted upon the working class by the ruling class in order to distract the former's attention from its own social and economic conditions.[23] British Communists believe in very strong measures to combat racial intolerance and discrimination, and thus fall into the pattern discovered by Dombrose and Levinson in which individuals who have the lowest E. scale scores also favour the most militant action against those who discriminate between races and ethnic groups.[24]

Apart from a handful of demented, moronic race haters everyone condemns the disgraceful behaviour of Colin Jordan and his nazi hooligans at Mr Gordon Walker's election meeting.

What will disgust many people is that race haters can go to public meetings, shout their filthy propaganda and get away with it. . . . What is needed is a law on the lines of what is known as the Brockway Bill. This would protect the community by making incitement of racial hatred, as well as discrimination, an offence.[25]

While Communists are highly intolerant of intolerance, Fascists are highly intolerant of tolerance. The two groups, if tested, should appear quite separately at the 'rigid low' and the 'rigid high' ends of the E. scale. In the ethnocentric and antidemocratic aspects of authoritarianism, then, Communists emerge as being anti-authoritarian and Fascists as authoritarian.

For the most part when British Communists are called authoritarians the reference is to their desire for a highly centralized economic system,[26] and to their attitude towards inner-Party discipline which is linked, in turn, to the structure of the Party. It is most usually assumed that Communist Parties are not democratic, and that Communists are themselves anti-democratic.[27] However, rarely has there been any attempt to compare what is known about the internal workings of Western Communist Parties with what is known about democracy as it operates in most other political organizations. It is widely acknowledged by most political scientists that most political organizations are oligarchical to a greater or lesser extent, and that an ideal democracy is not possible.[28] In spite of this, Communist Parties have usually been compared implicitly and quite unjustly with models of perfect democracies, and not with actual 'democratic' organizations. A significant exception is Grainger's article, 'Oligarchy in the British Communist Party', which he concludes by saying:

It perhaps needs to be said that lacking a carefully documented comparison, it should not be assumed that the C.P. is more 'oligarchical' than either the Conservative or the Labour Party, in the sense in which the word is used by Dr Robert McKenzie in his able analysis.[29]

At a number of points in his article Grainger points out that the B.C.P., at least in theory, is no less democratic than the Labour Party.

A great deal of the information supporting the view that the B.C.P. is an authoritarian organization comes from ex-Communists. Their accounts of the anti-democratic procedures within the Party *may* be quite accurate but there is no reason to treat their views without caution. It is possible that ex-Communists, and particularly the middle-class idealists, compare the actualities of the B.C.P. with a somewhat unrealistic and text-book ideal of political democracy, and leave the Party when they discover that the two do not square. Or they may leave over some policy disagreement, firmly convinced that the Party did not give them sufficient hearing and is not democratic when, in fact, their policy had very little support from the rest of the membership. Michael McCreery, of the C.D.R.C.U., left the Party complaining that he had never been given sufficient chance to publish his views in the Party press. In fact quite a number of his articles and letters had been printed, although, perhaps, only a small proportion of his prolific output.

All those who were interviewed firmly believed that the B.C.P. is the most democratic political organization in Britain.

Local branches have quite a lot of influence on the national policy and decision-making of the Party as a whole. We're always sending Resolutions and delegates to Congresses. . . . The ideas that animated the Minority Report (on Inner Party Democracy) were incorporated into the Majority Report. They were mistaken in not recognizing this. If their Report had been put into practice it would have weakened the Party very seriously. [Teacher]

The Party is the most democratic in the country. This branch does not have as much influence in the Party as it could have because we don't give enough thought to policy and don't send up enough resolutions. . . . [When asked about the Minority Report] I've forgotten all about it. [Electrician]

We're always arguing the toss about policy here. There's constant discussion throughout the Party from top to bottom. . . . I opposed the Minority Report and agree with the Majority's one. I was at the Conference. [Housewife]

All the branches have considerable influence on policy-making. It's a stupid, foolish question. [Full-time Party worker]

Most spoke of democracy in 'bourgeois liberal' terms and not in Marxist–Leninist democratic centralist terms. Only one respondent raised the distinction between bourgeois liberal democracy and Communist democratic centralism, and he was also the only one to speak on the need for 'a highly organized and disciplined Party – which the Labour Party is not'.

However, there is also evidence to show that the B.C.P. is actually less democratic than some other parties. Probably the issue will never be finally settled since it is unlikely that reliable and conclusive evidence will appear which will firmly establish the extent of democratic or anti-democratic practices within the Party. It is the author's opinion that the British Party is actually more democratic than most people believe, but somewhat less democratic than most Party members would claim. But it must be emphasized that this is only an opinion based on conflicting evidence and not a firm conclusion which is unlikely to be altered by new evidence, should it ever appear.

Grainger concludes his article by summarizing the devices 'which ensure that effective power is retained by a narrow circle at the top of the hierarchy'.[30] They include the proscription of factions, the confinement of discussion of inner-Party matters to the Party press, the method of electing members of leading committees, and a 'permanent caucus of the leadership', plus the rule that an appearance of unanimity must always be maintained by the leading committee of the Party – even to members.

In a Party handbook it was written:

The Party demands that the strictest discipline should operate within the fractions. Any member who goes contrary to the decisions of the leading committee as accepted by the fraction or speaks or votes in opposition to the fraction, or who in any way breaks the unity of the fraction, commits a grave breach of Party discipline.[31]

The Party leadership can always claim that opposition to policy from within has the effect of splitting the united effort of Party work, and thus reduces the effectiveness of the Party's work. Serious criticism can always be defined as treacherous both to the Party and its leadership, and to the working class as a whole. One ex-Communist said in an interview:

British Communism is based on the notion that Russia is socialist, and thus any criticism of Russia means that the person cannot be a socialist, and therefore cannot be a proper member of the Party. This state of affairs leads to a complete break-down of communications between the Party and its critics. The Party is completely unable to understand any criticism.

The centralized organization and leadership of the Party seem to perform a valuable function in holding the Party together. Radical political and religious organizations are notorious for their tendency to split again and again in amoeba-like fashion to form a multiplicity of tiny factions. The Independent Labour Party worked under the crippling disability of 'an almost complete lack of discipline in the party'.[32] It could be argued very strongly that the Communist Party would have been torn apart by rival factions long ago but for its centralized structure and organization. But it must also be remembered that while the Party rule-book demands strict discipline, at the same time it states that

Members not only have the right but the duty to take part in the formation of the policy of the Party through their Party organizations and in the election of the leading committees.[33]

There can be little doubt that most Party members spend an enormous amount of time arguing about Party policy. Whether their decisions have any effect on the Party leadership is a different matter, and one on which only a little light can be thrown.

The reception of the Majority Report of the Commission on Inner Party Democracy showed that the largest part of the membership approved of the structure and functioning of the Party. It was the job of the commissioners 'to examine and report on the problems of Inner Party Democracy, including Congress procedure, and to make recommendations as a basis for discussion'.[34] The Majority Report was passed by the delegates to a special National Congress which was called to discuss the findings of the commissioners. The Majority, who were mainly full-time Party workers, reported that although the Party had its faults, it was the most democratic of British political organizations. The 'essential and appropriate' principle of democratic centralism, they said, 'is the combination in practice of working-class democracy with a strong centralized leadership'.[35] The phrase 'strong leadership' and implications for its desirability are repeated elsewhere in the Majority Report. Even so the Majority had some doubts about the Party structure and considered that 'our Party should now correct what we feel to be a serious error – too great an emphasis on centralism and insufficient emphasis on democracy'.[36] Its criticisms, however, were not at all serious or far reaching, and resulted in only a few minor reforms of the election machinery, and more space in the press for a freer discussion of policy and problems.

The Commissioners also included a dissident group of three members who produced their Minority Report. Acceptance of the Minority Report would have meant the complete restructuring of the Party organization along radically new lines.[37] It starts off by observing that there is much confusion about what democratic centralism means, but that whatever it means the recommendations of the Majority Report 'would perpetuate the bureaucratic centralism that has had such disastrous results in Eastern Europe'.[38] The 'iron discipline', it continues, which the Communists want to build would result only in 'resentment, disunity and indiscipline', while in the past, the unity of the Party had too often rested upon an uncritical toeing of the Party line. This applied as much to the leadership in their relationship to Moscow as to the rank-and-file in their relations with King Street.

The Majority of the Commission took the view that Comrades Pollitt and Campbell, both of whom supported the war in 1939, were right to sign recantations a month later; the Majority argued that even if Campbell and Pollitt did not really believe that they were wrong, it was more important to preserve the unity of the Party by confessing to error, than to divide the Party by continuing to fight for their point of view. We cannot accept the view that the distortion of truth and honesty in this way can do the Party any good at all: if Pollitt and Campbell had adhered to their original view it would have been far better if they had said so. . . . Truth has to be taken as a whole, and the more damaging truth may be the more necessary it is to know it, if mistakes are to be put right and injustices undone.[39]

The Minority Report called for greater freedom of discussion in the Party journal *World News* and for more honest reporting in the *Daily Worker*, as well as for a review of Party committees and a revision of their election machinery. Finally, it commented, there was a

> growing minority belief that the uncritical support given by the Executive Committee to Soviet policy divides, discredits and isolates the Party, identifies Communism in the eyes of the British people with the denial of personal freedom and with certain indefensible politics, and renders ineffective the Party's efforts to combat anti-Soviet tendencies.[40]

None of the Minority Commissioners were full-time Party workers. It is difficult to estimate the support the report was given by the rest of the membership. On the *Daily Worker*'s own admission, however, Hungary, the Twentieth Congress of the C.P.S.U., and the Commission produced 'the most intense crisis' in the history of the Party. Reluctance of the leadership to consider or print internal criticism, it was claimed, was one cause of the publication of three editions of the *Reasoner* which was headed with a quotation from Marx – 'To leave error unrefuted is to encourage intellectual immorality'.

Having come to believe that the B.C.P. was anti-democratic those who left it were not willing to tolerate similar characteristics in any other organization which they might otherwise have considered joining. One author of the Minority Report recounts how a number of ex-Communists joined the Socialist Labour League, but left as soon as they discovered it to be 'a miniature C.P., stalinism writ small'.[41] The same accounts are offered by others, one of whom wrote:

> we came into the Trotskyist movement from the C.P., hard on the heels of our experience of Hungary and our struggle with the Stalinist bureaucracy in Britain, were assured that in the Trotskyist movement we would find a genuine Communist movement, where democracy flourished, where dissenters were encouraged to express their dissent, and where relations between comrades were in all respects better, more brotherly, and more humane than in the party we had come from.[42]

With the exception of a few 'steel-hardened' cadres, British Communists are genuine and sincere democrats. The problem of authoritarianism never arises for them because they are rarely exposed to the esoteric doctrine of the classics. This is particularly true of the working-class pragmatists, who, even if they do come face to face with the esoteric doctrine, find it quite irrelevant to their needs as militant trade unionists. The Party continues to fight for higher wages, better houses, a lower cost of living, and for a better deal for the working class, so it matters little to them whether it is democratic or not. Foreign affairs do not have great significance for them and so they are not concerned with what goes on in Hungary or Moscow or any other part of the Communist world.

The more perceptive middle-class idealists, with their wider intellectual perspectives, are less willing to tolerate or follow changes in the Party line, tactics or ideology. In many cases, Hungary struck at the very roots of their belief in Communism and the Soviet Union. Very frequently they react against the esoteric doctrine when they are exposed to it. In 1922 the *Report on Organization* was produced with the aim of changing the Party from a Social Democratic Organization to a Bolshevik one, and it was opposed by a group of middle-class intellectuals.[43] One year before, another group of middle-class members left the Party when it changed to a United Front Tactic,[44] and the same thing happened because of the combined effects of the Moscow Trials, the Nazi-Soviet Pact, and the Soviet attack on Finland.[45] The largest and most recent defection was the result of Khrushchev's attack on Stalin at the Twentieth Congress of the C.P.S.U., the Hungarian events in 1956, and the Minority Report. Between February 1956 and February 1958, total membership fell from 33,095 to 24,670. The loss among middle-class members was 'proportionately far more than in the Party as a whole'[46] – a fact confirmed by three District officials. The French and Italian Parties also lost a disproportionately large number of middle-class and intellectual members after Hungary.[47] Earlier, the Dutch C.P. lost a number of members who were unable to reconcile their democratic beliefs with the Czechoslovakian *coup*.[48] In between these major events other middle-class members resigned from the British Party, saying that they could not tolerate its *realpolitik*, and the means it used to attain its ends, no matter how noble these ends might have been.

The Party's theories and its practice were in the flattest contradiction and proceeding in downright reverse directions. . . . A political party is a means to an end. The C.P. lost sight of the ends and became pre-occupied with the means. Eventually the means became an end in itself, and thus came the transformation of the party.[49]

The much-publicized ballot-rigging case in the E.T.U. is an example of such means. The C.P. headquarters disclaimed any connexion with the affair, and those found guilty in the trial were expelled from the Party, but both Haxell and Foulkes were members of the B.C.P. and the judge, in his summing-up, strongly implicated the Party's leadership in their guilt.[50]

It may be asked why some of the idealistic Communists are willing to use or tolerate such methods in trade-union, local or national politics. When events of the magnitude of Hungary in 1956, or the E.T.U. trial, or the Twentieth Congress occur, some Party members can easily explain them away using the 'shock-absorbing buffers' supplied by their psychological make-up and ideology.

The trouble in Hungary was engineered by dissatisfied groups inside Hungary who were in contact with the Americans who supported their aims of over-throwing Socialism. I do regret the errors of the Hungarian Party before 1956. [Teacher]

It was a counter-revolutionary movement and I supported the C.P.S.U. and its policy. The measures it took were radical but I don't see what else they could have possibly done in the situation. It was found out later that the Hungarian Communist Party had failings which made the counter-revolutionary situation much worse. [Office clerk]

I was upset the same as every one else but I didn't leave the Party. I didn't let the problem slide quietly. I wasn't against the C.P.S.U. but they couldn't do anything else against the counter-revolutionary movement. [Housewife]

Whatever mistakes were made before 1956 – and there were mistakes – the Hungarian people and their government were 100 per cent correct when they took steps against counter-revolutionaries both inside and outside the country, who were exploiting the genuine grievances of the workers in the hope of restoring fascist reaction in Hungary.[51]

Many Communists are convinced that the movement is good through and through, and that it is the reactionaries who must resort to slanderous and lying attacks in order to discredit it. The conspiracy theory of history is useful because it helps to explain why good does not prevail.[52] In short, they deny that the C.P. does use dubious means. Others, even the most honest and idealistic, see politics as the art of the possible and are prepared to use illegitimate means because they believe the cause for which they are fighting to be an undoubtedly good one in principle.

I lied, I cheated, acted under false pretences, obeyed and carried out orders from on high – this is called democratic centralism – denied all my inner ethical tenets and spiritual codes for the good of the cause, convinced myself that the end, the most glorious and worthy end, justified the means. I had not even had the pleasure from it or enjoyed doing it. I found it distasteful in the extreme and time and time again offensive to my natural bent and good sense, but once having joined the Party I persevered in its service with masochistic devotion. [53]

Some are not exposed to the esoteric doctrine until fairly late in their career, but when they discover it they often leave the Party under great emotional distress and disgust. The quotation from Charlotte Haldane's autobiography will also help to explain the orientation of the steel-hardened cadres who, however, are far more tough-minded and most probably more dogmatic as well, about the means that they are prepared to use. Professor Hyman Levy analysed the motives of the Party leaders just after he had resigned in 1957, and his explanation dove-tails with that of Charlotte Haldane.

Now it would be quite false to cast doubts on the genuineness of people like Gollan, Dutt and Pollitt. They are all highly able men who have sacrificed themselves for a cause in which they believe, and they are prepared, if necessary, to be victimized on its behalf. That is not the question. The point rather is that they regard themselves as the Chosen People, the People of the Book, the personal custodians of a trust that is part of a great international movement. While the rank-and-file may argue every aspect of democracy and democratic centralism, they themselves have a loyalty much deeper than to their members or to the working class *at any given moment in history*. They are timeless and so they and their bodyguard must always be re-elected. Democracy-cum-loyalty can always be made to work that way.[54]

As suggested before, the degree of commitment of the steel-hardened cadres is much greater than that of the rest of the membership. It is this deep involvement which seems to lie at the root of their ability to reconcile the principles of benevolence and manipulation.

The different reactions of the three types of Party member to the authoritarian strains are summed up by Cadogan.

To those people who were interested in ideas and who felt strongly and imaginatively about human values, Hungary was the end. In the case of those to whom the Party signified above all a means of organizing against the boss on the shop floor, Hungary was unreal. For those to whom the Party was the Church and the Kremlin infallible, Hungary was as much to be ignored as Khrushchev's speech [at the Twentieth Congress] was not to be read.[55]

It seems clear, then, that many middle-class idealists leave the Party because, in part, they claim that it is not democratic. What is not firmly established is whether their evaluation of the Party is accurate. As political idealists they may take into the Party unrealistic notions of what are feasible democratic procedures. Sooner or later the Party falls short of their expectations, as, in fact, would many other political organizations. Hence they react against the Party after defection and claim that the Party has an anti-democratic organization and power structure. They react the more strongly because the Party itself claims to approach the democratic ideal. Some of those who left the C.P. in the 1956–8 period joined a number of other left-wing movements but left them all because, they said, the movements were not democratic enough.

Somehow the idealist must close a psychological gap – either the gap between unrealistic expectations and actuality, or the gap between realistic expectations and actuality. In both cases the gap corresponds to the gap between the exoteric, democratic ideology and the esoteric, power-tactics ideology. Dogmatism is the psychological 'bridging' mechanism which makes expectations square with actuality. It helps the democratic Communist reject completely the view that the B.C.P. has an anti-democratic organization. The more dogmatic the Communist, the more easily will he be able to maintain his Communist beliefs against various pressures, but the more strongly will he react against his old beliefs if he ever does come to leave the Party. Usually Communists are assimilated into the Party in gentle, almost imperceptible, stages. Only gradually are they exposed to the esoteric ideology. Many, however, are not exposed to the esoteric ideology and practices at all. The isolation of one branch from another, and the tendency of some members to lose close contact with the non-Communist world allow them to form little pockets of genuine democratic humanitarianism. This, one ex-Communist suggested in an interview, is especially the case with the student branches.

The Party has its members who like to talk and think about liberal ideas but quite often they form their own little groups which are separate from the main body and activity of the Party and from King Street. They read Marx and Lenin and realize their intellectual power and like their ideas. But the students are in a way divorced from the Party. They don't know what goes on in King Street or even at the District level. They discuss their liberal-progressive ideas but they don't know really what the Party is about.

At intervals, however, some event in the Communist world brings the idealist face to face with the esoteric ideology – the Moscow Trials, Lysenko, the Twentieth Congress of the C.P.S.U., Hungary, Inner-Party Democracy, the Nazi-Soviet non-aggression pact. The shock of sudden exposure is too great, and there is a strong tendency to defect. It ought to be said that this tension between political ideals and the this-worldly means necessary to put them into practice is not a problem peculiar to the Communist Party. Peter Gay, in his study of German Democratic Socialism, has written:

A Democratic Socialist movement that attempts to transform a capitalist into a Socialist order is necessarily faced with the choice between two incompatibles – principle and power.[56]

It has been suggested that the real or perceived discrepancy between the exoteric and esoteric ideologies and the strains which it produces for the average member are causes of neuroticism among Communists.[57] The discrepancy may be one of the main causes of high membership turnover. In most cases the dissonant combination of anti-democratic Party structure and non-economic liberalism is resolved by reaffirming democratic values. Seventy-eight per cent of Almond's sample of British ex-Communists developed 'moderate left-wing' political attitudes, and only two per cent developed 'extreme right-wing' attitudes.[58] The Communist turned Fascist is a rarity.

1. Brown, 1965, p. 478. Chapter 10 of this book contains an excellent summary and evaluation of the work on the authoritarian personality
2. Adorno, *et al.*, 1950
3. Lipset (1960, p. 101) uses the word 'extremist' to refer to movements, parties, and ideologies, and 'authoritarian' to refer to attitudes and predispositions of individuals. He says that, other things being equal, authoritarians will be more attracted to extremist movements than to democratic ones, thereby assuming that extremist movements are necessarily anti-democratic. This is not a valid assumption for some 'extremist' organizations like the Anarchists or the Socialist Party of Great Britain are thoroughly democratic. Also the word 'extremist' has connotations of the undesirable, and so the more value-neutral word 'radical' has been used throughout this study.
4. Adorno, *et al.*, 1950, p. 971; see also Barker, 1963
5. Borkenau, 1940, p. 20
6. Gurian, 1952
7. In parts of Sweden, it seems, the Communist Party competes with severely puritanical and authoritarian radical religious sects for the allegiance of the same people – Phillips Davison, 1955

8. Lasswell, in Christie and Jahoda, 1954, p. 216; see also Pye, 1961; Brewster-Smith, 1958

9. Harris, 1956

10. Rokeach, 1960, p. 61

11. Rokeach, 1960, p. 80

12. Le Gallienne, 1951, pp. 35–6

13. Plamenatz, 1961, p. xv

14. Koestler, in Crossman, 1950, p. 68

15. Rokeach, 1960, p. 55

16. Hyde, 1952, pp. 177–8

17. Rokeach, 1960, p. 213

18. Cross, 1961, pp. 73–5

19. See, for example, Hannington, 1937, Chapter 12

20. Rokeach, 1960, p. 115; Adorno, 1950, p. 187; Christie, 1956. The E. scale was designed to measure Ethnocentricism, or the degree of racial prejudice. The F. scale measures the Potentiality for Fascism, or Implicit Antidemocratic Trends.

21. Christie, at least, believes that there is no evidence to show that they feigned low scores – in Christie and Johoda, 1954, p. 132

22. *End Racialism in Britain*, British Communist Party pamphlet, 1964, p. 3. See also, 'The Menace of Racialism', *Daily Worker*, 29 September 1964, p. 1; Jelf, 1964, p. 2

23. For a more complete analysis of this aspect of Marxist thought see Rennap, 1942

24. Dombrose and Levinson, 1950

25. *Daily Worker*, 9 January 1956, p. 1

26. It ought to be pointed out that this does not necessarily make for a totalitarian government

27. '*Working class authoritarianism is Communism*' – Lipset, 1961 (his italics)

28. See Michels (1960) and Lipset (1960, Chapter 12) for an analysis of the oligarchical tendencies within political parties and trade unions in general, and more specifically, Bell (1961, Chapter 9 and 10) for an account of American trade unions; Goldstein, (1952) for an account of a British trade union; McKenzie (1964) for an analysis of the power structure of the Conservative and Labour Parties; Levin (1960) for an account of politics in Boston. There is the other side of the coin, which suggests that certain types of organizations can be, and are, democratic – Cf. Lipset, Trow and Coleman, (1956)

29. Grainger, 1958

30. Grainger, 1958

31. *Handbook of Local Organisation*, Communist Party of Great Britain, 1927, p. 30

32. Dowse, 1966, p. 43

33. *Rules of the Communist Party*, July 1943, Rule 3 (c)

34. *Report to the Executive Committee of the Commission on Inner Party Democracy*, British Communist Party, 1963, paragraph 1

35. 'Democratic centralism means: the right of all members to take part in the discussion and formation of policy and the duty of all members to fight for that policy when it has been decided . . . the right of the elected higher organizations to make, between Congresses, decisions which are binding on lower organizations.' *Inner Party Democracy*, 1963, p. 4

36. *Inner Party Democracy*, 1963, p. 32

37. Grainger, 1958

38. *Report to the Executive Committee of the Commission on Inner Party Democracy*, December 1956, paragraph 7. The Party later published the Majority Report but not the Minority Report

39. *Minority Report*, 1956, paragraphs 27 and 33

40. *Minority Report*, 1956, paragraph 63

41. Cadogan, 1961; see also Behan, 1964, p. 169

42. *International Bulletin of the International Secretariat of the Fourth International*, December 1959, no. 7, p. 10
43. Gallacher, 1948, p. 33
44. Bell, 1937, p. 83
45. Wood, 1959, p. 182
46. J. Gollan, *World News*, vol. 7, no. 23, 4 June 1960
47. Cantril, 1962, p. 206
48. Stapel and de Yonge, 1948
49. McCarthy, 1953, pp. 263–4
50. For a full account of the trial see Rolph, 1962
51. Moffat, 1965, p. 153
52. Ferkiss, 1962
53. Haldane, 1949, p. 238
54. Levy, 1957 (his italics)
55. Cadogan, 1961
56. Gay, 1952, p. iv
57. Lindner, 1953
58. Almond, *et al.*, 1954, pp. 356–65. In France, 'Communist voters, who in any case are the most loyal, tend to vote only for the socialists when they cease to vote Communist.' – Stoetzel, 1955

CHAPTER 9

THE THEORY OF MASS POLITICS AND BRITISH COMMUNISM

As it has proceeded, this study has stopped now and again to comment briefly on William Kornhauser's book *The Politics of Mass Society*, which presents the most sophisticated and systematic theory yet available of the theory of mass or 'extremist' politics.[1] As Bell has pointed out, there is no single theory of mass politics,[2] but Kornhauser has successfully combined the variations on the theme to produce a set of interdependent propositions about the relationship between certain types of social movement and certain types of social structure.

Mass theorists argue that societies are integrated and bound together by a plurality of formal and informal social groups. These groups, including anything from a political party or a trade union to a local darts club or tenants' association, create a network of social relationships which relate individual members of society to each other and to the society as a whole. Formal and informal associations also act as channels of communication for the expression of social and political demands between the ordinary members of society and its élite. Societies which possess a whole range of stable and cohesive groups are called pluralistic societies. Those which lack these organizations are called mass societies, because they are made up of an amorphous mass of unrelated, undifferentiated, isolated and atomized individuals. Such individuals are alienated from their society and thus tend to support extremist political organizations, which act outside the normal constitutional rules of political conduct. The extreme case of such political organizations are totalitarian movements like Communism and Fascism, and therefore it follows that Communist and Fascist movements will gain their greatest support among atomized and isolated individuals who live in mass conditions. This is a brief and simple, and therefore crude, account of mass theory. In fact, the theory, as presented by Kornhauser, is subtle and comprehensive, and he presents a great deal of detailed empirical data to support his theory.

However, the author himself has said that a rigorous testing of the theory remains to be done, and although this cannot be accomplished on the basis of a single case study, it is possible to collect together the conclusions about British Communism and to compare them with some of the main themes in Kornhauser's book. The aim is nothing more than to compare the theory with one set of data about one particular Communist Party, as a preliminary step to building a better theory. Conclusions drawn from studies of other radical movements will confirm or modify different aspects of the theory. For instance, Rossi's work on the French Communist Party suggests that it conforms to the mass pattern in a number of ways in which the British Party does not.[3]

Before discussing some particular points of difference there are some general points to be raised, which lead to problems in the application of the theory to any concrete case. Alienation, Kornhauser states, is a central concept in the analysis of mass society. There is bewildering confusion about the meaning of alienation, but Kornhauser nowhere attempts a formal definition of the concept. At one point he equates it with inefficacy or powerlessness,[4] and at another he equates it with hostility towards the established political order – with extremism.[5] Similarly there are problems about the meaning of the term marginality, but Kornhauser does not offer a definition, although he does draw up a list of groups which can be described as marginal. Lastly, and most important, he insists that mass movements are not class based. Admittedly there may be only an arbitrary and thin line dividing class movements from mass movements, but a movement like the British Communist Party which draws roughly seventy to seventy-five per cent of its members from the working class, and which explicitly appeals to the class-conscious and to working-class interests, would seem, by almost any definition, to be a class-based political movement.

The particular points of comparison between the theory of mass politics and the single concrete case of the B.C.P. can be divided into three sections.

1. The style and political behaviour of the mass or totalitarian movement.
2. The social conditions which produce mass or totalitarian movements.
3. The social composition of mass or totalitarian movements.

According to the theory, the political style of mass and totalitarian movements tends to be one of direct, activistic, unconstitutional, anti-democratic, and violent political behaviour, which is focused on abstract symbols which are remote from personal experience and daily life. It has already been shown that the vast majority of British Communists have never used violence, or been in favour of using it, that they have little time for remote or abstract symbols (even during the worst economic and political crises), and that they will not condone unconstitutional or anti-democratic behaviour. The Party leadership may, on occasions, use unconstitutional means where it can, and some members of the rank-and-file may persuade themselves that such means are justified by the ends, but the majority either defect when they are convinced that such means have been used, or else they preserve their integrity by persuading themselves that such means never have been and never will be used by Communists. The political behaviour of British Communists is sometimes activistic and direct, but most usually the Party uses normal constitutional methods – writing letters to M.P.s, to the papers, lobbying M.P.s, drawing up petitions, attending political meetings, and contesting local and national elections.

One defining characteristic of the totalitarian movement is the availability of its non-élite and the inaccessibility of its élite. In other words, the leadership of a totalitarian movement is insulated from its rank-and-file, but the leadership is able to manipulate the rank-and-file. It is the composition of those who select the élite, and not of those who are selected for the élite, which determines the degree of inaccessibility. In this sense the B.C.P. does tend towards the totalitarian model for, according to Grainger and the *Minority Report on Inner Party Democracy*, the Party élite is more or less self-selected.[6] Party power is concentrated in the Political Committee which is appointed by the Executive Committee. However, in this respect the Communist Party seems to be only rather more oligarchical than the Conservative or Labour parties. McKenzie has said about the Labour and Conservative parties that

whatever the role granted in theory to the extra-parliamentary wings of the parties, in practice final authority rests in both parties with the parliamentary party and its leadership.[7]

A degree of oligarchy seems to be built into the constitution of the Communist Party both in theory and in practice. This distinguishes it from the two main parties, although the difference seems to be quantitative rather than qualitative. While there are oligarchical tendencies in both the Labour and Conservative Party, neither conform rigidly to Michel's iron law of oligarchy. Oligarchy in the Communist Party seems to be formalized into a fairly rigid, but not iron, pattern.[8]

However, the last chapter emphasized that, because of insufficient information, the totalitarian nature of the Party must remain a moot point. Perhaps the only possible conclusion to draw is that one ought not to assert or assume that the Party is totalitarian until it is proven to be so. This study has not been able to collect the necessary data to prove this, and it seems rather unlikely that the necessary data will be available in the fore-seeable future.

War and unemployment are thought to be events which create the social conditions which sustain mass movements because, if their effects are severe enough, they tend to destroy the stable pattern of social relation-ships and thus tend to destroy social organizations. Kornhauser cites Britain as an example to support his argument that war is often accom-panied by mass political activity. He shows that many more people voted Communist in the election immediately after the Second World War than in the election immediately before it.[9] It is true that the B.C.P. collected more votes in 1945 than it ever had done before, but, on the other hand, the Party put up twenty-one candidates, and it had only twice before put up more. In the last general election before the Second World War it put up only two candidates, and so it is scarcely surprising that its post-war vote was much higher than its pre-war vote. In other words, it is not possible to compare absolute election figures. Far more significant is the fact that the Party started to increase its membership in 1932, and con-tinued to do so even when unemployment had subsided. The membership figures continued to climb long before war was threatened, and then started to decline in 1943, with two years of war and its after-effects still to follow. First and Second World War conditions and their after-effects do seem to have contributed towards the creation of Communist sympathies, but the influence of the Second World War seems to have been over-ridden by other factors. Sympathy for the Communist Party was at its strongest in 1943, not because of the social effects of war, so much as because the Russians were fighting as British allies – 'the popular enthusiasm for all things Russian soared to unprecedented heights. . . . The party itself was suddenly borne up on the same wave of Russophile sentiment'.[10]

Widespread unemployment is also given as a factor which creates mass conditions and which thus provokes an extremist response. But perhaps both Kornhauser and Selznick (though the latter is more cautious) tend to overestimate the influence of unemployment.[11] The ranks of the radical left- and right-wing did swell as the number of employed grew larger in the 1930s, yet compared with the total number who were out of work, only a few saw radical politics, or politics of any kind, as a solution to their problem. In her study of an area with an extremely high proportion of unemployed, Hilda Jennings found that the strong local traditions and stability of interests were not broken by widespread unemployment.[12] It is worth quoting Bakke on this point again.

Political group action [he wrote] does not rank high among the tactics adopted by the unemployed as a means of solving their problems. In view of the limited part played by politics in the life of the employed this is not surprising.[13]

There is a strong connexion between radical politics and unemployment, but before anything more definite can be said, it is necessary first of all to decide which sections of the unemployed join radical political movements and why they do so, while other sections do not.

In the case of unemployment and war, mass theorists seem to have underestimated the ability of individuals and groups to maintain their old patterns of life, and to create suitable new ones when they are threatened by communal and social discontinuities.

One of the main themes in mass theory is that groups which are isolated from their wider society, and yet very cohesive in themselves and with good internal communications, form isolated masses which are well disposed towards radical politics. Chapter 4 concluded that Communist support is strong among some occupational groups which form largely undifferentiated and isolated communities, but that the Party does not draw the bulk of its support from such communities. Mining communities are a good example of undifferentiated and isolated masses, and although more than half the Party members in 1932 lived in the Scottish and South Wales coalfields, fewer than 100 lived in the Durham, Northumberland, Yorkshire, and Cumberland coalfields.[14] Many mass occupational groups are not radically inclined at all. Particularly conspicuous among these are merchant seamen. This information suggests that mass conditions may help to sustain and spread an ideology among members of isolated groups, but that mass conditions do not determine the content of the ideology as being either radical or moderate. This conclusion is based on an analysis of occupational situations alone. But the conclusion that mass occupational conditions are not responsible for the concentration of Communist support among certain industries also suggests that mass conditions may not be responsible for the concentration of Communist support in certain geographical areas.

A study of Communism in Finland has shown that mass theory is not helpful in explaining Communist strength in some areas. In his excellent work on Finnish politics, Allardt distinguishes between two types of Communism.[15] The first, which he calls 'expressive' or 'emerging' radicalism, can be explained in mass terms – in terms of anomie, alienation, insecurity, rapid social change and communal discontinuities, the absence of traditions, isolation, changes in deprivation conditions, and uprootedness. The second type, which he names 'instrumental' or 'traditional' radicalism, cannot be explained in these terms, but correlates with strong socialist traditions, social and economic stability, inequality and superimposed cleavages. Traditional radicalism is not supported by uprooted or unattached individuals, but on the contrary by individuals who are closely connected with their community and its radicalism, even though these communities may be isolated from the national political and social centres.

In its earliest years British Communism was closer to the emerging or expressive type of radicalism than to the traditional type. The Party gathered its initial membership and quite considerable voting strength in conditions of widespread unemployment and social disorganization. The after-effects of the First World War were more severe than those of the 1939–45 war; the population was already uprooted to a certain extent before the war, and the welfare state was in a relatively primitive stage of development. The severity of social disorganization and instability was reflected in the revolutionary nature of the Party's ideology. This period of emerging Communism lasted for only a short time, however. Social conditions improved and settled down into a stable and secure pattern. The ideology of the Communist Party became less revolutionary, and gradually the Party shifted from the emerging type of radical group to the traditional type. Its membership soon became concentrated in stable and closely-knit working-class communities in the East End of London, South Wales, and in Glasgow, which have long-established socialist traditions and clearly-defined class structures. There is no information which suggests that these communities are marked by weak intermediary associations or isolated primary relations. They do not form isolated masses. On the contrary their pluralist bases of secondary associations seem to be no less firm than any other areas in Britain. South Wales has a strongly unified local system of associations which has not been upset by large population movements,[16] and its strong local traditions and stability of interests were not disrupted by the very high unemployment figures.[17] The area has a whole range of intermediary associations in the form of trade unions, political parties, and religious and cultural organizations.

British Communists are not recruited from isolated masses. The Party itself forms a closely integrated organization, and it is most successful in areas in which individuals are firmly supported by a complete range of formal and informal social relationships. As one ex-Communist has written:

. . . a block of flats in the East End [of London] is a world of its own, closer knit than the luxury flats in the West End, where, I imagine, a man can lock his door on his neighbour.[18]

In Pollock (Glasgow) it was found that C.P. members were well-integrated members of the community,[19] and the same was true of those Communists interviewed for this study. The Party would find it difficult to recruit isolated individuals and atomized masses because they are difficult to contact and almost impossible to organize.

A number of people may have joined the Party in order to escape isolation from social and community life. But once inside the Party they find themselves within a social system in microcosm, with its own internal structure of local, intermediary, and national governing bodies, its own channels of communications, and its own associations which cater for a wide variety of interests and abilities – the historians' group, the teachers' group, organizations for various types of professional workers, organizations for trade union members, groups concerned with education, and groups concerned with promoting relations with other countries, peace committees, and tenants' associations. The Party also organizes its own social life in the form of bazaars, social evenings, lectures, discussion groups, films, jumble-sales, etc. The Party itself is not a mass of isolated individuals. It forms a community of its own which is tightly bound together by an intricate pattern of formal and informal relationships.

There is a tendency for some members to live their whole life within the Party, but the leadership is most concerned that the rank-and-file should not live a life of sectarian seclusion apart from the wider society. It insists that Communists should mix frequently and freely with non-Communists, talk to them, persuade them, sow Communist ideas among them, and recruit them. Front organizations not only collect unsuspecting support for the Party, they are also one way of establishing contact with a group of individuals who have at least one set of ideas in common with Communists and, quite possibly, therefore, a whole range more besides.[20] The Labour Party proscribes about thirty-five Communist front organizations. Front organizations are a way in which Communists mix with potential Communists and sympathizers, and a means of breaking down the tendency of the Party to isolate itself from the wider community. Yet the Party is faced by conflicting aims here. On the one hand it wants to establish maximum control over its members, and to do this it must isolate and indoctrinate them. On the other hand, its aim is to send members into the non-Communist world to proselytize and recruit.

In the leadership's view the ideal Communist should be fully integrated into the local community and its formal and informal occupational, educational, political and economic associations. Without extensive interviewing it is difficult to know to what extent the Party is successful in its aims, but it is obviously fairly successful in trade unions, peace committees and tenants' associations. Though the available information is scarce and unreliable, it can be said with a fair degree of certainty that the British Communist Party is not composed of 'people who cannot . . . be integrated into any organization based on communal interests, into political parties, or municipal government, or professional organizations or trade unions'.[21]

The respondents were asked to list the types of clubs, societies and organizations which they belonged to, besides the local C.P. branch. On average they belonged to 4·5 each (mainly trade-union, political, educational, and social welfare organizations) of which two were Communist organizations.[22] Most, however, said that their friends were members or sympathizers of the Communist Party. The middle-class respondents belonged to more Communist and non-Communist organizations than the working class. It is possible that a few new recruits feel themselves to be isolated, and join the C.P. in order to integrate themselves into some social group. Three respondents mentioned the atmosphere of common purpose and comradeship within the Party, and said how much they appreciated this.[23]

I had experience of a large number of political organizations in my own town, but most of all I admired and respected the Communists. That's one reason why I joined, I suppose. They were the most honest, and self-sacrificing. You could look up to them. [Railway worker]

You haven't asked how does the Party satisfy the needs of social relationships. There is a tremendous feeling of comradeship in the C.P. There is the occasional misfit, but the overwhelming majority do get the feeling of comradeship because its common aims preclude personal ambition. We're all striving for something that's bigger than any of us. All that is asked of members can be obtained voluntarily and willingly. [Teacher]

I've lots of friends with the same outlook and ideals. I didn't really have many friends of interest before I joined the C.P. [Student]

The Party does attract some isolated individuals, but what little evidence there is suggests that they form only a small proportion of the total membership. Even if these few do join the Communist Party to escape unwelcome feelings of isolation, it is still necessary to discover why they joined the Party, rather than any one of a hundred other organizations which would probably fulfil the function of social integration far more satisfactorily. It is, to be sure, difficult to arrive at any exact estimation of the pluralist and integrated nature of the Communist Party. But it is also easy to exaggerate the Party's dependence on atomized individuals and isolated groups. The data are in no sense conclusive, but they do indicate that it is wiser to lean towards the first characterization than the second.

The social composition of the B.C.P. is closely connected with the social conditions which sustain it. Again, the indicators point to the conclusion that the Party does not fit the mass pattern. Kornhauser's analysis of the personality type which tends to predominate in extremist political movements seems to apply only to a few British Communists. 'Extreme submission to the *élite*', he writes, 'and extreme hostility towards outsiders are characteristic of the totalitarian man.' Those in the British Party who are not submissive to the *élite* tend to defect sooner or later, and in the main the rest believe that the Party is democratic, that there is no *élite*, and that even if there were an *élite* they would not submit to it. And to say that British Communists are extremely hostile towards outsiders is far too strong. The literature of the Party is sometimes aggressively polemical, it is true, but it seems that most Communists get on rather well with outsiders. Those interviewed were asked, 'How does being a Communist affect your relationship with non-Communists?' The following is a typical range of replies:

Some of them are belligerent and want to argue all the time, but they get used to me. Others are interested at first but their interest soon subsides. [Student]

It doesn't affect anything. Some people are offended or surprised at first but then they forget. It doesn't destroy friendships or anything like that. [Full-time Party worker]

Not at all – in fact some of them like having a tame Communist around the place. [Student]

People are very tolerant. It doesn't affect anything. [Electrician]

Not adversely. There's very little antagonism, you know. I mean, you know what the English are about politics. When they hear I'm a Communist they say 'Oh yes', and then talk about the weather. Some people are interested. [Teacher]

I have to work a lot with non-Communists – Conservatives sometimes. We have a job to do and they don't mind that I'm a Communist and I don't mind that they're not. [Housewife]

Most people in Britain believe that Communists are given hostile treatment in face-to-face contacts with non-Communists, but from respondents' replies it seems that there is, in fact, little enmity. The real state of affairs does not correspond to the popular stereotype, and it is not true to say that the majority of British Communists are hostile to outsiders or that outsiders are particularly hostile to them.

It has already been seen that atomized individuals and isolated groups do not provide the Party with most of its working-class support. The same appears to be true of middle-class members who, in the main, are not free-floating intellectuals. School teachers form the Party's largest middle-class occupational group, and they are marked by none of the characteristics which Kornhauser suggests predispose the intellectual to take up radical political affiliations.[24] They are not dependent on anonymous and unpredictable markets, nor do they have few institutional responsibilities, their rewards are certain, most of them have full control over their audiences, and they do not suffer from severe competition for jobs. The analyses of Congress delegates suggest that few middle-class members can be classified as 'unattached' intellectuals.

About twenty-four per cent of 1963 Congress delegates had middle-class occupations:

	per cent
Teachers	8
Clerical and administrative workers	7
Professional and technical workers	5
Medical workers	2
Self-employed	1
Students	1

Even the most generous estimate of unattached teachers, professional workers, self-employed, medical workers and students would give a figure of only about seven per cent:

	per cent
Teachers	2
Professionals	2
Students	1
Medical workers	1

Only about 0·1 per cent of British people with the middle-class occupations that are classified by the Credentials Committee are Communists. Of these 0·1 per cent, the majority are attached to formal organizations in that they work in schools, universities, colleges, offices, laboratories, or hospitals. Many are also attached to a number of voluntary associations, because middle-class Communists are expected and required by the Party to be active in such organizations.

One of the main failings of mass theory is that it will not easily allow for a development of the theory which will account for the specific type of radical reaction to mass conditions. It attempts to account for radicalism in general, but does not attempt to explain why certain groups of people become left- or right-wing political radicals or members of radical religious groups. The theory takes those living in mass conditions to the threshold of radicalism, but not to the threshold of particular types of radicalism. Indeed, it can be argued that an extension of mass theory inevitably leads to the conclusion that all radical groups, left-wing or right-wing, religious or political, function as alternative and equally suitable vehicles for the same individuals. Information about British radicalism strongly suggests that this is not so. The B.C.P. appeals to fairly discrete social groups, and other radical organizations appeal to different social groups. A potential member of the C.P. is not a potential member of a radical group which is not a radical left-wing political one. There is some overlap of appeal and competition for members within this group of radical left-wing political organizations, but very little between completely different types of radical organizations.

The conclusions reached in this chapter may be criticized in two ways. Firstly; it can be argued that information about the Party is so scanty that any generalizations must necessarily be of a highly tentative nature. This criticism must be accepted. Most, but not all, of the available information bears a rather oblique relationship to the main problems dealt with. But if this criticism is accepted, then the same criticism of other statements about the British Communist Party must also be accepted. These statements must also be of a highly tentative nature, particularly since they are based on less complete, if not on less reliable, data than are presented here, and even though many of the conclusions are expressed with a fair degree of confidence and finality. Secondly; it might be argued that as a Communist Party the B.C.P. is small, unique and atypical. As such it does not provide an adequate test case for the theory of mass and totalitarian politics. This criticism must also be accepted. The B.C.P. certainly bears little comparison with the vastly larger Parties in other European countries. But, on the one hand, the B.C.P. seems to be similar to the American Communist Party in at least some important respects, and on the other hand, it seems to be similar in at least some important respects to parts of the much larger Finnish Communist Party. The uniqueness of the B.C.P. has yet to be adequately explored.

As Kornhauser suggests, radical political movements can develop in pluralist conditions although they are likely to be small, weak and relatively powerless compared with those developing in mass conditions. But, judging only from the case of the B.C.P., it seems that radical movements operating in pluralist conditions seem to lean towards the political style of their pluralist *milieux*. Radical movements operating in pluralist conditions may be very different from those in mass conditions. As Gusfield has suggested, radical politics can be 'developed and conducted by well-structured groups, representing discrete and organized parts of the social structure, acting to secure goals relevant to group needs'.[25]

Lastly; the membership of the B.C.P. and its ideology is class based. Far from drawing the bulk of its support from those with the weakest class ties, the strength of the class ties of most members is matched only by the strength of their class-conscious interests. Even middle-class Communists who have broken with their own class subscribe to an organization and an ideology which is wholly concerned with promoting the interests of one class. The most general conclusion must be that mass theory is not of great use in analysing British Communism. The evidence collected, if it points to anything, points to the conclusion that a class-based theory would be a far more useful line of approach.

1. Kornhauser, 1960
2. Bell, 1961, pp. 21–38
3. Rossi, 1955
4. Kornhauser, 1960, p. 108
5. Kornhauser, 1960, p. 49. Here he quotes and follows Shils
6. Grainger, 1958; *Ministry Report*, 1956
7. McKenzie, 1964, p. 635
8. For a member who sees that Party as thoroughly democratic see Hobsbawm, 1954
9. Kornhauser, 1960, p. 171
10. Pelling, 1958, p. 120
11. Kornhauser, 1960, pp. 159–67; Selznick, in Olson, 1963, pp. 13–29. Almond (1954, p. 207) comments that Selznick (1952) underestimates the ability of a population to overcome mass conditions. See also Kluckhohn, 1962, p. 229
12. Jennings, 1934, p. 54
13. Bakke, 1940, p. 46
14. *Communist Review*, vol. 4, no. 12, pp. 577–8

15. Allardt, *Acta Sociologica*, 1962; *Transactions of the Fifth World Congress of Sociology*, 1962; *International Journal of Comparative Sociology*, 1964; in Allardt and Littunen (eds.), 1964, pp. 78–131

16. Brennan, Cooney and Pollins, 1954

17. Jennings, 1934, p. 54

18. Darke, 1953, p. 8

19. Broady and Mack, 'The Pollock Study', unpublished. Lipset found the same in his study of Canadian Agrarian Socialism – Lipset, 1950, pp. 179–96

20. In the 1920s and 1930s the Communist Party attracted a steady trickle of recruits from the Independent Labour Party – Dowse, 1966, p. 206. In the late 1950s and early 1960s it has managed to recruit a number of its younger members by using its contacts with the Campaign for Nuclear Disarmament

21. Arendt, 1951, p. 305

22. Almond and Verba (1963, p. 264) report that only two per cent of British adults belong to four or more organizations. British Communists seem to be considerably more integrated into networks of associations than non-Communists.

23. See also *Discussion*, March 1937, p. 25

24. Kornhauser, 1960, pp. 186–7

25. Gusfield, 1963

CHAPTER 10

A METHOD OF
DUAL ANALYSIS

This chapter attempts to present a general theory of British Communism based on the data and conclusions presented in previous chapters. The theory is phrased mainly in class terms rather than mass terms, and uses the concepts of alienation, anomie, marginality and competence as explanatory tools. But before these concepts can be used to any great effect their meanings must first of all be clarified, for they have been used in a wide variety of different ways by an increasing number of sociologists and political scientists.

Of all the writings and research on any concept used in political sociology, those on alienation must, at one and the same time, rank among the most numerous and least satisfactory. There are as many, if not more, definitions of alienation as there are political sociologists who have used the concept. Nettler opens a paper on alienation by saying:

Humpty Dumpty once told us that words meant what he meant them to mean. There can be no objection to this Dumptean practice except as it makes dictionaries irrelevant and as it confounds the scientific requirements of clear value for our coins of conversation.[1]

In the work on alienation the same word has been given completely different meanings, and the same meaning has been given to completely different words. Alienation has been defined in the same terms as competence,[2] anomie has been defined in the same terms as competence,[3] and, to complete the full cycle of confusion, anomie has been defined in the same terms as alienation.[4] This ruinous confusion has arisen, in great part, because these closely connected and interrelated concepts have not been placed side by side and analysed as a whole. As a result their separate theoretical identities and relationships have not been ordered and defined. Yet the importance of the four concepts in sociological and political analysis, and particularly in the analysis of radical political groups, suggests that some effort should be made to clarify their meanings.

Anomie has been given its most useful definition by Merton.

Anomie is then conceived as a breakdown in the cultural structure, occurring particularly when there is an acute disjunction between the cultural norms and goals and the socially structured capacities of members of the groups to act in accord with them.[5]

Defined as such, anomie refers to an objective state of a social system, as both Merton and Brookes have pointed out with some force.[6] On this basis, anomie is to be distinguished from concepts which refer to subjective feelings although these feelings may or may not result from anomie states. Anomie may produce alienation, but not all alienation is the consequence of anomie. This is not to say that anomie does not have its psychological concomitants, or that alienation cannot have psychological causes.[7]

Anomie is often confused with normlessness. The former refers to a situation in which norms exist but in which normatively-defined ends do not mesh with, or are out of phase with, normatively-defined means. The possible consequences of widespread and severe anomie may be a complete disintegration of the cultural structure – a state in which there are no norms, or normlessness. In a state of complete normlessness there would be no rules governing social action, and behaviour, therefore, would be totally random.

Merton illustrates his treatment of anomie with examples taken from the American economic value system. He could, as he says, have given examples from other spheres of social life. Particularly important for this study is the possibility of an anomie situation occurring within the political system of a society, and the consequences for political behaviour and attitudes of such an occurrence. Following Merton, it is suggested that an anomic political system occurs when there is an acute disjunction between culturally defined political norms and goals, and the socially structured capacities of members of the group to act in accordance with them. The democratic political system is widely believed to be a form of government 'for the people, by the people, and of the people'. Some groups which accept democracy as a political principle have come to believe that their particular political system is not fully democratic, that it is defective, even fraudulent, and that culturally defined goals cannot be attained by using culturally prescribed means. For example, revolutionaries may develop their belief in revolution as a means to an end partly because they believe that their goals can be attained in no other way.[8]

In many ways Marx accepted the generalized political values of his time (liberty, equality and fraternity) but he rejected the peaceful and constitutional means it prescribed because he believed that the state, and its ruling class, denied the masses access to these means. The state, he claimed, rendered the masses powerless to achieve what, on the face of it, were society's prescribed goals. Groups or individuals in anomic situations may, then, develop feelings of powerless, inefficiency or low competence.

Low competence has sometimes been called inefficiency or powerlessness. In this case three different words have been defined in essentially the same terms and attached to essentially the same phenomenon. The authors of *The Voter Decides* have offered a definition of political efficacy which may be adapted to give a definition of general efficacy or competence.

Sense of political efficiency may be defined as the feeling that political action does have, or can have, an impact on the political process, i.e. that it is worthwhile to perform one's civic duties. It is the feeling that political and social change is possible, and that the individual citizen can play a part in bringing about this change.[9]

Anomic social systems may well be the cause of most alienation and feelings of low competence, but, as Nettler has pointed out, this is poor reason to confuse the concepts.[10] Individuals or groups in anomic situations may not perceive it, while other individuals may attribute their alienation to anomie, whereas, in fact, none exists. As defined and measured by Neal and Rettig, powerlessness, normlessness, and anomie emerged as separate and unrelated dimensions, indicating that '*a priori* assumption of congruence among these dimensions of alienation is unwarranted'.[11] However, if an individual perceives that there is an acute disjunction between what the central value system states ought to happen in the political sphere, and what social conditions actually allow to happen, then he is likely to develop feelings of low political competence. What is important is not that there is an acute disjunction between norms and the capacity to act in accordance with them, but that people should develop feelings of low competence and believe that an anomic situation exists. In such a situation it is possible that the individual will join a group whose aim is to bring political actuality into line with the culturally defined 'ideal'. In other words, an anomic political system may result in feelings of low political competence, and such feelings can, in turn, result in demands for political change, or in the extreme cases, in political radicalism.

Nettler defines the alienated person as 'one who has been estranged from, made unfriendly towards, his society and the culture it carries'.[12] Hajda's definition is very similar –

an individual's feeling of uneasiness or discomfort which reflects his exclusion or self-exclusion from social and cultural participation. It is an expression of non-belonging or non-sharing, an uneasy awareness of unwelcome contrast with others.[13]

Laswell's definition is also very similar (although he uses psychoanalytical terms[14]) as is Levin's where he describes alienation as 'the psychological state of an individual characterized by feelings of estrangement'.[15] It is, perhaps, worth repeating here that alienation, as defined by these writers, refers to subjective feelings of individuals, to a negative evaluation of something, and not, as in the case of the concept of anomie, to an objective state of a social system.

It is possible that most, but by no means all, political alienation results from a feeling of low political competence – the individual negatively evaluates and reacts against a system which denies him access to the means by which he can attain culturally defined goals. Thus, says Shils, 'an extremist group is an alienated group. This means that it is fundamentally hostile to the political order'.[16]

When dealing with alienation it is important to ask the question 'Alienation from what?'. A man may be alienated from one sphere of social life but quite happy with others. The *avant-garde* artist may be bitterly critical of the artistic 'establishment' but quite content with the political system. The workman may be alienated from his work situation but quite happy about the political system. It is probable that total alienation, estrangement from all or most aspects of social life, is rare. For all that is written about them, the 'Alienated Men', the 'Outsiders', the 'Men of the Wasteland' are not in any way common in this or in any other century. Hermann Hesse's Steppenwolf is rare and curious, and so all the more attention is paid to him:

I stood outside all social circles, alone, beloved by none, mistrusted by many, in unceasing and bitter conflict with public opinion and morality; and although I lived in a bourgeois setting, I was all the same an utter stranger to this world in all I thought and felt. Religion, country, family, state, all lost their value and meant nothing to me any more. The pomposity of the sciences, societies and arts disgusted me.

But just as the totally alienated man is a rarity, so also is his opposite, the totally non-alienated man. At any given time any individual is likely to be estranged from some aspect of his society and the culture it carries, albeit, perhaps, a mild form of estrangement from an unimportant aspect of his society.

Alienation, however, may be displaced from one sphere to another. A person who is alienated from his work situation may displace his feelings onto political life, even though there may be no real cause to do so, and even though he does not feel particularly powerless where politics are concerned. Such an occurrence would be a case of 'a generally disgruntled attitude expressing itself as negativism in spite of non-alienation with regard to political affairs'.[17] This area of 'projected' or 'referred' alienation has been termed the 'phobic sector' by Thompson and Horton.[18] One ex-Communist tells how some Communists flouted middle-class norms, not because they disapproved of the norms themselves, but because they were bourgeois and therefore to be broken.[19]

Alienation may also be generalized,[20] or particularized.[21] The Communist ideology being broad in scope and pervasiveness tends to produce a highly generalized form of alienation. The Communist criticizes bourgeois economics, the bourgeois political system, the bourgeois educational system, bourgeois religion and bourgeois art, in such a way that many of his points of contact with the world are points of alienation. The middle-class Communist who attempts to eliminate all traces of his middle-class culture and background will develop a highly generalized form of alienation from his middle-class environment. In a number of different social spheres he may move a considerable distance from the attitudinal centre of his social background, and if he tries to remove all traces of his middle-class origins he may develop phobic sectors of alienation. The working-class Communist, and particularly the skilled worker, remains quite close to his social background, and therefore his alienation tends to be more particularized.

In some skilled occupations Communist affiliation may be accepted, and seen by non-Communists as unusual but not deviant. In America, where Communists are spread more thinly than in Britain, Glazer has suggested that 'normal' Communists, who join the Party in the course of a relatively normal social and psychological development, far outnumber those who had exceptional psychological reasons for joining.[22] The middle-class Communist, however, has moved out of his own subculture and into a rather different one. All the middle-class respondents to the questionnaire can be said to have done this, except one who regarded herself as middle-class, whose level of competence was much higher than any of the others, and who, alone, regarded the Party's main function as that of a 'ginger-group' for the Labour Party, rather than as an independent Party in its own right. The middle-class Communist, it may be expected, follows the same pattern as that discovered by Nettler in the alienated woman.

If radicalism, nonconformity, innovation are, in this [Canadian] social system, masculine qualities, it follows that the alienated woman is 'farther out' than the alienated man. She has moved farther away from the attitudinal centre shared by her sex . . .[23]

The most influential paper on alienation is that by Seeman,[24] but his method of separating and classifying the five different meanings that have been given to alienation in the past does not bring us any nearer to a useful definition of the concept. He has documented but not resolved the confusion, and mistaken possible causes of alienation for possible definitions of the concept. The same criticism that Blau has used against Weber's definition of bureaucracy can be used against Seeman's definition of the variants of alienation; namely, that 'the relation between the attributes and consequences of a social institution is a question for empirical verification', and that both cannot be part of a definition.[25] The first two of Seeman's variations on the theme of alienation are normlessness and powerlessness. Possible connexions between these two and anomie and alienation have already been suggested. The close association of the concepts in any given concrete case is all the more reason why they should be theoretically distinguished from one another. Dean has taken a literal view of the term normlessness, and, like de Grazia, has divided it up into two sub-types. The first, the conflict of norms, or what de Grazia calls simple anomie, can produce the second, purposelessness, or what de Grazia terms acute anomie.[26]

The third of Seeman's types, meaninglessness, is defined as that state in which 'the individual is unclear as to what he ought to believe – when the individual's minimal standards for clarity are not met'. It is questionable whether meaninglessness is compatible with Nettler's definition, since alienation implies a conscious rejection of values, and hence implies a set of criteria by which to judge other values. 'The alienated is confronted with working out his own moral judgements.'[27] At any rate, meaninglessness is certainly not a characteristic of the British Communist who, to a greater or lesser extent, has internalized a total ideology, which gives him a most meaningful view of the world. It is possible that some individuals join social groups in order to escape meaninglessness, but most Communist recruits in contemporary Britain seem to have a fairly well-defined political ideology and world view before they join the Party. However, Communists may find certain areas of social life meaningless, as, for example, the man who performs a tedious, simple and routine task in a mass-production factory.[28]

Self-estrangement, the next of Seeman's types of alienation is defined as 'the degree of dependence of the given behaviour upon anticipated future rewards'. Again, this type of alienation is not generally to be found among British Communists. Their ability to emphasize and sympathize with minority groups in Britain and elsewhere, and their generally idealistic goals, strongly suggest that their behaviour and political activity are not dependent on anticipated future rewards. Communists are alienated because their ideals and expectations are frustrated, not because they believe that the actions they undertake have no intrinsic merits. Communists may be self-estranged or self-alienated in the sense that they believe society ('the logic of the situation') forces them to do things which they dislike – to work on capitalist-controlled mass-production lines in order to earn a living, or to pay taxes which are spent on H-bombs.

Lastly, there is the type of alienation which Seeman calls 'isolation'. This can be more usefully broken down into two sub-types – geographical or physical isolation, and social isolation. Either may be the cause or the consequence of the other. Hajda found that physical isolation does not always produce social isolation.[29] There is also some overlap and confusion in the way that the concepts of isolation and marginality have been used.

The isolation 'dimension' of alienation overlaps with the concept of marginality insofar as the latter has been used to refer to a state in which an individual or group is socially isolated, or insulated within a 'fringe' position in the social structure. In this sense the marginal man is a social outsider although he is not necessarily a deviant. He is in a marginal position in that he is unable, or feels himself unable, to gain access to the central areas of interaction of his social world. Unattached intellectuals, isolated industrial and farm workers, and owners of small businesses have been classified as marginal groups because they are in some way excluded, or feel themselves excluded, from political decision-making processes.[30] But marginality has another aspect also. The concept was first used by Park to refer to the person who straddles two or more cultures but who is not fully part of one or another. Park defines the marginal man as 'one whom fate has condemned to live in two not merely different, but antagonistic, cultures.[31] For example, the second-generation immigrant in America is part American, but only part American. If he retains some of the cultural traits of his parents he will straddle two cultures and will, therefore, be in a marginal position. Such people are 'doubly alienated, marginal men'.[32]

Just as it is possible to straddle two national cultures, so it is possible to straddle two subcultures of the same society. A man may be both working-class and middle-class if he came from the working class and has moved into the middle class. Thus Hughes has extended marginality to include the type of status dilemma which may result from a poorly crystallized status,[33] and Lenski writes: 'apparently the individual with a poorly crystallized status is a particular type of marginal man.'[34]

After a comprehensive survey of the literature on marginality, Dickie-Clark broadens the 'inconsistent ranking' approach to marginality to produce a general definition of the concept.

Marginal situations [he suggests] can be defined as those hierarchical situations in which there is any inconsistent ranking of an individual or stratum in any of those matters falling within the scope of the hierarchy.[35]

He points out that our understanding of many social movements would be enhanced if we knew more about 'how behaviour in marginal situations differs from that in non-marginal ones'.[36] But, as Dickie-Clark suggests, the barriers between hierarchies can be based on any one, or combination of, a large number of criteria – age, education, race, religion, class, status – and thus any one society is likely to contain a very large number of marginal individuals or groups. However, some barriers between hierarchies will be more important and permanent than others. It seems that class and status hierarchies will be the most important in an analysis of any social movement in modern Britain, although the division between superordinate and subordinate racial and ethnic groups is not unimportant, particularly when considering Jewish Communism.[37] For this reason the study will concentrate on the type of marginality produced by low status crystallization and the subordination of ethnic groups.

Low status crystallization may have a number of consequences. It may produce role strain and role conflict and an uneasy sense of disequilibrium and ambiguity in the individual who is torn between the conflicting loyalties, values, and cultures of two or more social groups. It may also produce social isolation, as in the classic case of the *nouveau riche* who are accepted by neither the well-established upper class nor the well-established lower class. But although marginality may produce isolation, isolation is not inevitably associated with marginality, for the isolated may not have poorly crystallized statuses. Marginality, as used here, therefore, is distinguished from isolation, and refers to a situation caused, in part, by inconsistent rankings and low status crystallization, and associated with status dilemma, role strain, and conflicting norms and values. As a result marginality may induce feelings of ambiguity, anxiety and uncertainty.[38]

Lastly, a marginal situation may be closely associated with an anomic situation. Most barriers between hierarchies are permeable in the sense that at least some members of the subordinate group will be exposed to, and internalize, the norms and values of their superordinate group. In this way they may come to accept the goals of the superordinate group, and yet be denied access to the socially prescribed means for attaining these goals. Mann concludes that marginal personality traits may appear wherever the individual faces 'the coincidence of something wanted and the denial of the want'.[39] Similarly, Brett's study of South African Negroes with a college education showed that they were a marginal group because they were members of a subordinate group who had received a white, European style, education. As a result of this education they had rejected their traditional tribal culture in favour of a European one, with its political values of 'liberty, equality and fraternity'. But being denied access to the legitimate means of attaining these goals – voting in elections, standing for election, effective expression of political dissent – they used the innovatory mode of adaptation to anomie, and developed a belief in the inevitability and desirability of violent political means.

Africans in South Africa have known a longer and more intense contact with Europeans than anywhere else in Africa. Although never fully admitted to this society, their contact has led to aspirations that are essentially derived from its values. This feeling has led to a rejection of all measures designed to treat their group as one apart from the society as a whole, a rejection intensified by the oppressive way in which they feel the present policy of separate development is being carried out. The government's complete rejection of all attempts at peaceful political action has led to an increasing militancy and acceptance of violent action.[40]

The importance of the four main concepts discussed above lies in their power to help the sociologist understand why certain individuals or groups develop certain patterns of attitudes and behaviour. The last part of this section of the chapter, therefore, is concerned with the types of behaviour which may be produced by anomie, marginality, low competence and alienation. Merton has formulated five types of behavioural adaptation to anomie,[41] and his typology has been elaborated by Dubin.[42] However, the mode of behavioural adaptation to a situation depends on how the actor perceives and evaluates his situation. For this reason, Merton's classification is used here as a typology of modes of adaptation to alienation and not to anomie directly.

Any mode of adaptation chosen by an actor may produce its own difficulties for him. A man who feels politically powerless may join the Communist Party if he feels that by doing so he may gain some measure of power. But this step may only result in his being isolated or marginal in some sense. In this case he may come to feel that this particular type of adaptation is unsuitable, and he may try some other mode of adaptation which he feels is more suitable.

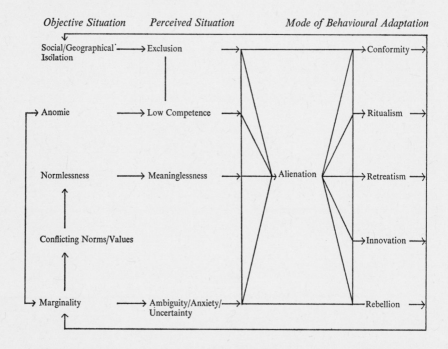

An attempt has been made to clarify a number of concepts which are frequently used in the analysis of political radicalism and of political life in general, and to outline the theoretical identities of these concepts. The diagram above summarizes this still tentative and incomplete picture of the possible causes of and paths to radicalism. However, as a heuristic tool the diagram has grave deficiencies. Movement from one horizontal or vertical level in the diagram to another is not inevitable or even probable. For example, some people may not realize that they are in an anomic situation, and so they will not develop feelings of low competence. Others may not be in an anomic position and yet still develop feelings of low competence. Others may prefer to be isolated from the wider society, and so they will not necessarily develop feelings of exclusion. Again, the geographically or socially mobile may not be isolated, or the conflict of norms and values in a marginal situation may not be prolonged or severe enough to result in normlessness. Dickie-Clark has shown that marginal individuals do not always develop feelings of ambiguity, anxiety, and uncertainty, and that even if they do acquire these marginal personality traits, their attitudes and behaviour do not differ markedly from non-marginal men.[43] In short, the arrows in the diagram represent possible, but by no means inevitable, movement. Much depends on the particular concrete situation, on its historical context, on how the actor perceives and evaluates the objective situation, and on the attitudes of others towards him and his situation.

For these reasons it is concluded that it is crucial to draw a sharp theoretical distinction between objective situations, the objective situation as it is defined by the actor, the feelings which the objective situation may induce in the actor, and the way in which the actor may evaluate the situation as he perceives it. Much of the existing literature on the concepts of marginality, alienation, anomie, and powerlessness has failed to draw these distinctions. Nettler has forcefully made much the same point:

How things really are 'out there', how one feels them to be, and how one feels oneself to be – regulated or purposeless – are disparate conditions: giving them the same name implies an equation that needs to be ascertained, not assumed.[44]

So far, this chapter amounts to nothing more than a preliminary step in devising categories and theoretical identities to align with these distinctions. The much more important job of discovering exactly what types of conditions result in exactly what types of attitudes and behaviour remains to be done.

However, given the theoretical identities of the concepts as they have been outlined above, it is now possible to construct a model of the particular objective situation – subjective orientation – behaviour sequence that results in Communist radicalism. But since the diagram (p. 120) is complex, and since its heuristic value is negligible, it will be broken down into its constituent parts before being re-assembled again to provide a more complete picture of the causes of and paths to Communist radicalism. The concern is with identifying a particular combination of causal variables and cultural–structural determinants which produce the specific outcome of Communism – Communsim being treated as one type of left-wing political rebellion. In Merton's typology there are five modes of adaptation to anomie. The problem to be faced is why certain groups or individuals choose one mode of adaptation rather than any other, and why one specific type of social situation will result in one specific type of behaviour. Lasswell has summarized the problem excellently.

Although political movements begin in unrest, all social unrest does not find expression in political movements. Under some conditions, a community which is visited by the plague may pray; under other conditions the community will demand the retirement of the health commissioner.[45]

Until very recently this 'choice of modes of adaptation' problem has not figured very largely, if at all, in the literature of sociology.[46] Sociologists are given to making such statements as – 'Political radicalism tends to increase during periods of unemployment', or – 'Membership of the Communist Party increased during this period because of the rapid urbanization and industrialization which took place'. Both statements may be accurate and sufficient for the writers' immediate purposes, but they overlook the fact that individuals can and do react in completely different ways to unemployment, and rapid urbanization and industrialization. They can join an other-worldly religious group, or a this-worldly left- or right-wing political group; they can commit suicide or take to alcohol or start wife-beating or become a tramp or a criminal or simply do nothing unusual at all.[47] Kornhauser's *The Politics of Mass Society* goes some way towards identifying a set of social conditions which induce radical ('extremist') attitudes and behaviour. Mass theory, in its present form, takes individuals and groups to the threshold of radicalism, but it does not take them to the threshold of particular types of radicalism – Fascist or Communist, religious or political, this-worldly, or inner-worldly, or other-worldly. And yet it is obviously important for both sociology and practical political life to understand why certain groups in certain situations join certain social movements. The 'choice of modes of adaptation' problem is immense. The present work is intended to be only a small first step towards an understanding of it. The method used is called the method of dual analysis, because it focuses on two types of variables, one of which causes radical attitudes and behaviour, and the other which directs attitudes and behaviour into particular channels. Two blocks of data will be used; the data collected about British Communism and the data collected about the concepts under discussion. Although the definitions of these concepts vary, even conflict, and although the reliability and validity of the scales designed to measure them have been questioned, the findings of the various studies are remarkably consistent.[48]

With the exception of Roberts and Rokeach,[49] writers have found that social and economic status (S.E.S.) and level of education correlate inversely with either anomie or alienation.[50] However, the bulk of the Party's membership, like that of so many other left-wing political groups, is made up of skilled and semi-skilled workers, and not of those with the lowest S.E.S. The low S.E.S. of the unskilled workers typically produces a combination of alienation and political apathy and fatalism.[51] The high S.E.S. of the middle-class individual tends to produce a combination of non-alienation and political activity. The skilled or semi-skilled worker, fitting as he does between these two groups, seems to take on characteristics of both. His S.E.S. may be sufficiently low to produce a certain degree of alienation and yet, at the same time, sufficiently high to equip him with the social and political skills which direct alienation into channels of political activism. His education, skill and intelligence enable him to fit his anomic situation into an ideological frame of reference. His energy, lack of fatalism, and ability to cooperate with others and to organize lead him to act positively in order to improve his social position and eliminate the sources of alienation. In short he is likely to choose rebellion or innovation as his mode of adaptation. This combination of causes and determinants can be summarized diagrammatically.

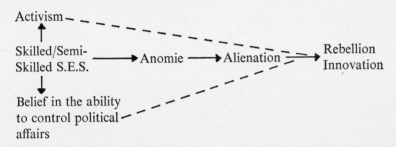

In this and subsequent diagrams, an arrow indicates the effect of causal variables – research indicates that low S.E.S. can cause anomie and alienation. Low S.E.S., therefore, is one variable which can act as a force generating social action. But this action may take any one of a number of different forms, so that it is still necessary to identify those factors which direct action into particular channels. A dotted line in the diagram indicates a structural or cultural factor which determines the particular channel along which action will be directed. In the diagram above, the activism and belief in the ability to control political affairs which are associated with skilled, and to a lesser extent with semi-skilled, S.E.S. tend to direct behaviour into channels of rebellion or innovation, rather than into channels of conformity, ritualism or retreatism. The unskilled worker tends to be fatalistic and apathetic, and so his alienation will usually be expressed in retreatist or ritualist forms. High S.E.S. produces non-alienation and also tends to be associated with activism and a belief that, in principle, political affairs can be controlled. In this case, therefore, conformity is the most likely mode of adaptation. These last two combinations of factors do not yield the outcome with which this study is concerned and so, for present purposes, may be set aside.

The diagrams, then, map out the likely effects of a combination of two types of factors – causal variables and structural-cultural determinants. Causal variables generate the dynamic force behind social action. Structural–cultural determinants are the factors which act as pressures directing action into particular channels. To use an analogy, causal variables are equivalent to the propeller which pushes a boat through the water, and structural–

cultural determinants are equivalent to the rudder which determines the direction in which the boat will move. In the rest of the chapter the terms causal variables and structural–cultural determinants will be abbreviated to causes and determinants.

The attitudinal consequences of an individual's low social and economic status may be strengthened and reinforced if the individual is socially and geographically immobile. What little information is available suggests that the bulk of working-class Party members are socially and geographically immobile. This immobility may aggravate the alienation associated with such factors as low S.E.S. and unemployment, because it cuts off the routes by which an individual may escape from them. Since the individual is prevented from moving into less alienative areas, his alienation may be said to be 'contained' or bottled up. There is no escape route or safety valve, and consequently the likelihood of a radical outcome is increased. In this case social and geographical immobility do not cause alienation, but act as factors which turn pre-existing alienation into contained alienation. However, social and geographical immobility may also act as causes of alienation where they prevent an ambitious person from moving up the social scale or from changing his occupation. One of the Communists interviewed had risen from an unskilled job to a semi-skilled one. He wanted a better job and thought he was capable of it, but could not improve his position within his trade and could not get as good a job outside it. Another said regretfully, if not bitterly:

I could have stayed at school until I was sixteen – I passed the exams which allowed me to, but there was a certain need to be earning although my parents did not put any pressure on me. . . . I couldn't get into an apprenticeship scheme. There was no room in any apprenticeship scheme. I became an office clerk – never did rise much beyond that level.

The influence of geographical and social immobility can be illustrated by the following diagram.

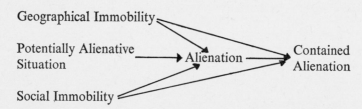

A higher proportion of middle-class than working-class Party members appear to be socially mobile. School teachers form the largest middle-class occupational group, and Bonham notes that school teachers are 'largely recruited from the lower middle class and working class'.[52] A Party official also suggested that many Communist school teachers have working-class and Communist backgrounds. Of the five teachers interviewed three were upwardly mobile, one of whom had a Communist background, and two were socially immobile, neither of whom had Communist backgrounds. It was not possible to tell whether this mobility produced anxiety about poor status crystallization and marginality.

Data collected by Allardt suggests that the combination of highly crystallized low status in a polarized two-class society is apt to increase the propensity towards political radicalism, while a poorly crystallized low status in the same society produces a propensity for moderate politics. In a multi-class society it appears to be a poorly crystallized status which tends to result in radicalism, and a highly crystallized one which results in moderate politics.[53] The largest section of Party members appears to have a fairly highly crystallized skilled or semi-skilled working-class status. Also Communists are concentrated in stable, old-established, relatively undifferentiated working-class communities, from which vantage point the class structure of the wider society is clearly 'visible'. It has also been found that high status crystallization correlates positively with class-status consciousness and class-interest consciousness.[54] High status crystallization in a two-class society may, therefore, be thought to increase the propensity for class-based, collective political action. Although Britain cannot be regarded as a polarized two-class society conforming to the Marxian model, there is a fairly well-documented tendency for working-class people to divide society into 'them' and 'us'. Britain also has relatively 'pure' class politics.[55] It would seem that many workers perceive the stratification system in two-class terms.

How is a highly crystallized skilled status in a perceived two-class society related to political radicalism? This combination of factors does not seem to create radical attitudes in itself. But if many members of a whole community have a highly crystallized status, the propensity for collective class-based action, rather than individual action, is increased. And if alienation is widespread in the community, that is if there is a need for radical action, then this collective action will take a radical form. This seems to be the case in the mining communities of South Wales and Scotland, in the East End of London, and in the working-class areas of Glasgow, where trade-union solidarity is intense, and where the C.P. is most successful. This pattern of variables produces the following diagram.

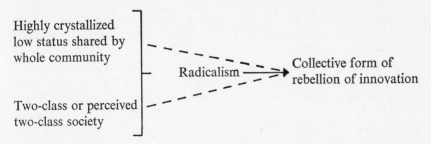

Highly crystallized low status shared by whole community

Two-class or perceived two-class society

Radicalism

Collective form of rebellion of innovation

While a highly crystallized low status does not produce radicalism on its own, a poorly crystallized status can produce radicalism if it results in feelings of ambiguity, uncertainty and anxiety.[56] It can result in maladjustment, or withdrawal,[57] or an attempt to eliminate the ambiguous position within the social structure by advocating political change of a left- or right-wing nature.[58] Quite a high proportion of school teachers are upwardly socially mobile and they may, therefore, have poorly crystallized statuses which, in turn, may produce radicalism. The activism and lack of fatalism generally associated with a school teacher's relatively high (if poorly crystallized) status will tend to direct their radicalism towards rebellion and innovation, rather than towards ritualism or retreatism. However, probably only a small minority of school teachers have a status which is sufficiently poorly crystallized to produce radicalism, and even then this factor probably does not create radical attitudes so much as add marginally to the tendency to develop them. It has been strongly argued that low status crystallization seems to have its strongest effect not so much when it is associated with class boundaries as when it is associated with ethnic boundaries.[59]

Only a small proportion of British Communists are members of ethnic or ethno-religious groups. The two largest groups seem to be the 750 members of the Cypriot branch in London and the Jewish Communists. No information is available about the Cypriots, but there is some information about the Jewish members. The Party was especially successful in recruiting Jews in the working-class communities of the East End of London. Here, Jews would be subject to many of the pressures, strains and frustrations of unemployment and poverty. Also, Jews have a strong desire to understand and control social and political affairs,[60] so that their radicalism would tend to be directed into channels of political rebellion or innovation, rather than conformity, ritualism or retreatism. Finally, the liberal economic and non-economic elements in Judaism and the immediate presence of Fascism and anti-Semitism would result in sympathy for, or membership of, the Communist Party. A combination of poverty, discrimination and the militant defence of minority rights on the part of the C.P. is not sufficient, on its own, to induce members of minority groups to join the Party. The American Communist Party campaigned militantly for American Negro rights but was not particularly successful in recruiting Negroes.[61] Members of minority groups must be predisposed towards left-wing political radicalism before the combination of poverty, discrimination and Communist egalitarianism will lead them to join the C.P.

Previous research indicates that unemployment can also be a powerful influence in the creation of radical political attitudes, particularly when it produces acute relative deprivation. It can create all the potentially alienative objective situations listed in the diagram on p. 120 – social and/or geographical isolation, anomie, normlessness, and marginality. However.

East End Jews

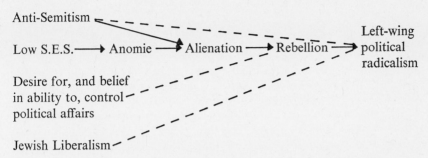

Anti-Semitism

Low S.E.S. ——→ Anomie ——→ Alienation ——→ Rebellion ——→ Left-wing political radicalism

Desire for, and belief in ability to, control political affairs

Jewish Liberalism

different individuals may react in different ways to the same objective situation, and therefore the next stage of the discussion will examine these objective situations and the subjective orientations of individuals to them.

Isolation and exclusion are treated here as a real and/or perceived situation in which an individual, group, or society is wholly or partially cut off from contact with other groups, societies, or individuals. Any measure of isolation should take into account the quantity and the quality of the interaction and expected interaction.

Few British Communists seem to be isolated as individuals. On the contrary, most appear to be well-integrated members of their local communities and associations. However, the social isolation of whole communities has been used to account for political radicalism.[62] It has also been said that the mining communities of South Wales have felt cut off from, and ignored by, the centres of political power in London. Social and geographical isolation do not necessarily produce radicalism in themselves, but may exacerbate pre-existing alienation. The community which feels itself to be isolated will feel itself to be excluded from the political decision-making processes, and unable to do anything to change the situation which causes their alienation. Thus the members of the community are likely to develop feelings of low competence. In short, geographical and social isolation are factors which may heighten feelings of alienation and which may help to create contained alienation.

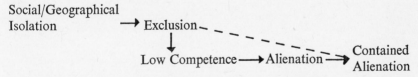

Social/Geographical Isolation ——→ Exclusion

Low Competence ——→ Alienation ——→ Contained Alienation

Objective states of anomie may also help to create feelings of low competence and alienation. Believing that the capitalist system is unable to produce the results which have been claimed and desired of it, Communists have resorted to a deviant ideology. The pattern of deviance has changed a little over the past forty years. In the 1920s the C.P.G.B.'s ideology could be typed as follows, in Dubin's elaborated version of Merton's schema.[63]

TYPE OF DEVIANT ADAPTATION	CULTURAL GOALS	INSTITUTIONAL NORMS	INSTITUTIONAL MEANS
Rebellion	Substitution	Substitution	Substitution

However, the gap between cultural norms and goals and the socially structured capacities to act in accordance with them has closed, or is believed to have closed, over the past forty years, and so also the pattern of Communist deviance has changed. All those interviewed believed that social and economic conditions have improved over the past forty years, and most thought that the democratic system had similarly improved. The position of the Communists is now more typically as follows:

TYPE OF DEVIANT ADAPTATION	CULTURAL GOALS	INSTITUTIONAL NORMS	INSTITUTIONAL MEANS
Institutional Invention	Acceptance	Substitution	Substitution

Such an alteration reflects a change in the pure, revolutionary element in the Party's ideology due to a weakening of anomic conditions (due, in turn, to an increase in economic and social security) and a heightened feeling of social, economic and political competence. The total result is that Communists in the 1960s are more prepared to work within the framework of the social order and are content to change mainly the institutional norms and means. It should be added that this is a shift of emphasis rather than a change from one discrete type to another.[64]

Political competence has been singled out as having a crucial role in the development of political attitudes,[65] and so a battery of four questions to estimate political competence was distributed at different points in the questionnaire administered to Communist respondents. The results were as follows:

	YES	NO	DON'T KNOW	OTHER
Would you say that ordinary people have any influence over the way the country is run?	20	6	0	1 (Only a little.)
Do you think the country is run by public opinion?	1	26	0	0

	AGREE	DIS-AGREE	DON'T KNOW	OTHER
It is sometimes said that the only people who have any real say in running the country are government leaders. Do you agree or disagree?	5	22	0	0

In general, what groups of people, (apart from political parties) have most influence over what the government does in this country?

Group	Number of times that a group was ranked from 1 to 4 in terms of the strength of its political influence

GROUP	FIRST	SECOND	THIRD	FOURTH
'Big business'	18	4	1	0
Trade unions	8	8	2	1
Churches (mainly Church of England)	0	2	6	1
'Mass pressure groups' (Mainly C.N.D.)	0	2	2	0
Middle-class consumers and businessmen	1	2	1	0
Military	0	2	0	0
Teachers and intellectuals	0	2	0	0
Tenants' Associations	0	2	0	0
Civil Service	0	0	1	0
Cooperatives	0	0	1	0
Press	0	0	1	0

(This table will not cross check because not all respondents were prepared to give as many as four influential groups.)

From these figures and from the comments of the respondents to the questions it seems that British Communists believe that the ordinary man does have some influence over the way the country is run, although they do not believe that the country is run by public opinion. They hold that it is not government leaders who are in control but 'big business' – variously called 'the industrialists', 'the City', 'bankers', 'monopolists', or 'the Employers' Federation'. The Conservative Party was identified with this group. Most felt that trade unions would have a greater share of political power under a Labour government. There was no difference between the middle-class and working-class responses.

People do have some influence, but it doesn't come through the official channels – elections and parliament – it comes through the trade unions. [Student]

Governments do have to take public opinion into account. For example, governments now recognize that mass unemployment would result in the end of their power. It's a big change from twenty years ago. But without any shadow of doubt it's the big associations of employers which have the biggest influence over the present [Conservative] government, and this can be substantiated in many ways. The people with the biggest say are the people with economic power – the employers. They are not always the government leaders but the two groups overlap – even in a Labour government. The Communist Party, you know, also has some influence because some of its ideas have been integrated into the ideas of the Labour Party and the trade unions. [Student]

Monopolists and big business have most power. The Churches also. The Church of England mostly. The capitalists control the means of propaganda – the press, T.V., orthodox economists, orthodox sociologists. [Student]

Ordinary people do have some influence but they ought to have a lot more. I mean they don't have as much as it's claimed they have, and even that wouldn't be enough. Mass feeling, if it's expressed does have some influence. It can move governments – look at the effect of C.N.D. But this can operate only to a little extent in capitalism. . . . The employers' federation dictate to the governments. Well, the Tory Party is the employers' federation. Religion also – especially the C. of E. It has its roots among the people and is powerful because of its official position within the establishment. [Research scientist]

Ordinary people have a certain influence when they express themselves in an organized way but most of the power lies with the employers. [Housewife]

Public opinion has some influence but it doesn't run the country. The Federation of British Employers and the monopolists do that. The trade unions, as well, a bit, and a variety of people's organizations also – peace movements, C.N.D., Tenants' Associations. [Teacher]

Under the Tory Party big business has all the influence. Trade unions don't have much in spite of what the papers are always saying. Public opinion can be influential but I wouldn't say any more than that. But any democratic organization has some influence – reform groups and things like that. Organizations like the Howard League for Penal Reform are often underestimated. And C.N.D. of course. [Bank clerk]

At the moment trade unions and employers' organizations are the most powerful. Things will change for the better under a Labour government. Most other groups are not cohesive enough to get a big pull. The Church has some influence. . . . Mostly the country is run by the middle class, certainly not public opinion. [Electrician]

Oh, no, ordinary people don't have any influence. It's all done by the bankers and people like that. The trade unions to a very limited extent. The country is run by public opinion at election time, but that's doubtful even. [Secretary]

Big business. The Tories are big business. The trade unions have some influence – but it's not important enough. Mostly, public opinion is created by those who run the country. It's forced on the country – look at the anti-nationalization campaign. It's not their fault. Pressure is put on them to conform from above.[66] [Full-time Party worker]

The quotations given in Chapter 2 (pp. 24–5) indicate that Communists themselves have a relatively high level of political competence. They believe that their own political competence, as members of the Party, is higher than that of the ordinary man, because they say that the Party wields influence in national and local affairs out of all proportion to its size. Most political sociologists would agree that they probably overestimate the Party's power, but joining the C.P. would appear to be one way of dealing with unwelcome feelings of low competence.

Most people in Britain maintain a comparatively well-developed sense of political competence.[67] And it seems that this is true of British Communists as well. Yet high competence is usually associated with moderate politics, and not with radicalism. The two sets of data seem to conflict with each other. However, it is important to distinguish between political competence, or the control a man believes he wields, and the desire for competence, or the control a man believes he ought to wield. What is important for the development of radical attitudes is not competence, but relative competence – the amount of control a man believes he has relative to the amount of control he believes he ought to have. High relative competence, therefore, will be used to refer to a man's belief that he wields enough control over social affairs, and low relative competence to the feeling that insufficient control is exercised. The Communist may believe that he and the ordinary man exercise limited control over social and political events and decisions, but he also believes that the ordinary man can and ought to wield more control. His relative control is low and hence his alienation. Almond and Verba's non-Communist respondents in Britain believed that they had some control over political affairs,[68] and probably believed, also, that they had enough control, particularly if they were deference voters. Their relative competence was high and hence their political conformism, if they were political activists, or their political apathy, if they were politically inactive.

Generally, the higher an individual's educational level and status the greater his sense of competence.[69] Since the vast majority of the population does not have a tendency towards political megalomania it will generally follow that the higher the level of competence the higher the relative competence. But just as the skilled status of the bulk of Communists is sufficiently low to produce alienation and sufficiently high to produce political activism, so also, it can be argued, their skilled status seems to be low enough to produce low relative competence and sufficiently high to produce the political skills which direct their behaviour into channels of organized political rebellion. In sum, skilled status seems to produce, on the one hand, a discrepancy between expectations and actuality, and, on the other hand, it is accompanied by social and political abilities which enable skilled workers to act positively in an attempt to reduce this descrepancy. This may be summed up diagrammatically.

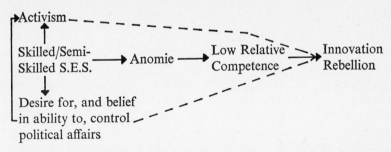

Marginality, the third objective state, may also contribute towards the development of a radical political consciousness. Marginality is probably not a malaise characteristic of most working-class Communists, but the concept can be used to help explain the relatively large numbers of school teachers and Jews in the Party. In Park's words: 'The emancipated Jew was, and is, historically and typically the marginal man . . .'[70] Ethnicity does not always produce marginality by any means, but the quotations from interviews with two Jewish Communists (p. 79) show definite signs of feelings of 'non-belongingness' and marginality. The Party gained much Jewish support in those areas where anti-Semitism threatened Jewish status in society. Even without the threat of anti-Semitism it is possible that some Jews might have joined the C.P., for it has been suggested that a satisfactory adaptation to marginality requires the fusion of two or more cultures. The resulting cross fertilization of old ideas may generate new ideas, or adherence to new ideas, and consequently an interest in social and political reform.[71] Thus a satisfactory adaptation to marginality will some-times result in a desire to change the culturally defined goals and means of society – that is, it might result in rebellion of which Communism is one form. Lastly; the Jewish culture is likely to act as a determinant which further limits the choice of type of rebellion, both because there is some small measure of congruity between Jewish political aspirations and Communist political aspirations and because the Communists campaigned militantly against anti-Semitism in Britain.

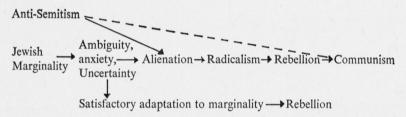

The marginality of some school teachers results from their social mobility and consequent low status crystallization. The widespread feeling among teachers that they are deprived of their proper status in society reinforces the effects of this marginality. In addition there is a low morale in the profession because of an inadequate supply of teachers, inadequate teaching facilities and overcrowded schools and classrooms. The resulting alienation is made inescapable, though not entirely so, because teaching skills are not easily transferable to other professions and because there are only limited chances for promotion within the profession. In spite of the conditions and strains of their profession, the teachers interviewed did not want to move into another job because they believed teaching to be the most worthwhile of occupations.

Oh, yes, I like the job very much. I like teaching and I like children. I'm very much concerned with youth in the country. But the schools in this area are terrible. They're bad for the children and they're bad for us as well – overcrowding – there are thirty-five in my class, but that's above average, I think – no equipment, little money. And there's not much chance of an improvement either. Quite a lot of money is being spent but it's only nibbling at the problem. You know the Party policy on this?

I was very lucky because I was promoted when I was young. That was excellent. . . . I like the job because I like working with people and I like young people.

You can't teach large classes properly, conditions aren't good in the profession. In fact they're very bad indeed in some parts of the country.

Only one of the five teachers believed that salaries were high enough to compensate for the job done and the training required, and none believed that they were high enough to solve the problem of the shortage of teachers. Again, it must be emphasized that this pattern of causes and determinants probably applies to only a minority of Communist school teachers.

School teachers

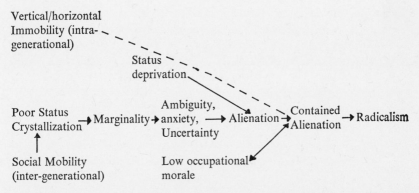

Lastly, there is the state of normlessness which may induce feelings of meaninglessness. Meaninglessness refers to a situation in which an individual believes that the continued existence of society and/or himself has no meaning because he feels either:

1. that there are no normatively defined goals and/or means, or
2. that there are no normatively defined goals and/or means to which he can adhere.

Normlessness may result in feelings of bewilderment and purposelessness. Prolonged or acute social disorganization on an individual or social scale can result in cultural disintegration and a state of mild normlessness. In Melanesia, a particularly acute culture clash produced a particularly unusual pattern of beliefs and behaviour.[72] A more mild clash of cultures may also produce a more mild pattern of deviance. Similarly, the man in a marginal position who is torn between two conflicting cultures or sub-cultures can try to solve his problem by joining a radical group of some kind. Experience of meaninglessness and purposelessness can induce an individual to join a group with a well-defined ideology in order to reintegrate and reorientate his life. One respondent who was half Jewish and was experiencing many of the problems of marginality found that joining the Party had given his life meaning and purpose.

Joining the C.P. can give the new member a sense of belonging which is frequently absent from the family and the job. By joining the C.P. branch you can immediately gain twenty or so friends who respect your opinions. Some people join the C.P. because of the personal understanding which is to be found in it. Just being a member relieves frustration and purposelessness. The C.P. gives people a place to meet and gives them friends, belonging and purpose. [Student]

Another respondent said:

Joining the C.P. was the biggest step forward I ever made in my life. It was like going from darkness into the light. I'm extremely interested in why people leave the Party but I can't understand why they do this. The Party gave me confidence in the future. It gave me courage to break with my husband – my marriage was going very badly at the time. I read a book about women and children in the Soviet Union, and I saw a new life for myself. I joined the Party and began a new life and got a host of new friends. [Office clerk]

Levin has suggested that the conspiratorial theory of history and charismatic leaders appeal to people in a state of normlessness.[73] Widespread unemployment in the thirties and the social disorganization produced by war are probably the most important causes of normlessness in Britain since 1920.

In the hectic times of the thirties, the disillusioned liberal scientist, who saw so many of his treasured liberal ideas shattered, could in his desperation push aside the others and make a fetish of science, a dogma of reason. The Communist emphasis upon control and manipulation, and upon the idea of a scientific society in which scientists would play a leading role, touched the Achilles heel of the nihilistic scientist. In a world in which science alone seemed to know what it was about, Communism held the hope that the rule of the scientist–king might become more than a dream.[74]

Rather oblique support for this argument is contained in a cautious conclusion of Struening and Richardson who suggest that their 'Perceived Purposelessness' factor measures a type of middle-class 'anomia', while their 'Alienation via Rejection' factor is more characteristic of the lower socio-economic classes.[75] This indicates that purposelessness may be one cause of middle-class radicalism and that rejection, or feelings of exclusion, may be a cause of working-class radicalism.

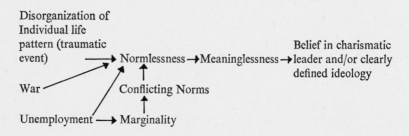

Now that all the causes and determinants which were planned out in diagram 1 have been discussed, a more complete picture of the causes of Communist radicalism can be assembled. The evidence suggests that three different configurations of causes and determinants account for the presence of skilled and semi-skilled workers, Jews, and teachers in the Party. From the data presented, Models 1, 2, and 3 can be assembled.

Three types of British Communist

Model 1 *(Skilled/Semi-Skilled Workers)*

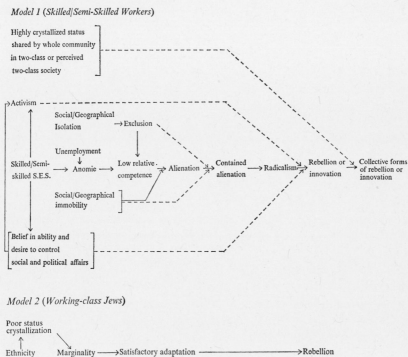

Model 2 *(Working-class Jews)*

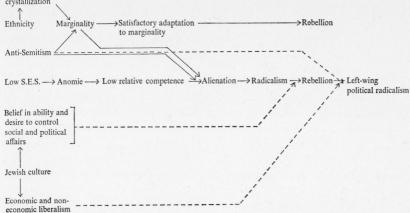

Model 3 (School teachers)

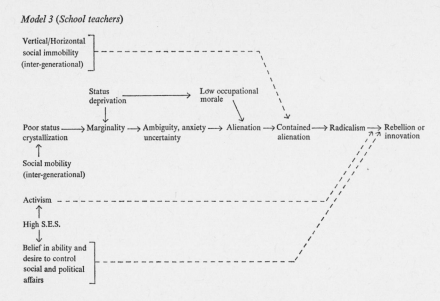

These models require some further explanation. They do not imply that only people subject to all the causes and determinants become political radicals, but that the larger the number of causes and determinants present in any concrete situation, the greater the tendency towards radicalism. The models also represent the pure, limiting cases in which all cross pressures have been removed. For example, the poor status crystallization of Communist school teachers and of marginal Jews may act as a cross pressure on their radical inclinations, because poor status crystallization in a two-class, or perceived two-class, society is usually associated with moderate politics. However, it is unlikely that Communist school teachers live in the same kind of undifferentiated communities as most working-class Communists, and so they may not perceive society to be divided so sharply into two classes – until they have assimilated the Party ideology, that is. The models do not take into account some important variables because no relevant data about them have been unearthed. Parental political influence is particularly important among these missing links. Lastly, it has not been possible to identify all the pressures which act upon some teachers and working-class individuals and which produce the specific outcome of left-wing political rebellion or Communism. But a radical left-wing political party like the C.P. will inevitably attract a relatively large proportion of skilled workers living in conditions which precipitate extreme alienation. All other things being equal, the more extreme the conditions the more radical the outcome. Very mild working-class alienation is likely to result in membership of the Labour Party rather than of the C.P. There is a significant positive correlation between support for the C.P. and the Labour Party in general elections.[76]

It seems that the same conditions which produce a high Labour vote will, in extreme form, produce a high Communist vote.

So far the method of dual analysis has been applied only to occupational, class, and ethnic groups. It is possible to apply the method as an explanatory device to geographical areas as well. The Party has contested the Rhondda East parliamentary constituency in each general election since 1929. In every one, except 1935 and 1951, the percentage of the Rhondda East population voting Communist has been about four times the Communist national average. In 1935 the Party contested only its two most successful constituencies, and although Gallacher was elected for West Fife, a slightly higher percentage of the electorate voted for Harry Pollitt in Rhondda East. In 1951 the percentage in Rhondda East was only twice the national Communist average. The Rhondda East voting figures have been exceeded only three times in all – in West Fife in 1929, 1950 and 1951. Rhondda East, together with West Fife, is the Party's most successful constituency and therefore should be marked by almost all the variables and pressures outlined in Model 1.

Rhondda East is a coal-mining constituency and miners are subject to almost all, if not all, the occupational variables which precipitate radicalism and which were discussed in Chapter 4. The area suffered very badly from heavy unemployment figures in the thirties. This produced unusually acute relative deprivation because the South Wales mining area had prospered during the post-1918 economic boom. Miners are geographically and socially immobile, and in their most depressed periods the South Wales mining communities have felt isolated from and ignored by the central government. The situation precipitating alienation was virtually inescapable, therefore, so that some form of radicalism was almost inevitable. There is a high proportion of skilled and semi-skilled workers among miners, whose activism and lack of fatalism is likely to direct their radicalism into channels of rebellion or innovation. Lastly, South Wales has a population which is more homogeneous in income range than any other region in Britain; a smaller proportion of its population is middle-class and most working-class people have similar incomes.[77] These considerations, together with the fact that South Wales mining villages form very tightly knit and unified communities, create conditions which prompt a two-class view of society and class-based collective political action. With widespread, acute, and contained alienation, the C.P. is the natural vehicle for the expression of unusually militant working-class political demands. In short, an unusual combination of causes and determinants has caused an unusually strong support for the Communist Party. Much the same configuration of factors will account for the strong support for Communism in the East End of London, in the working-class areas of Glasgow and in the Scottish mining villages.

The largest occupational group in the B.C.P. is formed by the engineers who are also subject to many of the occupational factors creating alienation. Blauner has found that the assembly-line worker feels powerless because he is unable to control his own work routine, finds his work meaningless because of the highly developed division of labour in the mass-production factory, and is socially isolated because the assembly line obstructs the formation of informal groups on the factory floor.[78] Unlike the miners, the engineers are not tied to a particular area, industry, or place in the social structure, although there is not much chance for promotion within the industry. But there is no reason why they should not be geographically or horizontally mobile and they are not, as a group, isolated.

The analysis may be taken a step further by linking some statements about alienation with some of those about authoritarianism. In the chapter on authoritarianism, closed-mindedness was treated as one dimension of authoritarianism. It is now possible to make some tentative propositions about the relationship between alienation and closed-mindedness. Two statements link the concepts. Rokeach has suggested that 'in the extreme, the closed system is nothing more than the total network of psycho-analytical defence mechanisms organized together to form a cognitive system and designed to shield a vulnerable mind'.[79] And Nettler has suggested that 'to be an extremist joined in a cause with others is ego-protective'.[80] It should follow, therefore, that radicals need both a closed ideological system and the comfort of close association with other radicals, for both act in an ego-protective capacity. This is a tentative proposition because it depends on a series of specific definitions, but it is, in principle, amenable to empirical verification.

The suggested connexion between closed-mindedness and alienation will also help to explain how the middle-class idealist manages to close a gap between his political demands and Party actuality. It has already been suggested that the middle-class Communist will be more alienated from his middle-class subculture than the working-class Communist from his sub-culture, because he has moved a greater distance from the attitudinal centre of his social background. If this is so, it may also follow that the middle-class Communist has a greater need for the ego-protective mechanisms than his working-class comrade, and thus he will tend to be more closed-minded. His closed-mindedness will help him to deal with the disagreeable aspects of Party ideology and activity, whether these disagreeable aspects are real or only perceived by him.

Research also indicates that the alienated may also be authoritarian, since both alienation and authoritarianism are associated with, or caused by, the same network of variables.[81] However, the problems associated with the concepts of alienation and authoritarianism make a bald statement of their association of dubious validity. The most that can be said at present is that some dimensions or causes of alienation may be associated with some dimensions or causes of authoritarianism – particularly dogmatism, non-economic illiberalism, anti-democratic feelings, self-estrangement, physical isolation, low competence, normlessness, and meaninglessness.

Feelings of alienation alone are insufficient to provoke political radicalism for the alienated may adapt to their situation in any one of a large number of different ways. The method of dual analysis represents an attempt to develop a general theoretical approach to the question of why certain types of individuals or groups use one mode of adaption rather than another. The method attempts to isolate two types of variables which are called causal variables and structural determinants. Causal variables generate the motivating power behind social action, and structural determinants influence the particular form which this behaviour will take. The existing literature on the sociology of social movements is mainly concerned with causal variables, and has only rarely attempted to provide any explanation of why social action takes particular forms.

The data presented suggest that Communist radicalism is rooted in a complex matrix of causes and determinants and that a large number of these causes and determinants must coincide in one concrete case before it will precipitate Communist sympathies. A combination of alienation and fatalism, which tends to be found in the lower social and economic status groupings, is not likely to result in political radicalism, but in some form of retreatism and mood of disgruntled, alienated helplessness. Before a man will join a radical political organization which aims at changing the social and political order he must first of all believe that national and international political events are man-made and man-directed, and not preordained in some mysterious and unknowable way by forces beyond his control. He must believe that social and political events can, in principle, be controlled by the people bound up with them. Radicalism also requires feelings of low relative competence – a discrepancy between the control a man believes he wields over political affairs and the control he believes he has a right to wield.

The degree of radicalism is dependent, in part, on the acuteness of the conditions provoking alienation. A very short spell of unemployment accompanied by mild relative deprivation may only result in a small shift of political attitudes, but a longer period of unemployment accompanied by acute relative deprivation may help to produce radicalism. The conditions which produce strong support for the Labour Party and trade unions may also produce, in extreme form, widespread support for the C.P. or other radical left-wing political groups. This is not surprising in itself and even less surprising when one considers the non-revolutionary, militant trade-unionist nature of the working-class Communist ideology.

The general impression received from a study of British Communism is that the concepts of marginality, poor status crystallization, normlessness and meaninglessness are not of much relevance to any explanation of why most members join the Party. Quotations from the interviews can be produced which show that some people become Communists in reaction to a marginal position in society or to a state of normlessness, but these are probably a minority of members. The small number of marginal Jews who become Communists do so not so much because of their marginality as because of a combination of poverty, anti-Semitism, and Jewish liberalism. Poor status crystallization probably accounts for the radicalism of only a small number of Jews or school teachers who become Communists. For, at the most, it seems to be no more than a minor and secondary factor.[82] The most important single combination of causes is the unemployment/low S.E.S. – anomie – low relative competence syndrome which applies to the vast bulk of the Party's working-class members.

Throughout the study it has been continually stressed and emphasized that the quantity and quality of data about the B.C.P. is far from satisfactory and that few hard and dependable conclusions can be drawn. Since the method of dual analysis is based on the data and conclusions presented in previous chapters, it is also tentative, and, in parts, rather speculative. But the uncertain nature of the method's empirical referent does not necessarily invalidate it as a general theoretical approach to the study of social movements. The method can be applied to the B.C.P. in what can only be described as a rule of thumb and probationary manner, but it may be that the method can be applied as an explanatory tool to better documented social movements in a more exact, satisfactory and productive manner. If it is at all useful the method will undoubtedly benefit from such application by way of clearer conceptualization, a more complete coverage of a wider range of empirical situations, and more exact specification of modes of behavioural adaptation to situations.

1. G. Nettler, 'The Alienated Man Revisited', mimeo
2. Clark, 1959; Pearlin, 1962; Thompson and Horton, 1960; Neal and Rettig, 1963; Levin, 1960, p. 59; Gouldner, 1950, p. 86; Dean, 1961; Meier and Bell, 1959
3. McDill and Ridley, 1962
4. McIver, 1950, pp. 84–5; Srole, 1956; Riesman, Denney and Glazer, 1950, p. 287
5. Merton, 1959, p. 162
6. Merton, 1959, p. 162; Brookes, 1951
7. See McClosky and Schaar, 1965. For methodological and theoretical critiques of this paper see Srole (1965) and Nettler (1965), and also McClosky and Schaar's reply (1965)
8. The two words 'may' and 'partly' are included in this sentence because revolutionary attitudes may be explained in other ways. Some people may be revolutionaries because they were dropped on their heads when they were babies. Or they may be revolutionaries because they have an Oedipus complex and hate all forms of authority. It has been suggested, not entirely seriously, that Marx was a revolutionary because he had a boil on his backside, and the pain it gave him as he sat in the British Museum Reading Room caused him to develop an angry and violent political philosophy. At any rate, it is not claimed here that all revolutionary attitudes are caused by anomie, or that all anomic results in revolutionary attitudes
9. Campbell, Gurin, and Miller, 1954, p. 187

10. Nettler, 1957
11. Neal and Rettig, 1963
12. Nettler, 1956
13. Hajda, 1961. It may be said that uneasiness may not always accompany alienation and is not, therefore, a necessary part of the definition
14. Laswell, in McIver, 1952
15. Levin, 1960, p. 59. See also Lane, 1962, p. 161
16. Shils, 1956, p. 231
17. Thompson and Horton, 1960
18. Thompson and Horton, 1960
19. Hyde, 1952
20. Davids, 1955
21. Dean, 1960
22. Glazer, 1961, p. 6
23. Nettler, 'The Alienated Man Revisited', mimeo
24. Seeman, 1959
25. Blau, in Peterson, 1958, pp. 252–3
26. Dean, 1960; de Grazia, 1948, pp. 72–4
27. Nettler, 'The Alienated Man Revisited', mimeo
28. Blauner, 1964
29. Hajda, 1961
30. Kornhauser, 1960, pp. 183–222
31. Park, 1950, p. 373
32. Herberg, 1960, p. 16
33. Hughes, 1949
34. Lenski, 1954
35. Dickie-Clark, 1966, p. 39
36. Dickie-Clark, 1966, p. 47
37. Mitchell, 1964; Kelly and Chambliss, 1966
38. Kerckhoff, 1958; Dickie-Clark, 1966
39. See Dickie-Clark, 1966, p. 16
40. Brett, 1963, p. 8
41. Merton, 1959, Chapters 4 and 5
42. Dubin, 1959. See also Harary, 1966. While the work of Dubin and Harary may add sophistication to the theory of anomie, it is felt that the limited data about the C.P. did not merit the use of their distinctions
43. Dickie-Clark, 1966
44. Nettler, 1965
45. Lasswell, 1931
46. For two notable and admirable exceptions see Neil Smelser's *Theory of Collective Behaviour* (London: Routledge & Kegan Paul, 1962) and Howard Becker's *The Outsiders* (New York: Free Press, 1963) in which they develop their respective 'value added model' and 'sequential model'. Merton (1959) has already offered some illuminating comments on the choice of modes of adaptation to anomie, and his work has been usefully extended by Cloward (1959) in his discussion of the 'availability of illegitimate means'. See also de Grazia, 1948
47. The deviant in the deviant situation has received considerable attention, but not the non-deviant in the deviant situation
48. Nettler, and Bell and Meier are convinced that Srole's scale measures despair and not anomie
49. Roberts and Rokeach, 1956
50. Dean, 1961; Thompson and Horton, 1960; Meier and Bell, 1959; Erbe, 1964; Mizruchi, 1960; Haer, 1956; McDill and Ridley, 1962; Clark, 1959; Pearlin, 1962

51. McDill and Ridley, 1962; Clark, 1959; Hajda, 1961; Bell, 1957; Mizruchi, 1960; Kornhauser, Sheppard and Meyer, 1956

52. Bonham, 1954, p. 64

53. Allardt, in Allardt and Littunen, 1964, pp. 105–7

54. Landecker, 1963

55. Alford, 1963

56. Seeman, 1956; Jackson, 1962

57. Lenski, 1956

58. Lenski, 1954; Malewski, 1963; Notestein, 1963; Goffman, 1957; Ringer and Sills, 1952. Kenkel's (1956) findings do not support Lenski's, but Lenski claims that Kenkel's study was not a true replication. See also, Kelly and Chambliss, 1966

59. Mitchell, 1964; Kelly and Chambliss, 1966

60. Glazer, 1952; Strodbeck, in McLelland, 1958, p. 155

61. Glazer, 1961; Chapter 5

62. Phillips Davison, 1955

63. Dubin, 1959

64. Lipset has noted a similar shift of emphasis in the ideology of the Italian Communist Party – Lipset, 1964

65. Almond and Verba, 1963; Cantril, 1962, pp. 168–71

66. For an elaboration of these points made in the interviews see Harvey and Hood, 1958; Aaronovitch, 1955, 1961

67. Almond and Verba, 1963

68. Almond and Verba, 1963

69. Almond and Verba, 1963, p. 213

70. Park, 1950, p. 354

71. Sanua, 1962; Seeman, 1956; Park, 1950

72. Worsley, 1957

73. Levin, 1960, pp. 66–8

74. Wood, 1959, pp. 150–51

75. Struening and Richardson, 1965

76. Nicholas, 1951, p. 325

77. Brennan, Cooney, and Pollins, 1954, pp. 60–61

78. Blauner, 1964

79. Rokeach, 1960, p. 70

80. Nettler, 'The Alienated Man Revisited', mimeo

81. Martin and Westie, 1959; Janowitz and Marvick, 1959; MacKinnon and Centres, 1956; Kornhauser, Sheppard and Meyer, 1956

82. About a year after this was written, some evidence to support the statement was produced by Kelly and Chambliss (1966). Their findings, they conclude, 'raise serious doubts as to the explanatory utility of the concept of status consistency. As a matter of fact, the results of this study indicate that social class membership and ethnic background of the respondents are far more important determinants of political attitudes than the degree to which persons are status consistent or inconsistent'

CHAPTER 11

SIX POLITICAL PROFILES

Inevitably any study of a social group tends to get lost in a collection of minute details. In the process of assembling and piecing together information about this and that point, the total picture becomes obscured by a mass of detail. To restore the balance, to illustrate some of the points made, and to bring them to life, six of the Communists interviewed will be used as case studies. The first two have been selected because they seem in general to be fairly typical of the working-class pragmatists. The second two correspond quite closely to the middle-class idealists in the Party, and the last two are not typical as Party members, but they illustrate some of the points made about marginality, isolation, poor status crystallization, and alienation. In all six cases the identities of the respondents have been carefully obscured so that the anonymity promised them is preserved.

Mr Brown

'My father was a railway man. Both my parents left school when they were twelve – the earliest age in those days. They always voted for the Labour Party. Father was a trade unionist – he was a union member, but I wouldn't say he was a militant one. We lived in a town just outside Glasgow. We lived in extreme poverty. We were always extremely conscious of it. I'll give you two examples. I remember going one day to some better-off relations. My mother took some jewels with her – worthless trinkets they were – hoping that they would buy them. It was a very humiliating experience. The other one – we had to make frequent visits to the local poor relief for clothing. My mother was in tears for days before we went. Everybody knew you had parish clothes. A terribly humiliating experience.

'I left school when I was fourteen, but I'd started to get interested in politics about a year before that. I had no immediate friends in the C.P. when I joined – that was in 1940. Most were members of the Labour Party or else they voted Labour. I had experience of a large number of socialist organizations in my home town, but I had most respect and admiration for the people who were Communists. They were the most honest and self-sacrificing, and you could look up to them. Joining was a big step because I never felt I had the moral strength and ability to live up to their standards. My reasons for being a Communist are a bit different now. I've changed from emotional reasons to a knowledge of Communism. Being in the Party has brought political maturity and understanding. I suppose most people join because they've had lousy living conditions. The rest because they are idealists – they're fairly well off themselves, by my standards anyhow, but they know something of the conditions of the rest of the country.

'I started off in a pretty poor job – delivering goods. I like my job now. I don't think I'd change it. I've considerable freedom and there aren't many restrictions. I've a free hand in all that I do. I think I'm capable of a better job and more responsibility. I'm in charge of a few men now and I regard myself as a skilled worker, but I'm not officially regarded as a skilled man. The union doesn't recognize me. Wages are bad. That's my main complaint. After I've paid for fuel, light, and rent I reckon I've got half the public assistance allowance left.

'My living conditions are better now than they've ever been. There's no doubt about that. But there's always that considerable degree of uncertainty. I've had about three years of unemployment and I don't want any more. This place has a decontrolled rent. I don't know what I'd have to do if the rent went up. I can't afford to pay any more for it.

'Everybody is much better off now than when I started working – better houses, better food, cars. The problem now is mental illness. That's an enormous social problem. Present day life produces an enormous mental strain. The only way to solve this problem is by planning. You've got to attack the whole system. All problems are political problems. The biggest world problem is peace. That's vital. We are drifting into war and it's a very, very dangerous situation. The answer is a complete change of British policy and a complete change from British colonialist policy. After peace, the big problem is monopolies. Monopolies make every social problem difficult to solve. The people who run the country are the people who own industry – employers and monopolists. They're the people who take the basic decisions which affect every-day life. The Conservatives are part of this group. There are 400 people who decide what is happening. The country certainly isn't run by public opinion, but the government must take account of public opinion to a certain extent. What they try to do is get public opinion to think their way by advertisements, radio and the press. Thousands and thousands of pounds are spent every year on propaganda, and very intelligent people do it. It's an advanced science and they are experts. They maintain the ideas they want in a very subtle way. For example the colonial wars. Working-class people want the colonies – Aden, Cyprus, Malaysia. They believe in troops to keep them for Britain.

'What disgusts me about the Tories is their snobbishness, their pomposity. They believe they are superior. I don't like anything about the Conservative Party. The Labour Party is a working-class Party with a majority of working-class members. It doesn't have selfish aims. It wants to advance the people as a whole. But I don't like the political dishonesty and spinelessness of Labour's leaders. They're not geared to winning socialism. The Communist Party is not merely a ginger-group for the Labour Party. Our job is much bigger than that. I believe that the left wing of the Labour Party will join up with the Communist Party to make a true socialist party. The Labour Party stands instinctively for the working class and for progress. The future development to socialism depends on the Labour Party, but it can't be done without the Communists as well.

'We don't want a revolution. Not a violent one. I don't think there will be a revolution. It's not necessary and we don't want it. You can get socialism in the normal way – by elections. I spend almost all my non-working time on Party work. I've been a Party candidate in a large number of different elections. Politics is my main interest. I said this before, but everything is related to politics. I'm a member of three other organizations besides the Party – my trade union and what you class as social welfare organizations. I come into contact with a lot of people who aren't Party members. Being a Communist does affect my relationship with them. It tends to sharpen antagonisms and aggravate them, but some like you because you are a Communist. People tend to have black or white attitudes – they're either very much for you or against you. I lost one job because of my politics and I know a number of others who lost theirs as well. From time to time there is severe political discrimination. I don't want to give you the idea that everyone hates us or anything like that, but it can be very annoying when it does come up – even tragic.

'My father and my mother were members of the Scottish Presbyterian Church. The teaching of the Scottish Church and Sunday School had a great influence on my social conscience. Religion has a very strong basis. It's not phoney or artificial – it attempts to explain what some people can't understand. We must respect the genuine religious sentiments of millions and millions of people. But our inability to understand is decreasing and therefore religion is becoming less and less necessary.'

Mr Smith

'My father was a counter-hand – he served in a shop. Mother was just a housewife. Both left school when they were thirteen as far as I know. They voted Tory, although my father swung to the Labour Party in later years, although he was never very strongly committed. Conditions were typical of the working class at that period. My father was earning a wage. He was unemployed for pretty long periods – twice for six months and once for about a year in the thirties. Money was tight but our life was wholesome. We were short of many things – clothes were handed down to the younger children in the family. At the time I didn't realize the shortage. It was like that all round us. There's no question about it, there was plenty of shortage but I didn't realize it then. We didn't have holidays. One day at the seaside was the most. No eggs. Jam and cakes were considered luxuries. It was a healthy diet but there was plenty of restriction. I left school when I was fourteen. That was the earliest you could then. I trained to be an electrician and became a skilled worker in an aircraft factory. My living conditions are now very fair. We have a semi-detached house. It isn't our own but it's clean and well furnished and up to modern standards.

'I first took an interest in politics when I was twenty. I was in hospital and had plenty of time to reflect about things. I was going to have my first vote and that brought about an interest in politics. There were lots of ex-servicemen in the ward and they were always talking about politics. There were a number of people who were very sharply for the Labour Party. I started reading history books. Then I met some Communists in the rehabilitation centre, and they gave me the *Daily Worker* to read. Pretty soon I swung to the C.P. That was the first political party I had any connexion with. I went straight into the C.P. when I joined in 1948.

'It was an awareness of the poverty of other people and of my own background that led me to join. That and the effect of the war. The two World Wars had a great influence. Especially what I knew of the First World War with its ferocity and the millions who died. My father fought in the First World War and then struggled to bring up three sons to see them go off to the Second War.

'Joining wasn't a big step really – I joined in a kind of vacuum. It was the political discussion in the ward that prompted my interest. My understanding of politics while I've been in the Party has broadened immensely. I knew nothing about the world or about history before. I've also developed a bit of feeling for culture which I never had at school. It wasn't part of my education.

'Politics is my main interest. I've got no deep-rooted hobbies. I like swimming. The C.P. takes up most of my time. I like gardening and reading too, and I'm interested in science-for-the-layman books.

'I haven't got a desire for anything of a violent character. I'd work to avoid it. I don't think there will be a revolution – not of the kind you mean. There'll be big changes certainly, but no guns or bloodshed or anything like that. The Party certainly doesn't want it.

'Ordinary people do have some influence over governments but they could have a lot more. Mass feeling if it is expressed can move governments but this only operates to a limited extent in capitalism. Without any shadow of doubt the Employers' Federation dictates to the government. After them I think religion has a big influence. It's part of the establishment – especially the Church of England. Trade unions do have some influence, but they don't really have much influence over this [Conservative] government. The Tory position in politics is clear but not Labour's. The Labour Party has lost its way. It's not faithful to its original ideas. It's betrayed the basic ideas of socialist founders in Britain.

'Peace is the main problem today. Peace undoubtedly. Obviously peace is most important because without it there are other problems. Then the technical changes which are combined with the world socialist upheaval. After that there are the problems of social inequalities. Social conditions have improved very much but the relative difference between the two classes is increasing. Most people think that social differences are getting less and less but this isn't true. They're widening. You can't do anything about this unless you attack the power of the employers. After that there's children's education, housing and old age pensions. The old age pensions are a terrible bloody thing. But none of these can be solved without solving the problem of war fever.

'I reject the mysticism of religion. It serves a purpose for some people. I would say it's misguided but I don't think it harms society. It's all part of the battle of ideas. The right to worship must be guaranteed.

'There's very little antagonism shown to me when people know I'm a Communist. Some are a bit wary on the first meeting but most become friends in the same way as anyone else. They even show respect and admiration. One of the great things about the Party is the combination of interests in a community spirit. This must be one of the important facts in the education of the people. Our aim is to create a Communist man with philosophical, ethical and cultural standards. The members become educated in life – in civilized behaviour – they become much superior in civilized life. The Party makes something of them as people.'

Mr Green

'My father was a teacher. He voted Conservative. In fact both my parents voted Conservative. They weren't deeply committed to the Conservative Party. They just voted for it. My childhood living conditions? I'd say that they were good. I mean we were never short of food or clothes. Not luxurious by any means, but good. I left school to go to university and then started work in industry. I lost that job because I was a Communist. It was decidedly because of my politics. Then I became a teacher. It's a good job. I wouldn't change it and I've been very lucky because I was promoted early. There just happened to be a gap in the department and I was the only one who could fill it. That was very lucky. I wouldn't change the job. I like working with people and I like the young and teaching them. I wouldn't change except maybe to do full-time work for the Party. I'm only part time on Party work at present. I'd say my present living conditions are good – about average. Again nothing luxurious, but nothing really to complain of.

'My parents were uneasy at the time I joined but they were tolerant. Gradually they became more open-minded and started to read the Party literature. . . . I don't think any single event aroused my interest in politics. The Second World War had great influence and so did reading the Dean of Canterbury's *The Socialist Sixth of the World* – that book has converted a lot of people. I joined on my eighteenth birthday. There was no Y.C.L. where I lived. Most of my friends were Conservative plus a few Labour supporters. As a child I used to read widely. The first thing that interested me about the Party was the idea of a scientifically planned society but now the emphasis of my interest has shifted and I'm more concerned with human happiness. I think the Party talks a bit too much about economics and efficiency and leaves ordinary human happiness out of things a bit. I want to see man rise to his full stature and to eliminate the barriers which prevent him from doing it in this society. People are stunted – literature and art should flourish freely – this is where I part company with the Russians. The idea of the full development of the individual is the mainspring behind all the little, mundane tasks we undertake – struggles over wages and rents. It's so that people can have the things that they are denied now – books, concerts, plays, sport, freedom, happiness. Understanding as well. This is our universe and we can explore it. That's what we're working for. My reasons for being a Communist have changed since I joined. My horizons have widened from wanting a scientifically planned society to wanting the maximum happiness for people. And there's a great deal of clarity of thought to be gained from a study of dialectical materialism and great satisfaction from the feeling of solidarity with workers in all countries. There's great comradeship and loyalty in the Party and we all experience it in full measure.

'Atheism is one of the basic feelings in my character. Religion gives a false impression of human dignity. It thwarts the destiny of man.

'Marxism, politics and economics are my main interests. I take an interest in many things but I can't find time to give to them – music, astronomy, novels, films – we're back to the whole human being again. I have to ration my time for films and the theatre. To get more done I learnt to read very fast and trained my memory.

'We can establish socialism by peaceful democratic means. No force will be used. The development of any feeling sufficient to overthrow a government by force would have a peaceful outcome before any revolutionary situation was reached.

'The most powerful groups in Britain at the moment, I would say, are the trade unions and employers' organizations. Most others are not cohesive enough to exert any great influence. The Church for instance does have some influence but not as much as trade unions or the employers. The country is run by the small group who handles the bulk of capital – economic power, that is.

'Peace, above all. That's the most important problem at present. I can't stress that enough. We should all be concerned with that first and foremost. But all political problems are connected. Really, I suppose it's a question of monopoly power versus socialist organization. That's what it all boils down to in the end. Housing and education are the two most pressing practical problems.

'Both the Labour Party and the Communist Party have a working-class composition and socialist aims, but the differences are more important than the similarities. The Communists have fought consistently against capitalism – the Labour Party has changed its course. The democratic centralism of the Party is important too. I would say that the real hallmark is our international solidarity with other working people. It's insufficient to say that we're a ginger-group for Labour. That comes into our work, but the C.P. is much more. It's a political party with its own identity and its own policy. The Labour Party is not enough on its own. It falls far short of what is required on some points of policy.

'The Party's influence is quite significant at times of foreign crisis but not on general foreign policy in this country. But we have inspired much that finally comes from the Labour Party and the trade unions. It has the same influence on domestic policy but more persistent effect.

'The ideas that animated the Minority Report were incorporated in the Majority Report and they were mistaken in not recognizing this. If their Report had been put into effect it would have weakened the Party very seriously.

'The trouble in Hungary was engineered by dissatisfied groups inside Hungary who were in contact with the Americans who supported their aims of overthrowing socialism. I do regret the errors of the Hungarian Party before 1956.'

Mr Jones

'My father was a doctor, he was originally an Irish Nationalist and a socialist but then he became a Liberal like my mother. My grandfather was a foundation member of the Fabian Society. There were always anarchist ideas in the family. I suppose they came from my grandfather originally. I think there is some connexion between Anarchism and Communism. There certainly used to be and there still is. Our home was comfortable. We lived on a large over-draft – a good standard of living but always with a sense of no money. I'd say my present living conditions are perfectly adequate. They always have been.

'It was really a sense of social injustice that brought me into the Party. At first it was the romantic view – the two nations. The Hunger Marches tipped the balance. I think lots of people join because of an idealistic notion of a reasonable, humane world. I knew jolly little about Communism at first, but I did know that people were being exploited. . . . Yes, joining the C.P. was a big step. I knew I would lose contact with most of my friends – most of them were Labour supporters. I regard it as an honour to be asked to join. My reasons have changed slightly. I don't believe in perfect justice any longer. Perfect justice just isn't feasible, but the C.P. is on the right lines.

'I'm a third generation rationalist, and I've an instinctive prejudice against religious people, but it doesn't stop me from cooperating with them and working with them on a number of different social problems, although we don't share the same fundamental beliefs.

'I'm still convinced that the Labour Party is a good party – a socialist party. At some point a Labour government will form a socialist party so that revolution isn't necessary. The Labour Party has the right policy but the wrong reasons. The 1945 programme was good but they sold out on it. The C.P. wants socialism but the Labour Party is prepared to settle for an improved version of capitalism. And the Labour leadership has such a stodgy image. I dislike the Conservatives' arrogance and their assumption that the ruling class deserves a better life. It's a strange thing to say I suppose but one of the things I like about the Conservatives is their politeness.

'The danger of nuclear war. That's the most important problem. I spend about four hours a week on political work and most of that is for C.N.D. After that housing and education are the most important problems.

'Yes. Ordinary people definitely do have some influence. I would say that the most influential groups are the trade unions and the intellectuals in the country. The trade unions because of their size and their organization, and the intellectuals because of the influence they have in the press. Intellectuals have an important place in the Party, for instance.'

Mr Clark

'My father was a teacher. He wasn't a political animal, and nor was my mother. They weren't religious in any way either. My mother is Jewish, but she doesn't practise that now. I had an average sort of life at home. We lived near a housing estate and I think that affected my political opinions. Our standard of living wasn't 'posh', but not bad. We had what I'd call an 'extremely nice house' in a mixed area. I can't say that this period had much influence on my opinions. But one thing was important. The headquarters of the British National Party were near my home, and I can remember the slogans 'Juden Raus' and 'Communists are Jews' painted on the walls. My sisters were Presbyterians and under their influence I used to go to church classes. It didn't go on very long and I wasn't confirmed, and I left because I disagreed with the theology. When I was thirteen I remember I wanted to be English rather than Jewish. I didn't want to go to Israel but I was very impressed by the kibbutzim when I got there. In the last three or four years I've felt myself increasingly Jewish, but it's not the religion which gives me this feeling of belongingness.

'I joined the Party because I believed in the life made possible by the Communists. It can't be done by the Labour Party. I had friends in all the political parties including Conservatives, but some of the Communists forced me to think about new things. It was a slow process of involvement which led me to join, so it wasn't a sharp break with the past. I'm less idealistic than I was then and my political ideas have a closer correspondence to economic conditions. I visited some of the Communist countries and was very impressed. I didn't join the Party because of a desire to belong. There is some connexion between the community spirit and this feeling of belongingness. The C.P. is no more idealistic and happy than any other group – some of the members get in your teeth, but you can find friendship in the Party and other people who have the same ideas. I value the intellectual ability and the community spirit of the Communists I suppose.

'Political change will come slowly. There's no need for revolution. That won't happen because I don't think the necessary preconditions exist in Britain now. Conditions have improved too much. Economic conditions will continue to improve but I don't think that social conditions will necessarily. For example, you can build housing estates but still be left with a delinquency problem. More money doesn't necessarily lead to better social conditions. People must be taught to use their money and their leisure.'

'I suppose I'm upper middle-class or lower middle-class. Somewhere in those categories anyway. It's a bit difficult to put students in a class, but using my social background as a criteria I would say definitely that I'm middle-class. But I've lots of working-class friends and when I've finished being a student I suppose I will become working-class. Most of my friends are Communists, that's both here at the university and at home. I think the Party members at home distrust the middle-class intellectuals because they have no experience of working-class conditions. Students here feel their intellectualness and they react against the university and its culture. But I don't think there ought to be any difference between the intellectual and the non-intellectual.'

Mrs James

'My parents were always quarrelling about money. There was never any unemployment at home but we lived on a very limited income, although we children were never short. My parents weren't political in any sense. My father was generally very reactionary. When I joined the Party they stopped me going home. But now my mother is very sympathetic towards the Party. I left school when I was fifteen. I passed the eleven-plus but my father couldn't afford to send me to the grammar school. I was trained as an office clerk, and that's what I am now. I don't like the job, but it's all I am trained for and I have to make a living. I hate sitting behind a desk. I'd sooner work with people. I always wanted to be a carpenter. I always felt oppressed as a woman. Had I been a man I could have been a carpenter. I don't like sitting in an office. I've always wanted a more active job where I could meet people.

'I didn't take any interest in politics until I was almost thirty. Most of my friends were non-political. The C.P. is the only Party I've been a member of. I went straight from being non-political into the C.P. Joining the C.P. was the biggest step forward I ever made in my life. It was like going from darkness into the light. I'm extremely interested in why people leave the Party but I can't understand why they do this. The Party gave me confidence in the future. It gave me courage to break with my husband – my marriage was going very badly at the time. I read a book about women and children in the Soviet Union, and I saw a new life for myself. I joined the Party and began a new life and got a host of new friends.

'My understanding of Marxism has matured now. I've been to some of the Party schools which taught me a lot. I've come to understand scientific socialism. That's what distinguishes the Communist Party from the Labour Party. The Labour Party isn't based on scientific socialism. Communists know that social problems can't be solved within a capitalist system. The Labour Party represents the working class but its leadership is capitalist. I don't like the leadership but I do like the rank-and-file. The leaders always betray them – always. You can get Tory policies into the Labour Party via the middle-class trade unions, that's what makes it so wishy-washy.

'I'm an atheist now. Mother was quite strongly religious, but not my father. I used to be a Sunday School teacher but now I dislike any form of religion. I've a number of Roman Catholic friends but all of my close friends are Communists. I get on well enough with people outside the Party – the same as anyone else I suppose, although before the Twentieth Congress relationships were a bit rigid – uncomfortable they could be. During the war I lost a job. But then I was reinstated by a tribunal. I lost about two or three others as well, but I wasn't reinstated with those. I worked full time for the Party at one time – for quite a long time, but now I do very little – I've got lazy although I'm still a confirmed Communist.'

CHAPTER 12

CONCLUSION

Although the study has been able to draw on some reliable information published in Party sources, answers to many important questions cannot be attempted because no relevant data are available. For example, there is no information about the political and religious background of Party members, although it is interesting to note here that a few of those interviewed had considerably influenced the views of their non-Communist parents. There is very little information about the age distribution of Party members. It has been suggested that the pre-war average was under thirty, and that it is now over forty,[1] but there is no way of checking the reliability of this information. It would also be useful to know how long most people stay in the Party. The high rate of membership turn-over suggests that the Party life of many is short. Does the Party ever manage to re-recruit some of these people for another short period? What social characteristics distinguish those who stay from those who leave after only a few months?

It is important to know the exact occupational composition of Party members. The 'engineers' category used by the Credentials Committee is vague. Are Communist engineers concentrated in mass-production factories or in particular trades within the industry, and are the Party's factory branches concentrated in a small number of very large factories? With the exception of the London Cypriot branch, there are no figures about immigrant or ethno-religious composition. What social groups rise to leading positions within the Party and to what extent has the élite assimilated and accepted the ideology of the power-oriented tactician? What little evidence there is suggests that most working-class Communists are socially and geographically immobile but the evidence is far from conclusive. How many Communist school teachers are upwardly socially mobile, and is poor status crystallization an important factor in the creation of their radical attitudes? Few of those interviewed had frustrated occupational ambitions, but then most respondents were middle-class with fairly good and secure jobs. Is vertical immobility a source of alienation among working-class Communists?

The units of totalitarian organizations are frequently rigidly separated from each other, so that channels of communication run only from the élites to the non-élites, and not between non-élites. One ex-Communist said that this was the case with the Party as well.

I never realized this until I had left the Party, but local branches have little or no contact with one another. You can contact the next highest level in the hierarchy but you can't contact other branches very easily, I don't know why this is. Not like the C.N.D. where there's an enormous amount of contact between different people and groups – nationally and internationally.

However, evidence about the separation of units within the Party is too flimsy to draw any conclusions, This, and some other questions, will probably remain unanswerable, and it is doubtful whether the Party would ever allow the systematic sampling and interviewing necessary to cull data relevant to other questions.

Nevertheless, some firm conclusions can be drawn from the quite considerable body of data which the Party has provided. Most British Communists do not correspond to the picture of Communists drawn by many political sociologists. This picture is to be found in a simple, black and white, caricature form in Hoffer's often-quoted book *The True Believer*. British Communists are not 'true believers'. They are not psychologically imbalanced revolutionary fanatics, riddled with hatred and intolerance. They are certainly deeply committed to a cause and an ideology, but they tend to be pragmatic, tentative, idealistic, humanitarian, and sometimes surprisingly cautious in their opinions. The Party exercised a moderating influence over two of the more revolutionary and intolerant members who were interviewed.

I've been more tolerant of them [religions] since joining the C.P. Perhaps because I'm a bit older. Before I dismissed them as cant and humbug. [Student]

I used to be committed to revolution in an emotional sort of way. You know, the blow-'em-all-up kind of attitude, but I changed my mind as a result of an understanding of Marxism-Leninism. [Teacher]

In fact the more revolutionary left-wing critics of the Party are fond of saying that it is old and tired, moribund and stagnant, and that to all intents and purposes its ideology and political platform is indistinguishable from that of the Labour Party. Hoffer's book is a caricature of the radical. It is plausible because it is a mixture of truths and half-truths and based on selected evidence.

British Communists do not seem to have much in common with the Russian élite as it has been analysed and described by Leites and Selznick.[2] They are not power-oriented tacticians and they do not believe in the use of violence in pursuit of power. For all of them violence is both unnecessary and wholly undesirable. Most British Communists do not believe in unconstitutional or illegitimate methods. In the past twenty years or so they have come to accept the principles of British parliamentary democracy, although they believe that the present economic system permits the ruling class to maintain its hold on the political system.

The process of investigating why certain people join the B.C.P. has been broken down into three steps. The first step identifies an alienated section of the whole British population which is radically inclined, and ascertains the causes of their alienation and radicalism, whether it is of a political or religious, left-wing or right-wing nature. The second step attempts to describe a line around those radicals who are predisposed towards left-wing political radicalism and also to ascertain why they are not inclined towards other types of radicalism. That is, in order to answer the question 'Why do people join the B.C.P. ?' it is also necessary to answer the question 'Why do other radicals join radical religious or radical right-wing political groups?' The third step narrows the field even more and identifies a pool of potential Communist recruits – that is, radicals who are likely to join the B.C.P.

The entire process can be seen in terms of three concentric circles. The outer circle marks off that section of the entire population which is radically inclined. Within this circle is marked off the smaller group which is disposed towards left-wing political radicalism, and finally the smallest circle in the middle includes only potential Communist recruits. An identification of the people within each circle requires also an identification of the causes and determinants acting upon them.

Given a number of left-wing political radicals, purely organizational factors are important determinants of which of them will join a particular radical left-wing group. All potential Communist recruits have a strong desire for social and political change of a left-wing nature, but few of them have a preference for Communism over and above other radical left-wing ideologies. Most Communist Party members are not Communist ideologists at the time of joining, and, indeed, few become so even after a considerable time in the Party. In fact it is possible that many potential Communist recruits do not become Communists at all, but become left-wing members of the Labour Party or join some radical left-wing organization other than the C.P. – the Socialist Labour League, the Independent Labour Party, the Socialist Party of Great Britain, the Syndicalist Workers' Federation, the Committee to Defeat Revisionism for Communist Unity, or perhaps an Anarchist group. In fact few people fall 'naturally' within the ambit of Communist operations. Public opinion is weighted solidly against the Party so that its general appeals for support are usually fruitless. The Party has to go out and find its recruits. It cannot afford to wait for recruits to approach it on their own initiative. It has to recruit mainly by personal contact followed by long and careful persuasion. This can be most easily and successfully accomplished by using previously established channels of communication and by contacting likely members through organizations of which they are already a member – factories, trade unions, or a tenants' association. Communists may try to infiltrate such organizations not only because they serve as useful Communist adjuncts, but also because they may function as vehicles which carry people who might become Communists with a little persuasion.

It is because of this organizational factor that the Party can recruit factory workers as against geographically mobile labourers; truck drivers who work for a factory as against 'peripatetic' truck drivers who work for a road haulage firm; workers concentrated in large factories as against thinly distributed and inaccessible agricultural workers; white-collar workers attached to a factory as against white-collar workers in a city-centre office. Some non-Communist sections of the population may be marked by the same set of social characteristics as Communists, but are not members of the Party because, no matter how alienated they may be, they cannot join unless the Party is available to them and they are accessible to the Party. This is not to say that the number of potential recruits enormously exceeds the number of actual recruits, although about eight times as many vote Communist as become Communist, but only that a number of people might become members if they were given the opportunity. The same is true of any social group whether it is religious, political, or recreational. The organizational factor is particularly important when it comes to deciding the incidence of membership of a social group which is small like the B.C.P. and which has to break through the barriers of public opinion. Such heavy stress on the importance of organization and organizations runs contrary to the suggestion that radical groups are populated by atomized, isolated individuals who are detached from formal and informal groups in society.

In some branches one or two unusually able organizers with a great deal of initiative, drive and energy will be able to make the best of the available resources and monopolize the area for the Party, giving it a firm organizational foundation and preventing other competing groups from entering the arena. In this way they may be able to collect all the potential recruits and even some more recruits besides, so that there is no room for another radical left-wing political organization in the area. In Manchester quite the opposite happened. In the 1920s the branch was run by a group of middle-class intellectuals who were more interested in discussion of ideological points than in political action. The local membership was never up to strength, and for a while after this local leadership had gone there was no leadership in the area at all.[3]

Many of the statements made by political sociologists about radicalism in general will not apply to British Communism. Concepts like normlessness, meaninglessness, isolation, marginality, poor status crystallization and deracination are not particularly useful in explaining its social basis. These concepts apply to the small section of Party members who are school teachers or Jews, but even then probably only as secondary factors. Jews join the Party because of a combination of relative economic deprivation, liberal economic and non-economic values, and anti-Semitism, and not so much because they may be regarded as a marginal group with a poorly crystallized status. Ironically it is the anti-Semites who daub 'Jews are Communists' on walls, who drive some Jews into the Party, although the number of Jews in the Party is relatively small.

The British political culture is essentially non-radical. The political system does not encourage the formation of third parties and even less does it encourage radical politics. The wary tolerance with which most radical ideologies are viewed and the considerable social pressures against Communism, probably direct alienated, frustrated behaviour into non-political channels. Again the relative economic and social security which has prevailed in Britain for most of the century has not provided a firm or continuous basis for radical politics or radicalism of any kind.

The British Party's lack of substantial success has resulted in its being both isolated and insulated at the fringe of the political structure. In this respect it forms a peculiar type of radical political movement which has settled into a routine. It has lost its original dynamic and has ceased to be revolutionary in the usual sense of the word. In order to maintain its continued existence and its numerical strength it has had to compromise with the world so that smaller but more active and revolutionary groups have taken over its role as the spearhead of the revolutionary movement. Normally a party as small and powerless as the B.C.P. would have collapsed and disintegrated in its earlier years, but helped by its association with a vastly larger and more powerful world organization it has been kept alive. Hence its rather strange nature as a radical movement. Unlike most small revolutionary movements it has been given time to accommodate to the world.

1. *What's Wrong With Our Communist Party*, A Forum Publication, June 1965
2. Leites, 1951, 1953; Selznick, 1952
3. Pelling, 1958, pp. 61–2; McCarthy, 1953, pp. 71–4

APPENDICES

APPENDIX 1A

Official Membership Figures of the British Communist Party

DATE	MEMBERSHIP	SOURCE
1920 (August)	4,000	Macfarlane, 1966, p. 302
1921 (January)	2,000–2,500	Macfarlane, 1966, p. 302
1922	5,116 (fees for 2,300)	E.C.C.I., *4th Congress Report*, 1922 p. 289
1924 (May)	3,000	Macfarlane, 1966, p. 302
1924 (September)	4,000	C.I. *Between 5th/6th World Congress* (1928) p. 30
1925 (June)	5,000	C.I. *Between 5th/6th World Congress* (1928) p. 30
1926 (April)	6,000	C.I. *Between 5th/6th World Congress* (1928) p. 30
(October)	10,730	*8th Congress Report*, C.P.G.B., p. 39
1927 (January)	9,000	Macfarlane, 1966, p. 302
1927 (October)	7,377	*Inprecorr*, vol. 7, p. 1288
1928 (March)	5,500	Macfarlane, 1966, p. 302
1929 (January)	3,500	*Communist Review*, vol. 4, p. 383
(December)	3,200	*Inprecorr*, vol. 12, p. 446
1930 (November)	2,555	*Inprecorr*, vol. 11, p. 680
1931 (June)	2,724	*Inprecorr*, vol. 12, p. 447
(November)	6,279	*Inprecorr*, vol. 12, p. 447
1932 (January)	9,000	*Communist Review*, vol. 4, p. 383
(November)	5,600	*Communist Review*, vol. 4, p. 577
1934 (December)	5,800	*Inprecorr*, vol. 15, p. 1053
1935 (July)	7,700	*Inprecorr*, vol. 15, p. 1053
1936 (October)	11,500	*Discussion*, November 1936, p. 12
1937 (May)	12,250	*Daily Worker*, 27 May 1937
1938 (September)	15,570	*Daily Worker*, 19 September 1938
1939 (July)	17,756	*Report of E.C. to 16th Congress*, p. 13

DATE	MEMBERSHIP	SOURCE
1941 (December)	22,738	*World News and Views*, vol. 22, p. 206
1942 (December)	56,000	*World News and Views*, vol. 23, p. 221
1943 (December)	55,138	*World News and Views*, vol. 24, p. 63
1945 (March)	45,435	*Report of E.C. to the 18th Congress*, p. 17
1946 (April)	42,123	*World News and Views*, vol. 26, p. 198
1947 (June)	38,579	*World News and Views*, vol. 28, p. 99
1948 (April)	43,000	*Daily Worker*, 1 May 1948
1950 (May)	38,853	*Report of E.C. to 22nd Congress*, p. 17
1952 (March)	35,124	*Report of E.C. to 22nd Congress*, p. 17
1953 (March)	35,054	*Report of E.C. to 23rd Congress*, p. 12
1954 (April)	33,963	*For a Lasting Peace*, 13 April 1956
1955 (March)	32,681	*For a Lasting Peace*, 13 April 1956
1956 (February)	33,095	*For a Lasting Peace*, 13 April 1956
1957 (February)	26,742	*World News*, vol. 4, 13 April 1956
1958 (February)	24,670	*Daily Worker*, 11 February 1958

The above figures are collected in Pelling, 1958, p. 192 and Macfarlane, 1966, p. 302. Other, and in some cases slightly different, figures are to be found in different sources.

1926 (October)	12,000	*Communist International*, 1927, p. 154
1931 (September)	3,927	*Communist International*, 1932, p. 168
1942 (March)	47,932	*World News and Views*, 1943, vol. 22, p. 206
1943 (January–July)	46,643	*Report of E.C. to 17th Congress*
1944 (March)	47,513	*Report of E.C. to 17th Congress* p. 9
1949 (March)	40,161	*Report of E.C. to 21st National Congress*
1959	25,313	*26th Congress Report*
1960	26,052	*27th Congress Report*, 1961, p. 21
1961	27,541	*27th Congress Report*, 1961, p. 21
1962 (May)	32,492	*World News*, 1962, vol. 9, no. 26
1963	33,008	*28th Congress Report*, 1963, p. 16
1964 (February)	34,281	*Daily Worker*, 7 February 1964, p. 1
1965 (February)	33,734	*Daily Worker*, 12 February 1965, p. 1

APPENDIX 1B

Official Membership Figures of the Young Communist League

DATE	MEMBERSHIP	SOURCE
1921	Founded	
1924	500	*Report of the Central E.C. to National Party Congress*, 1924, p. 11
1926	Claimed 9,000 but had only 5,000	*International Press Correspondence*, 1 August 1928, vol. 8, no. 42
1928	1,000	*International Press Correspondence*, 1 August 1928, vol. 8, no. 42
1934	660	*International Press Correspondence*, 7 October 1935, vol. 15, no. 51
1935	2,000	*International Press Correspondence*, 7 October 1935, vol. 15, no. 51
1938	4,600	*Report of E.C. to 15th Party Congress*, 1938, p. 37
1942	10,000	*World News and Views*, 1942, vol. 22, p. 335
1947	2,000	*World News and Views*, 1947, vol. 27, no. 44
1951	5,000	*Newsletter*, vol. 2, no. 76, p. 239
1952	4,950	*World News and Views*, 1953, vol. 33, no. 44
1955	3,500	*Newsletter*, 1958, vol. 2, no. 76, p. 239
1956	2,623	*World News*, 1956, vol. 3, no. 3
1958	1,387	*Newsletter*, 1958, vol. 2, no. 76, p. 239
1961	2,702	*World News*, 1961, vol. 8, no. 17
1962	4,019	*World News*, 1962, vol. 9, no. 26
1963	3,989	*Report of E.C. to 28th Party Congress*, 1963
1965	4,276	*Daily Worker*, 12 February 1965, p. 1

APPENDIX 2

Occupational and Industrial Composition of National Congress Delegates, 1944–63

Year	1944	1947	1948	1949	1952	1954	1956	1957	1959	1961	1963	Average per cent 1944-63	Calculated total of Communists in each occupational group
Number of Delegates	789	665	762	405	520	615	486	547	492	455	461		
Occupations						Percentage of total delegates							
Engineering	27	25	25	20	26	23	25	18	22	25	25	23·0	8,280
Building	7	8	10	8	6	8	10	7	10	9	8	8·0	3,000
Teaching	?	?	?	3	6	6	7	11	9	8	8	7·0	2,520
Mining	7	5	7	4	6	6	7	6	8	10	5	6·5	2,340
Transport and Rails	7	6	6	3	7	7	6	6	5	4	6	5·5	1,980
Housewives	8	5	5	7	5	6	6	6	5	5	4	5·5	1,980

												%	Total
Clerical and Administrative	7 ⎱	20	6	6	3	7	5	4	3	6	7	5·0	1,800
Professional and Technical	10 ⎰		10	?	2	4	2	5	3	3	5	3·0	1,080
C.P. officials	?	5	5	?	14	7	8	8	6	?	5	5·0	1,800
Clothing and Textiles	3	2	3	3	3	4	3	3	4	2	2	3·0	1,080
Distribution	2	2	4	1	2	2	2	3	2	2	1	2·0	720
Medical	?	?	?	?	1	0	1	1	1	1	2	1·0	360
Printing	1	?	?	1	2	2	2	1	1	2	2	1·5	550
Agriculture	2	1	1	1	1	1	1	1	1	?	?	1·0	360
Unemployed	2	4	?	?	?	?	?	?	?	1	1	2·0	720
Women delegates	23	16	15	15	14	15	14	15	15	14	15	14·5	5,200
											Total	96·5	28,570

Figures are taken from the Reports of the Credentials Committee which are published in each *Congress Report*.

APPENDIX 3

Occupational Composition of South Midlands District 1964

Agriculture	5 or 1·5 per cent		Iron and steel	0
Boot and shoe	0		Mining	0
Leather	0		Postal	2
Building: Architects	0		Professional: Lawyers	1
Woodwork	6		Scientists	0
Furniture	3		Teachers	23 or 7·2 per cent
Bricklayers	3		Others	3
Labourers	3		Total	27 or 8·4 per cent
Others	7			
Total	22 or 7·0 per cent			
Chemicals, oils, plastics	0		Printing and paper	3 or 1·0 per cent
Clerical and administrative	12 or 4·0 per cent		Self-employed	23 or 7·2 per cent
			Students	32 or 10·0 per cent
Clothing	0		Textiles: Cotton	0
Distribution	2 or 0·6 per cent		Hosiery	0
Electrical: Contracting	1		Wool	0
Engineering	3		Others	0
Supply	3		Total	0
Others	3			
Total	10 or 3·0 per cent			

Engineering: General	16
Shipbuilding	0
Vehicles	30
Others	4
Total	50 or 15·3 per cent

Entertainments: Actors, films, musicians,	0
Others	0
Foremen	0
Food, drink, tobacco	6
Foundries	0
Gas	0
Health: Doctors	0
Dentists	0
Nurses	0
Others	2
Total	2 or 0·6 per cent

Transport: Air, docks	0
Rails	5
Road (Haulage)	2
Road (Passengers)	3
Seamen	0
Others	2
Total	12 or 4 per cent

Retired and old-age pensioners	16
Unemployed	1 or 0·5 per cent
Housewives	51 or 16·0 per cent
Miscellaneous	16
Women	73 or 22·8 per cent
District Total	320 (excluding 'Women' category)

APPENDIX 4

The Communist Party in the General Elections 1922–66

	1922	1923	1924	1929	1931	1935	1945	1950	1951	1955	1959	1964	1966
Number of candidates	7	9	8	25	26	2	21	100	10	17	18	36	57
Total vote	52,819	77,641	55,296	50,622	74,824	27,117	102,780	91,736	21,640	33,144	30,897	44,567	62,112
Average vote	7,545	8,627	6,937	2,025	2,870	13,558	4,894	917	2,164	1,950	1,716	1,236	1,089
Average percentage of the electorate voting Communist in constituencies contested	23·2	25·3	19·0	4·3	6·5	29·9	11·0	1·0	3·8	3·4	3·1	2·4	2·1

Percentage of the Electorate Voting Communist in the General Elections, 1922–66

Constituency	1922	1923	1924	1929	1931	1935	1945	1950	1951	1955	1959	1964	1966	Average
London Boroughs														
Battersea North	28·6	32·2	37·5	13·0	6·0			1·5				1·3	1·9	13·2
Bermondsey West					2·6									2·6
Bethnal Green	19·5							1·4						10·5
Bethnal Green North-East	21·2													21·2
Bethnal Green South-West		24·9	28·0	5·0	10·7									17·15
City of London and Westminster								1·2						1·2
Clapham								1·0						1·0
Deptford								1·1						1·1
Fulham								0·9					0·6	0·8
Greenwich					3·2									3·2
Hackney Central										2·3				2·3
Hackney South				0·7			16·2	2·9	2·3					5·5
Hammersmith North					1·5									1·5
Hampstead								2·3						2·3
Islington South-West								1·3				2·6	1·5	1·7
Kensington North								1·0						1·0
Lewisham South								1·1	1·0					1·0

Constituency	1922	1923	1924	1929	1931	1935	1945	1950	1951	1955	1959	1964	1966	Average
Mile End							31·8							31·8
Paddington North								0·9						0·9
Peckham								1·4						1·4
Poplar								1·1						1·1
Southwark								0·9		1.4	2·2	2·7	2·6	2·2
Stepney								10·0	5·2	4·4	4·0	4·0	3·7	4·6
Stepney: Limehouse				0·6										0·6
St Pancras North					0·9			1·5		2·1	2·2	2·1	2·4	2·1
St Pancras South-East					0·8									0·8
Stoke Newington and Hackney North										2·3			2·3	2·3
Streatham			10·6											10·6
Vauxhall								1·0						1·0
Westminster: Abbey Division							10·3							10·3
Whitechapel					7·0									7·0
Woolwich East								1·2						1·2
English Boroughs														
Acton								1·3						1·3
Ashton-under-Lyne		24·9						0·9						12·9
Bexley								0·7						0·7
Birkenhead								1·5					1·1	1·3
Birmingham: Duddeston					0·8									0·8

Constituency	1922	1923	1924	1929	1931	1935	1945	1950	1951	1955	1959	1964	1966	Average
Handsworth							2·4							2·4
Northfield								0·8					1·1	1·0
Perry Bar										1·8	0·5			1·1
Small Heath												2·0	1·1	1·6
Sparkbrook							5·1	0·7						2·9
Stechford													1·8	1·8
West Divison			19·0											19·0
Yardley								0·7						0·7
Bradford East								0·9						0·9
Brentford and Chiswick								0·8						0·8
Bristol South-East								0·8						0·8
Bristol North-West													1·0	1·0
Burnley					0·7			0·8						0·8
Chesterfield								0·7						0·7
Coventry East							5·0	0·8				1·5	1·8	2·3
Croydon West								0·6						0·6
Dagenham								1·3				1·5	2·0	1·6
East Ham South								0·9						0·9
Eccles													2·2	2·2
Erith and Crayford													1·0	1·0
Eton and Slough								1·2						1·2
Harrow							4·5							4·5
Harrow East								1·0						1·0
Hayes and Harlington								1·3		2·0	1·1	1·9	1·5	1·6
Hendon North								1·7						1·7

Constituency	1922	1923	1924	1929	1931	1935	1945	1950	1951	1955	1959	1964	1966	Average
Hornsey							16·4	1·6		2·0	1·6	1·8	1·8	4·2
Ilford South								1·4						1·4
Leeds North-East								1·3						1·3
Leeds South												1·9	1·5	1·7
Leicester North East								0·6						0·6
Liverpool: Scotland					3·9			1·2				1·7	2·0	2·2
Luton												1·0	1·0	1·0
Manchester:														
Blackley								1·0						1·0
Gorton					2·1			1·4						1·7
Openshaw												3·6	2·9	3·3
Platting			0·8											0·8
Rusholme		17·2	16·2											16·7
Wythenshawe								1·1						1·1
Middlesbrough East								0·7						0·7
Mitcham												1·0	0·9	1·0
Newcastle West								0·8						0·8
Newcastle Central												1·3		1·3
Nottingham East			8·1					1·7						4·9
Nottingham North										1·5	2·3	2·4	1·6	2·5
Oldham West								0·8						0·8
Oxford								0·7						0·7
Portsmouth West								0·4						0·4
Preston North							5·8	0·7						3·3
Rossendale							3·8							3·8

Constituency	1922	1923	1924	1929	1931	1935	1945	1950	1951	1955	1959	1964	1966	Average
Sheffield:														
Attercliffe				4·1	6·6									5·3
Brightside					3·3		1·0	2·0	2·0	2·5	2·4	2·5	1·9	2·2
Hallam							5·1							5·1
Hillsborough								1·2						1·2
Park								1·8					2·2	2·0
Southall								1·4						1·4
South Shields								0·6						0·6
Stockton-on-Tees													1·4	1·4
Stoke-on-Trent													3·6	3·6
Sunderland							4·9							4·9
Swindon								0·6				1·6	1·5	1·2
Tottenham South				1·6				1·1						1·4
Wallsend				1·5										1·5
Warrington								1·0						1·0
Wembley								0·8						0·8
West Ham South								1·1						1·1
Wigan				2·4				2·3		2·7	1·7	1·9	1·7	2·1
Willesden West								1·4			2·1	1·9	2·0	1·9
Woodford								1·1	1·1					1·1
English Counties														
Beds: Bedford								0·4						0·4
Berks: Abingdon							2·8	0·7						1·7
Bucks: Wycombe								0·4						0·4

Constituency	1922	1923	1924	1929	1931	1935	1945	1950	1951	1955	1959	1964	1966	Average
Devon: Totnes								0·7						0·7
Durham: Seaham				2·4	11·0								6·7	6·7
Glos: Cirencester and Tewkesbury								0·7						0·7
Gloucester City	30·4	32·0												31·2
Kent: Dover								0·8						0·8
Sevenoaks							1·2							1·2
Lancs: Huyten								0·7						0·7
Northants: Kettering								1·0						1·0
Notts: Mansfield				0·9				0·8					1·0	0·9
Suffolk: Eye								0·6						0·6
Yorks: Don Valley								1·7						1·7
Goole												2·2	1·7	2·0
Shipley								0·5						0·5
Spen Valley				0·5										0·5
Welsh Boroughs														
Aberdare				13·0				2·7					4·9	3·8
Rhondda East					24·0	30·6	37·5	11·2	7·6	11·6	12·1	9·0	6·6	16·3
Rhondda West					10·4								5·9	8·2
Swansea East													1·6	1·6
Welsh Counties														
Aberavon												2·2	2·8	2·4
Caerphilly				1·8										1·8

Constituency	1922	1923	1924	1929	1931	1935	1945	1950	1951	1955	1959	1964	1966	Average
Llanelly												1·7	2·0	1·9
Neath								3·6			3·8	4·8		4·1
Ogmore								3·1						3·1
Pontypool												2·8	1·9	2·4
Scottish Burghs														
Aberdeen North				3·6	8·2			2·0					1·2	3·8
Bothwell													2·1	2·1
Dundee East	7·6	13·4	10·6	6·5	10·5			2·0						8·5
Dundee West									2·3	2·1	1·3	2·0	2·0	5·8
Dumfermline				4·8										4·8
Edinburgh:														
Central					3·4			1·2						2·3
Leith													0·8	0·8
Glasgow:														
Bridgeton								2·0			2·0			2·0
Central							7·6							7·6
Gorbals					5·5			4·6	4·8	4·4	4·0	3·6	2·5	4·2
Govan								3·1			3·7	3·0	2·7	3·1
Kelvingrove		24·4												24·4
Provan													1·7	1·7
Scoutstoun								2·2					4·0	3·1
Shettleston							8·2	2·5						5·4
Springburn					5·6			3·2		3·7	3·2	2·4	2·5	3·4
St Rolox				1·4										1·4

{ The 1922, 1923, 1924 and 1931 figures against Dundee are bracketed across Dundee East and Dundee West (two-member constituency). }

Constituency	1922	1923	1924	1929	1931	1935	1945	1950	1951	1955	1959	1964	1966	Average
Greenock	29·3	31·2	22·4	16·0	14·6		11·8	2·5					1·6	14·9
Scottish Counties														
Dumbartonshire East									3·6	4·0	3·4	1·6	2·0	2·9
Dumbartonshire West								2·5						2·5
Fife West				14·4	14·8	29·2	32·5	18·5	9·2	10·1	6·8	5·4	2·8	12·3
Kilmarnock								2·0						2·0
Kinross and West Perthshire												0·4		0·4
Kircaldy							6·4							6·4
Lanarks: Bothwell				3·9	5·1									4·1
Hamilton				1·4										1·4
Ogmore				6·3										6·3
Rutherglen				1·9										1·9
Motherwell	25·9	27·5		2·7				2·2			3·1		3·0	10·7
Stirling and Falkirk								1·5					1·3	1·4
West Lothian								1·8				1·0	0·9	1·4

APPENDIX 5

Published District Membership Figures, 1925–49

DISTRICT	1925	1930	1931	1937	1938	1939	1940	1947	1949
South Wales	450								
Manchester	335								
Lancashire		101					2,000		
Birmingham			500						
Midlands					489	928	1,000		2,200
Yorkshire									
West Riding							500		
Scotland		423	1,396			3,000	3,000		
Sussex							300		
North Midlands							954		
Eastern Counties						330	460		
London				5,000		7,102	8,000		16,500
Surrey						400			
Tyneside							500		

Published District Membership Figures, 1952–61

DISTRICT	1952	1953	1954	1955	1956	1957	1958	1959	1960	1961
South Wales	5,600	2,100	1,319		1,444					
Yorkshire			1,800	2,300						
Scotland						4,700	4,662	4,852	5,465	6,120
London				8,993	8,464	7,186				
Kent			970	913	785					
West Middlesex	1,425				1,349	1,023				

Membership of the Communist Party Districts, 1926–7

DISTRICTS	1926			1927			
	LOCALS	MEMBERSHIP	PERCENTAGE OF NATIONAL MEMBERSHIP	LOCALS	FACTORY OR PIT GROUPS	MEMBERSHIP	PERCENTAGE OF NATIONAL MEMBERSHIP
London	36	1,560	14·6	37	13	1,321	16·8
South Wales	41	1,500	14·0	38	43	2,300	31·5
Scotland	45	1,607	14·8	45	11	1,500	20·3
Lancashire	42	1,256	11·7	35	8	638	8·7
Yorkshire	24	1,450	13·4	21	10	420	5·6
Tyneside	39	1,900	17·7	22	12	737	10·0
Birmingham	18	326	3·5	13	0	180	2·4
Cumberland		Not Given		4	3	55	0·8
Unattached locals		Not Given		12	0	196	2·7
National Group		Not Given		0	0	30	0·4
Total	245	10,730	90·7	227	100	7,377	100

1. *Sources*: 8th and 9th C.P.G.B. *Congress Reports* (1926 and 1927)

2. Manchester and Liverpool have been combined to give a figure for Lancashire. Bradford and Sheffield have been combined to give a figure for Yorkshire in 1926. There is no figure available for the membership of the Bradford District in 1927 and so the figure for Sheffield has been used. However, this figure does not indicate the true strength of the District in 1927. Fife, Glasgow, Dundee, Edinburgh have been combined to give a figure for Scotland.

Membership of Communist Party Districts, 1942

DISTRICT	MEMBERSHIP	PERCENTAGE OF TOTAL PARTY MEMBERSHIP
London	16,500	29·0
Scotland	6,300	13·1
Lancashire	4,800	10·0
Midlands	4,600	9·6
South Wales	2,200	4·6
Bedford	1,800	3·5
Sheffield	1,500	3·1
North East	1,500	3·1
Merseyside	1,400	2·9
West Riding	1,200	2·5
Nottingham	1,200	2·5
Reading	1,100	2·3
Bristol	1,100	2·1
Kent	800	1·9
Hants	500	1·1
East Anglia	300	0·6
Sussex	300	0·6
Devon	300	0·6
North Wales	200	0·4
Total 47,900		*Total* 99·5

Membership of Communist Party Districts, 1943–4

DISTRICT	1943		1944	
	MEMBER-SHIP	PER-CENTAGE OF TOTAL	MEMBER-SHIP	PER-CENTAGE OF TOTAL
London	16,963	30·5	17,537	33·5
Scotland	9,088	16·5	8,407	16·0
Lancashire	6,830	12·4	5,541	11·5
Yorkshire	3,581	6·5	3,092	6·0
Midlands	not available		3,237	6·5
North Wales	246	0·5	2,724	5·0
South Wales	2,579	4·5		
East Midlands	3,519	6·5	2,225	4·0
South East Midlands	3,678	6·6	1,460	3·0
West of England	1,374	2·5	1,427	3·0
South Midlands	1,286	2·3	1,338	2·5
North-East	1,449	2·7	1,114	2·0
Kent	1,189	2·1	1,016	2·0
Hants and Dorset	644	1·2	850	1·5
East Anglia	737	1·3	644	1·2
Teesside	515	1·0	567	1·0
Devon and Cornwall	383	0·7	387	0·7
Sussex	274	0·5	339	0·5
North-West	not available		250	0·5
Total	55,138	98·7	52,207	100·7

Sources: *World News and Views*, 19 February 1944
World News and Views, 9 December 1944

APPENDIX 6

General Analysis of Communists Interviewed

1. *Geographical Distribution*

London (mainly Hampstead)	13	Norwich	2
Cambridge (all students)	6	Leeds	1
Southall	4	Oxford	1

2. *Party Position Held at the Time of Interviewing*

National Executive Committee	3
District Committee	4
Branch, Borough or Area Committee	7
Rank-and-File	13

3. *Occupations*

Students	6	Office clerk	1
Full/Part Time C.P.	4	Publishers' reader	1
Teachers (Secondary)	3	Research scientist	1
Teachers (Primary)	2	Railway worker	1
Journalists	2	Bank clerk	1
Housewives	2	Architect	1
Secretary	1	Electrician	1

4. *Parental Political Preference*

Both apolitical	10	Both Conservative	4
Both Communist	8	One Labour	3
Both Liberal	8	One Conservative	2
Both Labour	6	Both unknown	2
One apolitical	5	One Liberal	2
One Communist	4		

Total   54

APPENDIX 7

Questionnaire

---

*YOU ARE NOT REQUIRED TO GIVE EITHER YOUR OWN NAME
AND ADDRESS OR THE NAME AND ADDRESS OF ANY OTHER
PERSON OR ORGANIZATION*

The object of the questionnaire is strictly scientific and it has no connexion
whatsoever with any commercial or political organization. The answers you
give will be strictly confidential.

1. Date
2. Age
3. Sex
4. Marital Status
5. Average Net Wage, (i.e. after any deductions for income tax, national
   insurance, etc.)
6. Number of dependants, that is people who are dependent on you and
   who are not receiving a pension or earning a wage. Do not include your
   wife if she has a full- or part-time job.

Questions 7–26 do not apply to students

7. Present occupation (in detail, but do not give the name of the firm for
   which you work)
8. Is this a skilled job?
9. If you are a union member, in which section of the union are you classified? If this question does not apply to you please write 'none'.
10. In what kind of place do you work, e.g. office, factory, shop, school,
    etc.?
11. How many are employed at your present place of work?
12. How many members of the Communist Party are employed at your
    place of work?
13. If you have not held your present job for a year or more, would you
    please state what your previous job was?
14. What was your first job?
15. Are you pretty free to work as you like in your job with no one in
    charge of what you do?
16. How good are your chances for advancement in your present job?
17. Would you prefer a job with more responsibility and authority?
18. Do you now hold, or have you held a position of responsibility in your
    job? If 'yes', would you please say what kind of position.

19. Do you like your job?
20. Would you like to change your job if, for instance, it did not mean moving house? If 'yes' what kind of job would you prefer?
21. Compared with other jobs in Britain do you think yours is paid well enough? Why do you say this?
22. At what age did you leave school?
23. What type of school was this, e.g. grammar, technical, etc?
24. Would you say what is the highest educational qualification you have, e.g. G.C.E. 'O' or 'A' levels?
25. Have you attended any educational or vocational courses since you finished your full-time education?
    If 'yes', what have you been studying?
    Why did you decide to continue studying?
26. Do you think you have ever lost a job, or lost the chance of promotion because of your political opinions?

Questions below apply to all respondents, including students

27. What are (were) your parents' occupations (in detail)?
28. At what age did they finish their full-time education?
29. Have your parents ever been members of, or sympathetic to, the Communist Party?
30. If your parents were members of, or sympathetic to, any other political organization, would you say which one?
31. If your parents were *not* members of, or sympathetic to, the Communist Party before you joined, how your membership influenced them?
32. Are any other of your relations members of the Party?
    If 'yes' would you say which relations?
33. Was your father a member of a trade union?
    If 'yes', would you say he was very militant, militant, not very militant?
34. If your parents were members of, or sympathetic to, a religious organization would you say which church or denomination?
35. How would you describe the social and living conditions of your childhood, say between the ages of five and eighteen?
36. How many years have you been living in your present home town, district or area?
37. How would you describe your present social and living conditions?
38. At what age did you take an interest in politics?
39. What would you say prompted your interest?
40. In what year did you join the Communist Party?
41. Which political party did most of your friends prefer just before you joined?
42. Why did you join the Communist Party?

43. Do you now have different reasons for being a member?
    If 'yes', how would you say your reasons have changed?

44. Did joining the Party seem to be a big step for you?
    Why do you say this?

45. Apart from the satisfaction of helping to achieve socialism in Britain, what other sorts of personal satisfactions would you say you get out of being a member of the C.P.?

46. For what sorts of reasons do you think people generally join the C.P.?

47. Do you now hold, or have you held, an official position within the Communist Party?
    If 'yes', what positions have you held?

48. How many hours a week would you say you spend on Party work, excluding your own private reading?

49. Are you now a member of a religious organization?
    If 'yes', would you say which church or denomination?
    If 'no', would you say which church or denomination lies closest to your sympathies?

50. What is your present attitude towards religion?

51. Some people say that most people can be trusted while others believe that you can't be too careful in your dealings with others. How do you feel about this?

52. It is also said, sometimes, that life as most people live it in Britain is quite purposeless and meaningless.
    How do you feel about this?

53. To which class would you say you belong?

54. What do you understand by the word 'class'?

55. What are your main interests in life?

56. Of these which would you say is your main interest?

57. Besides the Communist Party are you a member of any other clubs, societies or organizations?
    If 'yes', how many would you say you belong to? Would you say which of the following types they are?
    Trade Union, Social Welfare, Political, Sports, Social, Educational, Vocational, Hobby, Other.
    How many of these are Communist organizations?

58. Do you think that a forcible overthrow of the government is desirable in Britain?
    Why do you say this?

59. Do you think that the government will be overthrown by force in the near future (say in the next twenty years or so)?
    Why do you say this?

60. Do you think that the democratic system in Britain has improved over the past sixty years?
    Why do you say this?

61. Do you think that social and economic conditions have improved in Britain over the past sixty years?
   Why do you say this?
62. Would you say that ordinary people have any influence over the way that the country is run?
   Why do you say this?
63. In general, what groups of people, apart from political parties, have most influence over what the government does in this country?
64. What would you say are the main problems facing Britain today?
65. How do people who are not Communists react to you as a member of the Party?
66. What would you say are the main differences and similarities between the Communist Party and the Labour Party?
67. Do you think that the country is run by public opinion?
68. Some people have suggested that the Communist Party ought to act primarily as a 'ginger-group' for the Labour Party.
   Do you agree or disagree?
69. What do you think is the attitude of most Communists towards the intellectuals in the Party?
70. Which political party do most of your friends prefer?
71. It is sometimes said that the only people who have any real say in running the country are the government leaders. Do you agree or disagree?
72. In general how much influence do you think your own Party branch has on the national policy and decision-making of the Party as a whole?
73. In general, how much influence do you think the B.C.P. has on trade unions?
74. In general, how much influence do you think the B.C.P. has on the country's foreign policy?
75. In general, how much influence do you think the B.C.P. has on the country's domestic policy?
76. In general, how much influence do you think the B.C.P has on local affairs?
77. Do you think that in some political situations the end justifies the means?
78. Are there any aspects of the Communist policy or life that you dislike?
79. Have you, or your father, ever been unemployed?
   If 'yes', on how many separate occasions, for how long each time, and in what years?
80. What is your opinion of the Minority Report on Inner Party Democracy of 1957?
81. What is your opinion of the events in Hungary in 1956?

82. What is your opinion of the Committee to Defeat Revisionism, for Communist Unity – Michael McCreery's group?

Questions 83–5 apply only to Students

83. What kind of job or career do you think you will go into?
84. What kind of job or career would you most like?
85. What subject are you reading?

All respondents, including Students

86. Do you have any comments on the questions that have been asked here or on the answers that you have given? For example, do you think that any of the questions have been unfair or 'loaded' or phrased poorly? Would you like to qualify any of the answers you have given now that you have had second thoughts on them? Do you think that there are any aspects of the Party, its policy and life, that have been overlooked?

SELECT BIBLIOGRAPHY

Communist and Non-Communist Periodicals

Challenge (Y.C.L.)
Comment
Communist (continued as *Workers' Weekly*)
Communist International
Communist Review
Daily Worker
Discussion
Forward
The Free Oxford – A Communist Journal of Youth
Industrial Research and Information Services News
International Press Correspondence (continued as *World News and Views*)
Labour Monthly
Left News
Mainstream (London students)
Marxist Quarterly
Modern Quarterly
Music and Life (Musicians' Groups)
New Leader
Newsletter
Our History (Historians' Group)
Out of Work (Journal of the N.U.W.M.)
Party Life
Party Organiser
Plebs
Realm (Artists' Group)
The Reasoner
Solidarity
Sunday Worker
Vanguard
Workers' Life (continued as *Daily Worker*)
Workers' Weekly (continued as *Workers' Life*)
Working Woman
World News (continued as *Comment* and *Party Life*)
World News and Views (continued as *World News*)

Books, Pamphlets and Articles

Aaronvitch, S., *Monopoly*, (London: Lawrence and Wishart, 1955)
    The Ruling Class, (London: Lawrence and Wishart, 1961)
Abrams, M., 'Social Class and British Politics', *Public Opinion Quarterly*,
    1961, pp. 342–50

Abrams, M. and Rose, R., *Must Labour Lose?*, (Harmondsworth: Penguin Books, 1960)

Adorno, T. W. *et al.*, *The Authoritarian Personality*, (New York: Harper & Row, 1950)

Aldred, G. A., *Communism – The Story of the Communist Party*, (The Strickland Press, 1943)
Socialism and Parliament, (The Strickland Press, 1942)

Alford, R. R., *Party and Society*, (Chicago: Rand McNally, 1963; London: John Murray)

Allardt, E., 'Community Activity, Leisure Use and Social Structure', *Acta Sociologica*, 1962, pp. 67–82
'Institutionalised Versus Diffuse Support for Radical Political Movements', *Transactions of the Fifth World Congress of Sociology*, 1962, pp. 369–80
'Social Sources of Finnish Radicalism: Traditional and Emerging Radicalism', *International Journal of Comparative Sociology*, 1964, pp. 49–72
'Patterns of Class Conflict and Working Class Consciousness in Finnish Politics', in E. Allardt and Y. Littunen, (eds), *Cleavages, Ideologies and Party Systems: Contributions to Contemporary Political Sociology*, Transactions of the Westermarck Society, 1964, pp. 97–131
'Working Class Consciousness and Alienation: A Preliminary Ecological Analysis', (University of Helsinki, Institute of Sociology, Publication no. 35)

Allen, G. C., *The Structure of Industry in Britain*, (London: Longmans, 1961)

Allen, V. L., *Trade Union Leadership*, (London: Longmans, 1957)

Allinsmith, W. and B., 'Religious Affiliations and Politico-Economic Attitudes', *Public Opinion Quarterly*, 1948, pp. 377–89

Almond, G. A. *et al.*, *The Appeals of Communism*, (Princeton: Princeton University Press, 1954)

Almond, G. A. and Verba, S., *The Civic Culture*, (Princeton: Princeton University Press, 1963)

Arendt, H., *The Origins of Totalitarianism*, (New York: Harcourt, Brace, 1951; London: Allen & Unwin)

Aris, S., 'The Jewish Entrepreneur', *New Society*, no. 70, 30 January 1964, pp. 8–10

Arnot, R. Page, *Twenty Years: The Policy of the C.P.G.B. from its Foundation, July 31, 1920* (London: Lawrence & Wishart, undated)

Aron, R., *The Opium of the Intellectuals*, (Garden City, N.Y.: Doubleday, 1957)

Ashley, M. P. and Sanders, C. T., *Red Oxford: A History of the Growth of Socialism in the University of Oxford*, (Oxford University Labour Club, 1933)

Baker, B., 'Today's 18-Plus Problem', *Daily Worker*, 14 September 1963, p. 2

Bakke, E. W., *Citizens Without Work*, (New Haven, Conn.: Yale University Press, 1940)

The Unemployed Man, (Welwyn Garden City: Nisbet & Co., 1933)

Barbu, Z., *Democracy and Dictatorship*, (London: Routledge & Kegan Paul, 1956)

Barker, E., *Principles of Social and Political Theory*, (Oxford: Oxford University Press, 1961)

Barker, E. N., 'Authoritarianism of the Political Right, Center, and Left', *Journal of Social Issues*, 1963, pp. 63–74

Becker, H. S., *Outsiders: Studies in the Sociology of Deviance*, (New York: Free Press, 1963)

Behan, B., *With Breast Expanded*, (London: MacGibbon & Kee, 1964)

Bell, D., *The End of Ideology*, (New York: Collier Books, 1961)

Bell, T., *Pioneering Days*, (London: Lawrence & Wishart, 1941)

John McLean: A Fighter for Freedom, (C.P. Scottish Committee, 1944)

'Arthur MacManus', *Workers' Life*, 4 March 1927

The British Communist Party: A Short History, (London: Lawrence and Wishart, 1937)

Bell, W., 'Anomie, Social Isolation, and Class Structure', *Sociometry*, 1957, pp. 105–16

Benney, M., Gray, A. P. and Pear, R. H., *How People Vote*, (London: Routledge & Kegan Paul, 1956)

Benney, M. and Guise, P., 'Social Class and Politics in Greenwich', *British Journal of Sociology*, 1950, pp. 310–27

Bescoby, J. and Turner, T. A., 'An Analysis of Post War Labour Disputes in the British Car Manufacturing Firms', *The Manchester School*, May 1961, pp. 133–60

Birnbaum, N., 'Monarchs and Sociologists', *Sociological Review*, 1953, pp. 125–41

'Protest Movements in Developed Areas', in M. A. Kaplan (ed.) *The Revolution in World Politics*, (London: John Wiley, 1962)

Blauner, R., *Alienation and Freedom*, (Chicago: University of Chicago Press, 1964)

Blondel, J., *Voters, Parties and Leaders*, (Harmondsworth: Penguin Books, 1963)

Bloombaum, M., 'The Mobility Dimensions and Status Consistency', *Sociology and Social Research*, 1964, pp. 340–47

Bonham, J., *The Middle Class Vote*, (London: Faber & Faber, 1954)

Borkenau F., *The Communist International*, (London: Faber & Faber, 1938)

European Communism, (London: Faber & Faber, 1953)

World Communism, (Ann Arbor, Mich.: University of Michigan Press, 1962; London: Cresset Press)

The Totalitarian Enemy, (London: Faber & Faber, 1940)

Bradbury, M., 'Uncertainties of the British Intellectual', *New Society*, no. 117, 24 November 1965, pp. 7–9

Braddock, J. and B., *The Braddocks*, (London: MacDonald, 1963)

Brennan, T., *Reshaping a City*, (Maidenhead: The House of Grant Ltd, 1959)

Brennan, T., Cooney, E. and Pollins, H., *Social Change in South West Wales*, (London: Watts & Co., 1954)

Brett, E. A., 'How South Africa's Africans React', *New Society*, no. 61, 28 November 1963, pp. 6–8

Brewster-Smith, M., 'Opinions, Personality and Political Behaviour', *The American Political Science Review*, 1958, pp. 1–25

British Communist Party, *The British Road to Socialism*, (London: B.C.P., 1958)
  Report to the Executive Committee of the Commission on Inner Party Democracy, (London: B.C.P., 1963)

Broady, M. and Mack, J. H., *The Pollock Study*, unpublished

Brookes, R. H., 'The Anatomy of Anomy', *Political Science*, 1951, pp. 44–51

Brown, R., *Social Psychology*, (New York: Free Press, 1965)

Butler, D. E., *The Election System in Britain, 1918–1951*, (Oxford: Oxford University Press, 1963)

Cadogan, P., 'The B.C.P. in the Light of 1956', the *Review*, October 1961, pp. 26–44

Campbell, A., Gurin, G. and Miller, W. E., *The Voter Decides*, (Evanston, Ill.: Row, Peterson & Co., 1954)

Campbell, J. R., *Forty Fighting Years*, (London: B.C.P., 1960)
  Communism and Industrial Peace, (London: C.P.G.B., 1928)
  The Case For Higher Wages: The Incomes Racket Policy Exposed, (London: B.C.P., 1963)

Cantril, H., *The Politics of Despair*, (New York: Collier Books, 1962)

Carr, E. H., 'Mr Gallacher and the C.P.G.B.', Chapter II in *Studies in Revolution*, (London: Macmillan, 1950, pp. 166–80)

Caute, D., *Communism and The French Intellectuals*, (London: André Deutsch, 1964)

Central Statistical Office, 'Monthly Digest of Statistics', *Central Statistical Office*, July 1964, no. 223

Chinoy, E., *The Automobile Worker and the American Dream*, (Garden City, N.Y.: Doubleday & Co., 1955)

Christie, R., 'Eysenck's Treatment of the Personality of Communists', *Psychological Bulletin*, 1956, pp. 411–30

Christie, R. and Jahoda, M. (eds), *Studies in the Scope and Methods of 'The Authoritarian Personality'*, (New York: Free Press, 1954)

Clark, E. T., *The Small Sects in America*, (Nashville, Tenn.: Abingdon Press, 1959)

Clark, J. P., 'Measuring Alienation Within a Social System', *American Sociological Review*, 1959, pp. 849–52

Clegg, A. A., *Labour Relations in London Transport*, (Oxford: Blackwell, 1964)

Clegg, A. A., Killick, A. J. and Adams, R., *Trade Union Officers*, (Oxford: Blackwell, 1961)

Cloward, R. A., 'Illegitimate Means, Anomie and Deviant Behaviour', *American Sociological Review*, 1959, pp. 164–76

Cloward, R. A. and Ohlin, L. E., *Delinquency and Opportunity*, (New York: Free Press, 1960)

Cockburn, C., *In Time of Trouble*, (London: Hart-Davis, 1956)
 Crossing the Line, (London: MacGibbon & Kee, 1958)
 View From the West, (London: MacGibbon & Kee, 1958)

Cole, G. D. H., *A History of Socialist Thought*, vol. IV, Parts 1 and 2, *Communism and Social Democracy, 1914–1939*, (London: Macmillan, 1958), vol. V, *Socialism and Fascism*, (London: Macmillan, 1960)
 A Short History of the British Working Class Movement, 1787–1947, (London: Allen & Unwin, 1948)
 Socialism in Evolution, (Harmondsworth: Penguin Books, 1938)
 A History of the Labour Party from 1914, (London: Routledge & Kegan Paul, 1948)
 Labour and the Coal Mining Industry, Economic and Social History of the World War, (Carnegie Endowment for International Peace, Milford, 1923)

Cole, G. D. H. and M. I., *The Condition of Britain*, (London: Gollancz, 1937)

Cole, G. D. H. and Postgate, R., *The Common People:1746–1946*, (London: Methuen University Paperbacks, 1961)

C.P.G.B., *Report of the Party Commission on Organisation Presented to the Fifth Congress of the C.P.G.B. 1922*

Copeman, F., *Reason in Revolt*, (London: Blandford Press, 1948)

Coser, L. and Howe, I., 'Images of Socialism', in *Voices of Dissent*, (New York: Evergreen Books, 1958, pp. 17–33); 'Authoritarians of the "Left"', in *Voices of Dissent*, (New York: Evergreen Books, 1958, pp. 89–99)

Coupland, Sir R., *Welsh and Scottish Nationalism*, (London: Collins, 1954)

Crook, W. H., *Communism and the General Strike*, (Hamden: The Shoestring Press, 1960)

Cross, C., *The Fascists in Britain*, (London: Barrie and Rockliff, 1961)
 'Britain's Racialists', *New Society*, no. 140, 3 June 1965, pp. 9–12

Crossman, R. H. S. (ed.), *The God that Failed*, (London: Hamilton, 1950)

Cyriax, G. and Oakshott, R., *The Bargainers*, (London: Faber & Faber, 1960)

Darke, B., *The Communist Technique in Britain*, (London: Collins, 1953)

Davids, A., 'Generality and Consistency of Relations Between The Alienation Syndrome and Cognitive Processes', *Journal of Abnormal and Social Psychology*, 1955, pp. 61–7

Davies, B., 'Pages from a Worker's Life, 1916–1926', *Our History*, Autumn 1961, no. 23

Dean, D. G., 'Alienation: Its Meaning and Measurement', *American Sociological Review*, 1961, pp. 753–8

'Alienation and Political Apathy', *Social Forces*, 1960, pp. 185–9

Degras, J., *The Communist International, 1919–1922*
The Communist International, 1923–1928
(Oxford: Oxford University Press, 1960)

Dennis, N., Henriques, F. and Slaughter, C., *Coal is our Life*, (London: Eyre & Spottiswoode, 1956)

Dickie-Clark, H. F., *The Marginal Situation*, (London: Routledge & Kegan Paul, 1966)

Dombrose, L. A. and Levinson, D. J., 'Ideological "Militancy" and "Pacificism" in Democratic Individuals', *The Journal of Psychology*, 1950, pp. 101–13

Dowse, R. E., *Left in the Centre*, (London: Longmans, Green), 1966

Draper, T., *The Roots of American Communism*, (New York: The Viking Press, 1957)

American Communism and Soviet Russia, (New York: The Viking Press, 1960; London: Macmillan)

Dubin, R., 'Deviant Behaviour and Social Structure', *American Sociological Review*, 1959, pp. 147–64

Einaudi, M., Domenach, J. M. and Garoschi, A., *Communism in Western Europe*, (Ithaca, N.Y.: Cornell University Press, 1951)

Eisenberg, P. and Lazarsfeld, P. F., 'The Psychological Effects of Unemployment', *Psychological Bulletin*, 1938, pp. 358–90

Erbe, W., 'Social Involvement and Political Activity', *American Sociological Review*, 1964, pp. 198–215

Ernst, M. and Loth, D., *Report on American Communism*, (New York: Holt, Rinehart & Winston, 1952)

Evans, A. H., *Truth Will Out*, (C.D.R.C.U., 1964)

Evans, E. W., *The Miners of South Wales*, (Cardiff: University of Wales Press, 1961)

Eversley, R. and Little, I. M. D., *Concentration in British Industry*, (Cambridge: Cambridge University Press, 1960)

Eysenck, H. J., *Uses and Abuses of Psychology*, (Harmondsworth: Penguin Books, 1958)

Ferkiss, V. C., 'The Political and Intellectual Origins of American Radicalism, Right and Left', *Annals of the American Academy of Political and Social Science*, 1962, pp. 1–12

Foote, A., *Handbook For Spies*, (London: Museum Press, 1953)

Footman, D. (ed.), *International Communism*, St. Antony's Papers, no. 9, (London: Chatto and Windus, 1960)

Foulser, G., *Seaman's Voice*, (London: MacGibbon & Kee, 1961)

Francis, D., 'Miners Want More Than Kind Words', *Daily Worker*, 27 September 1963, p. 2.

Freedman, M., 'The Jewish Population of Great Britain', *The Jewish Journal of Sociology*, 1962, pp. 92–100

(ed.), *A Minority in Britain*, (London: Vallentine, Mitchell and Co., 1955)

Freeman, R. (ed.), *Principles of Sociology*, Henry Holt & Co., 1952

Friedrich, C. J. and Brzezinski, K., *Totalitarian Dictatorship and Autocracy*, (Cambridge, Mass.: Harvard University Press, 1956; London: Pall Mall)

Fuchs, L. H., 'American Jews and the Presidential Vote', *American Political Science Review*, 1955, pp. 385–401

The Political Behaviour of American Jews, (New York: Free Press, 1956)

Galenson, W. and Lipset, S. M. (eds.), *Readings in the Economics and Sociology of Trade Unions*, (London: John Wiley & Sons, 1960)

Gallacher, W., *Revolt on the Clyde*, (London: Lawrence & Wishart, 1936)

The Rolling of the Thunder, (London: Lawrence & Wishart, 1948)

Rise Like Lions, (London: Lawrence & Wishart, 1951)

The Tyrant's Might is Passing, (London: Lawrence & Wishart, 1954)

The Case For Communism, (Harmondsworth: Penguin Books, 1949)

The Last Memoirs of William Gallacher, (London: Lawrence & Wishart, 1965)

Le Gallienne, R., *The Romantic 90's*, (New York: Putnam and Co., 1951)

Gay, P., *The Dilemma of Democratic Socialism*, (New York: Columbia University Press, 1952)

Gerth, H. H. and Wright Mills, C., *From Max Weber*, (London: Routledge & Kegan Paul, 1957)

Gibbs, J. P. and Martin, W. T., *Status Integration and Suicide*, (Oregon: University of Oregon Books, 1964)

Glantz, O., 'Class Consciousness and Political Solidarity', *American Sociological Review*, 1958, pp. 375–83

Glazer, N., *The Social Basis of American Communism*, (New York: Harcourt, Brace & World, 1961)

'Why Jews Stay Sober', *Commentary*, 1952, pp. 181–6

Gleason, A., *What the Workers Want: A Study of British Labour*, (New York: Harcourt, Brace & Howe, 1920)

Goffman, I. W., 'Status Consistency and Preference for Change in Power Distribution', *American Sociological Review*, 1957, pp. 275–81

Goldstein, J., *The Government of British Trade Unions*, (London: Allen & Unwin, 1952)

Goldthorpe, J. H., 'Technical Organisation as a Factor in Supervisor-Worker Conflict', *British Journal of Sociology*, 1959, pp. 213–30

Gollan, J., 'Which Road?', *Marxism Today*, July 1964, pp. 198–216

'Britain's Future', *Twenty Eighth Communist Party Congress Report*, British Communist Party, 1963, pp. 3–21

'Labour in Power – What Next?' *Daily Worker*, 16 November 1964, p. 2

Gollancz, V., *The Betrayal of the Left*, (London: Gollancz, 1941)

Golovensky, D. I., 'The Marginal Man Concept: An Analysis and Critique', *Social Forces*, 1952, pp. 333–9

Gosling, R., 'Twistings in that Poor White Boy', *New Society*, no. 9, 29 November 1963, pp. 9–11

Gould, J. and Esh, S. (eds.), *Jewish Life in Modern Britain*, (London: Routledge & Kegan Paul, 1964)

Gouldner, A., *Wildcat Strike*, (London: Routledge & Kegan Paul, 1955)
(ed.), *Studies in Leadership*, (New York: Harper & Bros., 1950)

Grainger, G. W., 'Oligarchy in the British Communist Party', *British Journal of Sociology*, 1958, pp. 143–58

Graubard, S. R., *British Labour & the Russian Revolution, 1917–1924*, (Cambridge, Mass.: Harvard University Press, 1956; Oxford: Oxford University Press)

de Grazia, S., *The Political Community*, (Chicago: University of Chicago Press, 1948; London: Phoenix House)

Griffiths, W., *The Welsh*, (Harmondsworth: Penguin Books, 1950)

Guest, C. H., *David Guest*, (London: Lawrence & Wishart, 1939)

Gurian, W., 'Totalitarian Religions', *Review of Politics*, 1952, pp. 3–14

Gusfield, J. R., 'Mass Society and Extremist Politics', *American Sociological Review*, 1963, pp. 19–30

Haer, J., 'Social Stratification in Relation Towards Attitudes Towards Power', *Social Forces*, 1956, pp. 137–42

Hajda, J., 'Alienation and Integration of Student Intellectuals', *American Sociological Review*, 1961, pp. 758–77

Haldane, C., *Truth Will Out*, (London: Weidenfeld & Nicolson, 1949)

Hall, O. M., 'Attitudes and Unemployment', *Archives of Psychology*, 1934, vol. 25, no. 165, pp. 1–65

Hallgren, M. A., *The Seeds of Revolt*, (New York: Knopf, 1933)

Hannington, W., *The Problem of the Distressed Areas*, (London: Gollancz, 1937)

Unemployment Struggles, (London: Lawrence & Wishart, 1936)

Ten Lean Years, (London: Gollancz, 1940)

Harary, F., 'Merton Revisited: A New Classification for Deviant Behaviour', *American Sociological Review*, 1966, pp. 693–7

Hardy, G., *Those Stormy Years*, (London: Lawrence & Wishart, 1956)

Harris, C. D., 'Authoritarianism as a Political Variable', *Journal of Politics*, 1956, pp. 61–82

Harvey, J. and Hood, K., *The British State*, (London: Lawrence & Wishart, 1958)

Herberg, W., *Protestant – Catholic – Jew*, (Garden City, N.Y.: Anchor Books, 1960)

H.M.S.O., 'Communist Papers, Documents Selected From Those Obtained On The Arrest of Communist Leaders On 14th and 21st October, 1925', cmd. 2682, 1926

Annual Abstract of Statistics, 1964, no. 101, Table 141, p. 125

Historians' Group, 'British Communist Party, Labour – Communist Relations, 1920 – 1939', *Our History*, no. 5, Spring 1957

Hobsbawm, E. J., 'The British Communist Party', *Political Quarterly*, 1954, pp. 30–42

Primitive Rebels, (Manchester University Press, 1959)

Hodges, D. C., 'Social Oppression and Identification', *Il Politico*, 1963, pp. 316–31

Hoffer, E., *The True Believer*, (New York: Mentor Books, 1964)

Hoggart, R., *The Uses of Literacy*, (Harmondsworth: Penguin Books, 1959)

Hook, S., *World Communism*, (Princeton, N.J.: Van Nostrand, Anvil Books, 1962)

Horner, A., *Incorrigible Rebel*, (London: MacGibbon & Kee, 1960)

Howe, I. and Coser, L., *The American Communist Party, A Critical History*, (Boston, Mass.: The Beacon Press, 1957)

Hughes, E. C., 'Social Change and Status Protest: An Essay on the Marginal Man', *Phylon*, 1949, pp. 58–65

de Huszar, G. B. (ed.), *The Intellectuals*, (New York: Free Press, 1960; London: Allen & Unwin)

Hutt, A., *The Post War History of the British Working Class*, (London: Gollancz, 1937)

Hyde, D., *I Believed*, (London: The Reprint Society, 1952)

United We Fall, (Princeton, N.J.: Ampersand Books, 1964; London: Allen & Unwin)

Iverson, R. W., *The Communists and the Schools*, (New York: Harcourt, Brace & World, 1959)

Jackson, B. and Marsden, D., *Education and the Working Class*, (London: Routledge & Kegan Paul, 1962)

Jackson, E. F., 'Status Consistency and Symptoms of Stress', *American Sociological Review*, 1962, pp. 469–80

Jackson, T. A., *Trials of British Freedom*, Chapter 14, 'The Communists – The 12 of 1925', (London: Lawrence & Wishart, 1945)

Solo Trumpet, (London: Lawrence & Wishart, 1953)

Janowitz, M. and Marvick, D., 'Authoritarianism and Political Behaviour', *Public Opinion Quarterly*, 1959, pp. 579–81

Jarvie, J., 'Wage Restraint – This Hoary Old Idea', *Daily Worker*, 4 September 1963, p. 2

Jeffreys, J. B., *The Story of the Engineers*, (London: Lawrence & Wishart, 1945)

Jelf, G., 'Tackling the Roots of Racial Tension', *Daily Worker*, 2 October 1964, p. 2

Jennings, H., *Brynmawr: A Study of a Depressed Area*, (London: Allenson & Co., 1934)

The Joint Ford Shop Stewards' Committee, 'What's Wrong at Fords?', Joint Ford Shop Stewards' Committee, undated

Jones, J., *Unfinished Journey*, (London: Hamish Hamilton, 1937)

Jones, M., 'Why Britain Needs the Communists', *Twentieth Century*, Spring 1963, pp. 50–60

Just, W. C., 'With British Communists to Russia', *Twentieth Century*, 1957, pp. 16–27

Kelly, K. D. and Chambliss, W. J., 'Status Consistency and Political Attitudes', *American Sociological Review*, 1966, pp. 375–82

Kendall, W., 'Russian Emigration and British Marxist Socialism', *International Review of Social History*, 1963, pp. 351–78

Kenkel, W. F., 'The Relationship Between Status Consistency and Politico-Economic Attitudes', *American Sociological Review*, 1956, 365–8

Kerckhoff, A. C., 'Group Relations and the Marginal Personality', *Human Relations*, 1958, pp. 77–92

Kerr, C., Dunlop, J. T., Harbison, F. H. and Myers, C. A., *Industrialism and Industrial Man*, (London: Heinemann, 1962)

Kerr, M., *The People of Ship Street*, (London: Routledge & Kegan Paul, 1958)

Keynes, J. M., 'Democracy and Efficiency', *New Statesman and Nation*, 28 January 1939, p. 122

Klein, J., *Samples from English Cultures*, (London: Routledge & Kegan Paul, 1965)

Kluckhohn, C., *Culture and Behaviour*, (New York: Free Press, 1962)

Klugmann, J., 'The Foundation of the C.P.G.B.', *Marxism Today*, January 1960, pp. 1–10

'Education For the Main Debate of the Day', *World News*, vol. 7, no. 39, 1960

'The Fight For Work and Bread', *World News*, vol. 7, no. 28, 1960

'Get Your Ideas From the Sources', *Daily Worker*, 29 August 1963, p. 2

Knowles, K. G. J. C., *Strikes*, (Oxford: Blackwell, 1952)

Knupfer, J., 'Portrait of the Underdog', *Public Opinion Quarterly*, 1947, pp. 103–14

Koestler, A., *The Invisible Writings*, (London: Collins & Hamish Hamilton, 1954)

Kolarz, W., *Books on Communism*, (Princeton, N.J.: Ampersand, 1964; London: Allen & Unwin)

Kornhauser, A., Dubin, R. and Ross, A. R. (eds.), *Industrial Conflict*, (New York: MacGraw-Hill, 1954)

Kornhauser, A., Sheppard, H. L. and Meyer, A. J., *When Labour Votes*, (New York: University Books, 1956)

Kornhauser, W., *The Politics of Mass Society*, (London: Routledge & Kegan Paul, 1960)

Krausz, E., 'Occupational and Social Advancement in Anglo-Jewry', *The Jewish Journal of Sociology*, 1962, pp. 82–90

  Leeds Jewry: Its History and Social Structure, (The Jewish Historical Society of England, 1964)

Kuczynski, J., *Hunger and Work*, (London: Lawrence & Wishart, 1938)

Labedz, L. (ed.), *Revisionism: Essays on the History of Marxist Ideas*, (London: Allen & Unwin, 1962)

Landecker, W. S., 'Class Crystallisation and Class Consciousness', *American Sociological Review*, 1963, pp. 219–29

  'Class Crystallisation and its Urban Pattern', *Social Research*, 1960, pp. 308–20

Lane, R. E., *Political Ideology*, (New York: Free Press, 1962)

  Political Life, (New York: Free Press, 1961)

Lasswell, H. D. and Blumenstock D., *World Revolutionary Propaganda* (New York: Knopf, 1939)

Lasswell, H. D., 'The Measurement of Public Opinion', *American Political Science Review*, 1931, pp. 311–36

Lawrence, A., 'Revolutionary Unionism in English Trades', *Labour Monthly*, April 1923

Legget, J. C., 'Economic Insecurity and Working Class Consciousness', *American Sociological Review*, 1964, pp. 226–34

Leites, N., *A Study of Bolshevism*, (New York: Free Press, 1953)

  Operational Code of the Politburo, (New York: McGraw-Hill, 1951)

Lenin, V. I., *On Britain*, (Moscow: Foreign Languages Publishing House, 1959)

  On the International Working-Class And Communist Movement, (Moscow: Foreign Languages Publishing House, undated)

  Left-Wing Communism, An Infantile Disorder', *Selected Works*, vol. 2, (Moscow: Foreign Languages Publishing House, 1947)

Lenski, G. E., 'Status Crystallisation: A Non-Vertical Dimension of Social Status', *Ameriean Sociological Review*, 1954, pp. 405–13

  Social Participation and Status Cystallisation', *American Sociological Review*, 1956, pp. 458–64

  'Comment on R. E. Mitchell's, "Methodological Notes on a Theory of Status Crystallisation" ', *Public Opinion Quarterly*, 1964, pp. 325–30

Levin, M. B., *The Alienated Voter*, (New York: Holt, Rinehart & Winston, 1960)

Levy, H., 'A Blot on the History of Socialism', *Jewish Clarion*, July/August 1956, no. 9

'A Marxist Party?', *New Statesman*, 27 April 1957, pp. 535–6

Lindner, R. M., 'Political Creed and Character', *Psychoanalysis*, 1953, pp. 10–33

Lindsey, G. (ed.), *Handbook of Social Psychology*, vol. 2, Addison – Wesley, 1959

Lipman, D. V., 'Trends in Anglo-Jewish Occupations', *The Jewish Journal of Sociology*, 1960, pp. 202–18

Lipset, S. M., *Political Man*, (London: Heinemann, 1960)

Agrarian Socialism, (Berkeley, Calif.: University of California Press, 1950)

' "Working Class Authoritarianism": A Reply to Riesman and Miller', *British Journal of Sociology*, 1961, pp. 277–81

'The Changing Class Structure and Contemporary European Politics', *Daedalus*, vol. 93, no. 1, 1964, pp. 271–303

Lipset, S. M., Trow, M. and Coleman, J. S., *Union Democracy*, (New York: The Free Press, 1956)

Litt, E., 'Jewish Ethno-Religious Involvement and Political Liberalism', *Social Forces*, 1962, pp. 328–32

Lloyd Warner, W. and Srole, L., *The Social System of American Ethnic Groups*, (New Haven, Conn.: Yale University Press, 1945)

Lockwood, D., *The Black-Coated Worker*, (London: Allen & Unwin, 1958)

'The New Working Class', *European Journal of Sociology*, 1960, pp. 248–59

Lorwin, V. L., 'Working Class Politics and Economic Development in Europe', *American Historical Review*, January 1958, pp. 338–51

McCarthy, M., *Generation in Revolt*, (London: Heinemann, 1953)

McClosky, H. and Schaar, J. H., 'Psychological Dimensions of Anomy', *American Sociological Review*, 1965, pp. 14–40

McDill, E. L. and Ridley, J. C., 'Status, Anomia and Political Participation', *American Journal of Sociology*, 1962, pp. 205–13

Macfarlane. L. J., *The British Communist Party: Its Origin and Development Until 1929*, (London: MacGibbon & Kee, 1966)

McIver, R. M., *The Ramparts We Guard*, (London: Macmillan, 1950)

Conflict of Loyalties, (New York: Harper & Row, 1952)

McKenzie, R. T., 'Conservatism and the British Working Class' *Bulletin of the Society for the Study of Labour History*, 1963, no. 7, pp. 10–14

British Political Parties, (London Mercury Books, 1964)

McKenzie, R. T. and Silver, A., 'Conservatism, Industrialism and the Working Class Tory in England', *Transactions of the Fifth World Congress of Sociology*, 1962, vol. 3, pp. 191–202

MacKinnon, W. J. and Centres, R., 'Authoritarianism and Urban Stratification', *American Journal of Sociology*, 1956, pp. 610–20

McLelland, D. C., *The Achieving Society*, (Princeton, N.J.: Van Nostrand, 1961)

(ed.), *Talent and Society*, (Princeton, N.J.: Van Nostrand, 1958)

MacRae, D. G., *Ideology and Society*, (London: Heinemann, 1961)

Malewski, A., 'The Degree of Status Incongruence and Its Effects', *Polish Sociological Bulletin*, 1963, pp. 9–19

Manis, J. G. and Melzter, B. N., 'Some Correlates of Class Consciousness Among Textile Workers', *American Journal of Sociology*, 1963, pp. 177–84

Mann, G., 'The Intellectuals, 3, Germany', *Encounter*, June 1955, pp. 42–9

Mann, T., *Tom Mann's Memoirs*, (London: Labour Publishing Co., 1923) *Power Through the General Strike, A Call to Action*, (pamphlet) 1923

Marsh, A. I. and Coker, E. E., 'Shop Steward Organisation in the Engineering Industry', *British Journal of Industrial Relations*, 1963, vol. 1, pp. 170–90

Marshall, T. H., *Sociology at the Cross Roads*, (London: Heinemann, 1963) 'Work and Wealth', *Labour Management*, 1945, vol. 27, no. 282, pp. 98–104

Martin, J. G. and Westie, F., 'The Tolerant Personality', *American Sociological Review*, 1959, pp. 521–8

Meier, D. L. and Bell, W., 'Anomia and Differential Access to the Achievement of Life Goals', *American Sociological Review*, 1959, pp. 189–202

Merton, R. K., *Social Theory and Social Structure*, (New York: Free Press, 1959)

Mess, H., *Industrial Tyneside*, (London: Ernest Benn, 1925)

Micaud, C. A., 'The Basis of Communist Strength in France', *Western Political Quarterly*, 1955, pp. 354–66

Communism and the French Left, (London: Weidenfeld and Nicolson, 1963)

Michels, R., *Political Parties*, (New York: Collier Books, 1962; London: Constable)

Miller, S. M., 'The American Lower Class: A Typological Approach', *Social Research*, 1964, pp. 1–22

Miller, S. M. and Riesman, F., 'The Working Class Subculture: A New View', *Social Problems*, 1961, pp. 248–59

Milne, R. S. and MacKenzie, H. C., *Straight Fight*, (London: The Hansard Society, 1954)

Marginal Seat, 1955 (London: The Hansard Society, 1958)

Ministry of Labour, *Gazette*, 1962, vol. 70, no. 12.

Gazette, 1963, vol. 71, no. 4, p. 170

Mitchell, R. E., 'Methodological Notes on a Theory of Status Crystallisation', *Public Opinion Quarterly*, 1964, pp. 315–25

Mitrany, D., *Marx Against the Peasants*, (New York: Collier Books, 1961)

Mizruchi, E. H., *Success and Opportunity*, (New York: Free Press, 1964)

'Social Structure and Anomie in a Small City', *American Sociological Review*, 1960, pp. 645–54

Moffat, A., *My Life with the Miners*, (London: Lawrence & Wishart, 1965)

Monnerot, J., *The Sociology of Communism*, (London: Allen & Unwin, 1953)

Moore, W. E., *Industrial Relations and the Social Order*, (New York: Macmillan, 1957)

Morton, A. L., *Socialism in Britain*, (London: Lawrence & Wishart, 1963)

Muir, C., *Justice in the Depressed Areas*, (London: Allen & Unwin, 1936)

Murphy, J. T., *Preparing For Power: A Critical Study of the History of the British Working Class Movement*, (London: Jonathan Cape, 1934)

New Horizons, (London: The Bodley Head, 1941)

Neal, A. G. and Rettig, S., 'Dimensions of Alienation Among Manual and Non-Manual Workers', *American Sociological Review*, 1963, pp. 599–608

Nettler, G., 'The Alienated Man Revisited', mimeo

'A Measure of Alienation', *American Sociological Review*, 1957, pp. 709–16

'A Further Comment on "Anomy" ', *American Sociological Review*, 1965, pp. 762–3

Nettler, G. and Huffman, J. R., 'Political Opinion and Personal Security', *Sociometry*, 1957, pp. 51–86

Nicholas, H. G., *The British General Election of 1950*, (London: Macmillan, 1951)

Nichols, J. H., *Democracy and the Churches*, (Philadelphia, Pa.: The Westminster Press, 1951)

Nolan, W. A., *Communism versus the Negro*, (Chicago: Henry Regnery Co., 1951)

Notestein, R. B., 'Some Correlates of Right Wing Extremism Among Members of The Daughters of the American Revolution', *Wisconsin Sociology* (New Series), 1963, pp. 11–18

Nove, A., 'Jews in the Soviet Union', *The Jewish Journal of Sociology*, 1961, pp. 108–20

Olson, P. (ed.), *America as Mass Society*, (New York: Free Press, 1963)

Palme-Dutt, R., 'A Gain – Small But Precious', *Daily Worker*, 17 August 1963

'Intellectuals and Communism', *Communist Review*, September 1932, pp. 421–30

The Internationale, (London: Lawrence & Wishart, 1964)

Park, R. E., *Race and Culture*, (New York: Free Press, 1950)

Parkes, A., *A History of the Jewish People*, (Harmondsworth: Penguin Books, 1964)

Paul, W., 'Power of Persuasion', *Communist Review*, May 1921, vol. 1, no. 1.

The Path to Power, (London: C.P.G.B., 1925)

Paynter, W., 'Automation – Leisure or Dole?', *Daily Worker*, 2 October 1963, p. 2

Pearlin, I. L., 'Alienation From Work', *American Sociological Review*, 1962, pp. 314–26

Pelling, H., *The British Communist Party: A Historical Profile*, (London: Macmillan, 1958)

'The Early History of the C.P.G.B., 1920–1929', *Transactions of the Royal Historical Society*, Fifth Series, 1958, vol. 8, pp. 41–57

A History of the British Trade Union Movement, (Harmondsworth: Penguin Books, 1963)

A Short History of the Labour Party, (London: Macmillan 1962)

Perry, R. B., *Puritanism and Democracy*, (New York: The Vanguard Press, 1951)

Peterson, W. (ed.), *American Social Patterns*, (Garden City, N.Y.: Anchor Books, 1958)

Phillips Davison, W., 'A Review of Sven Rydenfelt's "Communism in Sweden" ', *Public Opinion Quarterly*, 1955, pp. 375–88

Philips-Price, M., 'The Communist International and the Labour Party', *Forward*, vol. 19, 1925

Piatnitsky, O., 'The Achievements, Tasks, and Shortcomings of the Communist Parties', *International Press Correspondence*, vol. 13, no. 16, 1933

Pilgrim Trust, *Men Without Work*, (London: The Pilgrim Trust)

Piratin, P., *Our Flag Stays Red*, (London: Thames Publications, 1948)

Plamentaz, J., *German Marxism and Russian Communism*, (London: Longmans, Green & Co., 1961)

Polanyi, M., *Personal Knowledge*, (London: Routledge & Kegan Paul, 1958)

'The Magic of Marxism?' *Encounter*, December 1956, pp. 5–17

Pollitt, H., *Answers to Questions*, (British Communist Party, 1945)

Serving My Time, (London: Lawrence & Wishart, 1950)

Pope, L., 'Religion and the Class Structure', *The Annals of the American Academy of Political and Social Science*, 1948, pp. 84–92

Pribićević, B., *The Shop Stewards' Movement & Workers' Control, 1910–1922*, (Oxford: Blackwell, 1959)

Prince, W., 'We Need a Say in Our Safety', *Daily Worker*, 29 September 1964, p. 2

Pritt, D. N., *From Right to Left*, (London: Lawrence & Wishart, 1965)

Brasshats and Bureaucrats, (London: Lawrence & Wishart, 1965)

Pye, L. W., *Guerrilla Communism in Malaya*, (Princeton, N.J.: Princeton University Press, 1956)

'Personal Identity and Political Ideology', *Behavioural Science*, 1961, pp. 205–21

Quelch, T. and Laine, W. M., 'Report as to the Communist Movement in Britain', *The Communist International*, nos. 11–12, pp. 2242–6

Radford, F. H., *Fetch the Engine: The Official History of the Fire Brigades' Union*, (Fire Brigades' Union, 1951)

Ransome, A., *Six Weeks in Russia in 1919*, (London: Allen & Unwin, 1919)

Record, W., *The Negro and the Communist Party*, (Chapel Hill, N.C.: University of North Carolina Press, 1951)

'Some Historical, Structural and Functional Differences Between the N.A.A.C.P. and the Communist Party', *Alpha Kappa Deltan*, 1959, pp. 10–75

Record, W., 'The Development of the Communist Position on the Negro Question in the United States', *Phylon*, 1958, pp. 306–26

Redman, J., 'British Communist History', *Labour Review*, July–August 1957, vol. 2, no. 4, pp. 106–10

'From Social Fascism to People's Front', *Labour Review*, September–October 1957, vol. 2, no. 5, pp. 148–53

'The Early Years of the C.P.G.B.', *Labour Review*, January–February 1958, vol. 3, no. 1, pp. 11–22

'The British Stalinists and the Moscow Trials', *Labour Review*, 1958, vol. 3, no. 2, pp. 44–52

Rennap, I., *Anti-Semitism and the Jewish Question*, (London: Lawrence & Wishart, 1942)

Revans, R. W., 'Industrial Morale and Size of Unit', *Political Quarterly*, 1956, pp. 303–11

Riesman, D., Denney, R. and Glazer, N., *The Lonely Crowd*, (New Haven, Conn.: Yale University Press, 1950)

Rimlinger, G. V., 'International Differences in the Strike Propensity of Coal Miners', *Industrial and Labour Relations Review*, 1959, pp. 390–405

'The Legitimation of Protest',*Comparative Studies in Society and History*, 1960, pp. 329–43

Ringer, B. B. and Sills, D. I., 'Political Extremism in Iran', *Public Opinion Quarterly*, 1952, pp. 689–701

Robb, J. H., *The Working Class Anti-Semite*, (London: Tavistock Publications, 1954)

Roberts, A. H. and Rokeach, M., 'Anomie, Authoritarianism and Prejudice: A Replication', *American Journal of Sociology*, 1956, pp. 355–8

Rokeach, M. *et al.*, *The Open and Closed Mind*, (New York: Basic Books, 1960)

Rolph, C. H., *All Those in Favour?*, (London: André Deutsch, 1962)

Romilly, G. and E., *Out of Bounds*, (London: Hamish Hamilton, 1935)

Rose, R., *Politics in England*, (Boston, Mass.: Little, Brown & Co. 1964; London: Heinemann)

Ross, A. M. and Hartmann, P. T., *Changing Patterns in Industrial Conflict*, (London: John Wiley & Sons, 1960)

Rossi, A., *A Communist Party in Action*, (New Haven, Conn.: Yale University Press, 1955)

Rossiter, C., *Marxism: The View from America*, (New York: Harcourt, Brace & World, 1960)

Roy, R. L., *Communism and the Churches*, (New York: Harcourt, Brace & World, 1960)

Rundquist, E. A. and Sletto, R. F., *Personality in the Depression*, (Minneapolis, Minn.: University of Minnesota Press, 1936)

Rust, W., *The Story of the Daily Worker*, (London: People's Press Printing Society, 1949)

Sansom, W. *et al.*, *Jim Brady, The Story of Britain's Firemen*, (London: Drummond, 1943)

Sanua, V. D., 'Minority Status among Jews and their Psychological Adjustment', *Jewish Journal of Sociology*, 1962, pp. 242–53

Schapiro, J. S., *Movements of Social Dissent*, (Princeton, N.J.: Anvil Books, 1962)

Schuman, H. and Harding, J., 'Sympathetic Indentification with the Underdog', *Public Opinion Quarterly*, 1963, pp. 230–41

Scott, J. D., *Life in Britain*, (London: Eyre & Spottiswoode, 1956)

Seeman, M., 'On the Meaning of Alienation', *American Sociological Review*, 1959, pp. 783–91
'Intellectual Perspectives and Adjustment to Minority Status', *Social Problems*, 1956, pp. 142–53

Segal, C., *Weekend in Dinlock*, (Harmondsworth: Penguin Books, 1962)
'Short Talk with a Fascist Beast', *New Statesman*, 4 October 1958, p. 440

Selznick, P., *The Organisational Weapon*, (New York: McGraw-Hill, 1952)

Shannon, D. A., *The Decline of American Communism*, (New York: Harcourt, Brace & World, 1959: London: Stevens & Sons)

Shils, E., *The Torment of Secrecy*, (London Heinemann, 1956)

Shils, E. and Young, M., 'The Meaning of the Coronation', *Sociological Review*, 1953, pp. 63–81

Simpson, R. L. and Miller, H. M., 'Social Status and Anomia', *Social Problems*, 1963, pp. 256–64

Sloan, P., *John Cornford: A Memoir*, (London: Jonathan Cape, 1938)

Smelser, N., *Theory of Collective Behaviour*, (London: Routledge & Kegan Paul, 1962)

Spinley, B. M., *The Deprived and the Privileged*, (London: Routledge & Kegan Paul, 1953)

Spinrad, W., 'Correlates of Trade Union Participation: A Summary of the Literature', *American Sociological Review*, 1960, pp. 237–44

Srole, L., 'Social Integration and Certain Corrolaries', *American Sociological Review*, 1956, pp. 709–16

'A Comment on "Anomy" ', *American Sociological Review*, 1965, pp. 757–62

Stagner, R., 'Fascist Attitudes', *Journal of Social Psychology* 1930, vol. 7, pp. 438–54

Stalin, J. V., *Selected Works*, (Moscow: Foreign Languages Publishing House, 1943)

Stapel, J. and de Yonge, W. J., 'Why Vote Communist?', *Public Opinion Quarterly*, 1948, pp. 390–8

Stoetzel, J., 'Voting Behaviour in France', *British Journal of Sociology*, 1955, pp. 104–22

Street, D. and Leggett, J. C., 'Economic Deprivation and Extremism', *American Journal of Sociology*, 1961, pp. 53–7

Struening, E. L. and Richardson, A. H., 'A Factor Analytic Exploration of the Alienation, Anomia, and Authoritarianism Domain', *American Sociological Review* 1965, pp. 765–76

Tawney, R. H., *Religion and the Rise of Capitalism*, (Harmondsworth: Penguin Books, 1961)

Thompson, E. P., *The Making of the English Working Class*, (London: Gollancz, 1963)

Thompson, W. E. and Horton, J. E., 'Political Alienation as a Force in Political Action', *Social Forces*, 1960, pp. 190–5

Tighe, J., 'Automation at the Coal Face', *Daily Worker*, 12 July 1963, p. 2

de Tocqueville, A., *Democracy in America*, (New York: Vintage Books, 1956)

Toole, M., *Mrs. Bessie Braddock, M.P.*, (London: Robert Hale, Ltd., 1957)

Torr, D., *Tom Mann*, (London: Lawrence & Wishart, 1936)

Trist, E. L. and Bamforth, K. W., 'Some Social and Psychological Consequences of the Longwall Method of Coal-Getting', *Human Relations*, 1951, pp. 3–38

Turner, H. A., *Trade Union Growth and Structure: A Comparative Study of the Cotton Unions*, (London: Allen & Unwin, 1962)

U.S. Department of State, Office of Intelligence Research, *World Strength of the Communist Party Organisations*, Intelligence Report no. 4489, R–15

Utley, F., *Lost Illusion*, (London: Allen & Unwin, 1949)

Way, E. L., '70 Stepney Families', *The Tablet*, 14 February 1959

Weaver, H., 'The Building Employers Have a Nerve!', *Daily Worker*, 16 August 1963, p. 2

Webb, L., *Communism and Democracy in Australia*, (New York: Frederick A. Praeger, 1955)

Wellisz, S., 'Strikes in Coal Mining', *British Journal of Sociology*, 1953, pp. 346–66

Whitehead, E. T., 'Apathy and the Class Struggle', *Communist Review*, vol. 3, no. 6, November 1921

Wigham, E., *What's Wrong With the Unions?*, (Harmondsworth: Penguin Books, 1961)

Wilkinson, E., *The Town That Was Murdered*, (London: Gollancz, 1939)

Williams, C. R., 'The Welsh Religious Revival', *British Journal of Sociology*, 1952, pp. 242–59

Williams, J. E., *The Derbyshire Miners*, (London: Allen & Unwin, 1962)

Williams, T., 'He's Picked For the Job – By His Mates', *Daily Worker*, 22 October 1963, p. 2

Willmott, P., *The Evolution of a Community*, (London: Routledge & Kegan Paul, 1963)

Willmott, P. and Young, M., *Family and Class in a London Suburb*, (London: Routledge & Kegan Paul, 1960)

Wilson, A. T. M., 'Some Aspects of the Social Process', *The Journal of Social Issues*, Supplementary Series, no. 5, November 1951, pp. 5–22

Wilson, B. R., *Sects and Society*, (London: Heinemann, 1963)

Wood, N., *Communism and the British Intellectuals*, (London: Gollancz, 1959)

'The Empirical Proletariat: A note on British Communism', *Political Science Quarterly*, 1959 pp. 256–72

Woodward, J., *Management and Technology*, (London: H.M.S.O., 1960)

Worsley, P. M., *The Trumpet Shall Sound: A study of 'Cargo' Cults in Melanesia*, (London: MacGibbon & Kee, 1957)

Young, M. and Willmott, P., *Family and Kinship in East London*, (Harmondsworth: Penguin Books, 1962)

Zawadski, B. and Lazarsfeld, P. F., 'The Psychological Consequences of Unemployment', *Journal of Social Psychology*, 1935, vol. 16, pp. 224–51

Zinoviev, G., 'Survey of the Class War', *Communist Review*, vol. 3, nos. 8 and 9, 1923

Zweig, F., *The British Worker*, (Harmondsworth: Penguin Books, 1952)

INDEX